Rothmans

WORLD RALLYING 2

1979-80 Annual review of national and international rallying

Martin Holmes and Hugh Bishop

OSPREY

Published in 1980 by Osprey Publishing Limited, 12-14 Long Acre, London WC2E 9LP
Member company of the George Philip Group

ISBN 0 85045 343 7

Editor Tim Parker

Typeset by NHK Offset Plates Ltd., Birmingham, and printed by Ebenezer Baylis and Son, Limited, Worcester and London.

All photographs and illustrations used in this book are those of the authors unless a special credit is given with the particular photograph or illustration

CONTENTS

Björn Waldegård
Ticksta Gård, RÖ

Telefon 0175/62011

Rö den 20 september 1979

Jag har följt Martin Holmes och Hugh Bishops rally-böcker sedan de kom till för ett par år sedan. Det är alltid lika roligt att ta fram ett exemplar då och då och bläddra i.

Jag vet att Hugh är ute på de flesta tävlingarna, om inte samtliga. Jag ser honom då och då skymta förbi när vi kommer farande i våra rallybilar. Han har liksom blivit en av familjen i vårt kringflackande gäng. Jag vet att han har tiofalt mer bilder hemma på sina hyllor mot vad han får publicerat i olika tidningar världen över. Vad kan då vara mer perfekt än att få se alla dessa fantastiska foton från hela världens olika rallytävlingar samlade för ett helt år i den här årsboken.

Martin känner jag sedan många år tillbaka. Jag imponeras alltid av hans stora kunnande och hans vetgirighet. Det är aldrig tal om att inte skriva något som han inte är riktigt säker på. Det mest talande är nog när han gör en intervju med en icke engelsman, mig själv t.ex. Då återger han i engelsk text min egen skolengelska, vilket jag själv ler lite åt. Men vilket väl säger i vilken anda han arbetar med motorsporten.

Den här speciella upplagan av Rallying kommer jag säkerligen att plocka fram extra många gånger. Det har varit ett stort år för mig. Hittills, jag skriver det här förordet efter Kanada-tävlingen, har det blivit VM-segrar i Grekland och Kanada.
Jag leder förar-VM och ser ut att ha stora chanser att bli världsmästare. Jag har ännu inte riktigt lärt mig hur ordet världsmästare smakar. Hur det klingar i öronen. Det är nästan för fantastiskt att det kanske blir verklighet om några månader.

Men nu när Ni kära läsare har öppnat den här föträffliga boken vet vi alla svaret på denna fråga - och alla andra frågor som också kan tänkas dyka upp i dag eller i framtiden om rallyåret 1979.

Björn Waldegård

FOREWORD

I have read all of Martin Holmes' and Hugh Bishop's books since they started to have them published a couple of years ago. I have really enjoyed them every time I have looked at them.

I know that Hugh visits most of the major rallies, if not all of them. I sometimes see him out of the corner of my eye when we are driving flat out on the special stages. He has come to be, nowadays, part of our big family travelling around the world. I also know that he has many, many more photographs at home some of which have been published in magazines throughout the world. What could be more perfect than for others of *his* photographs to be used in this year book.

I have known Martin for a long time now. I have always been impressed by his understanding of the sport and his desire for more knowledge within it. He never writes anything he is not absolutely sure about. Take this example for instance. When he interviews a non-English speaking driver, like me for example, he writes their own schoolboy English, which they, of course, have to smile about. But it says a great deal about him and his writing philosophy.

I will certainly take this 'special' edition of *World Rallying* down from my bookcase many times. It has been a great year for me. Up until now, and I am writing this just after the Canadian rally, I have won two World Championship events, in Greece and Canada and it looks as though I am in the running for the World Champion crown. But I am not there yet . . . How it rings in my ears. It is just too fantastic if the reality of it comes about in a couple of months.

But, dear readers, by the time you have opened this excellent book you will know the answer to the question — and to all other questions about what has happened during the 1979 rally year.

Ford Motor Company competitions department

A depot at one side of the disused Boreham airfield in Essex has gradually become the hub of British rallying activity. This is where the competitions department of Ford Motor Company is situated. Nowadays a large warehouse houses the workshops and stores, while at the rear, a huge yard is filled with the relics of competition cars whose lives are finished and the unfinished bodies of cars which still have their active lives in front of them. From this base the official rallying activities of Ford are operated, directly in the case of the international World Championship rallies and either directly or independently in the case of others.

The head of the department is Peter Ashcroft, Competitions Manager, whilst the direct responsibility for rallying lies with the rallies manager, Charles Reynolds. The development of the group 4 (Escort RS) cars is the work of Alan Wilkinson, while that of group 2 (Fiesta) and group 1 (Escort RS2000) cars is under the guidance of John Griffiths. The mechanics probably have more experience than those in any other team currently in rally competition, most of them working both on rallies as well as in the workshop between events. The workshop foreman is Mick Jones.

The complete assembly of rally cars does not take place at Boreham, for initial construction is the work of a variety of contracted companies. The most important of these is Brian Hart Limited, the official suppliers of competition engines. Hart himself has been an international racing driver of considerable repute in Formula 2, but now he works full-time with the preparation of both racing and rally engines. His 420R 2-litre Formula 2 engines are, together with those of BMW, the only competitive units available, while his 2-litre BDA engines have gained an enviable reputation for quality and strength. He is also responsible for development work with the push-rod 1600 cc engines for the Fiesta. Hart's factory is at Harlow, about one hour's drive to the west of Boreham. Other important suppliers include Maurice Gomm in Woking, who send ready-prepared bodyshells, duly strengthened where permitted and fitted with the necessary safety equipment, to Boreham.

Ford have gradually been building up their international rallying activity over the past few years, so that the remark-

The only indication as to the whereabouts of Britain's most important rally headquarters is this small sign beside a picturesque Essex lane

Despite an appearance as an aircraft hangar the rally department workshop was, in fact, purpose built

General view of the inside of the Ford competition workshop, showing Roger Clark's rough-road Fiesta being built alongside group 4 Escorts

Norman Masters, longtime the personal mechanic for Roger Clark, left, with Mick Jones — at work on Bjorn Waldegard's Portugal Rally car

Robin Vokins, left, discussing an engine mounting problem with Alan Wilkinson on a new car being built for Russell Brookes

able sporting career of the Escort (which began in 1968) will end on just as high a note as it started. No other type of car has been so successful in rallying for so long. In 1980 it is expected that the Escort rear-wheel-drive model will cease production, and it is the policy of Ford not to continue in competition with a model which is not available for purchase by the general public. Much of the strength of Ford competition rallying lies in the private use of their cars.

Throughout the world, Escorts are used mostly in groups 1 and 4. However, this is a market which Boreham cannot handle. Most of the sales to foreign.buyers are handled by David Sutton Cars Limited, who also operate (with a similar company run by the former driver Tony Maslen) an international rally car rental service. In Britain most of the rally cars are constructed by the teams themselves, using parts that have been developed by the official teams and marketed

THIS PAGE *Wide wings on the rear of an asphalt-specification Escort. The rules about wings being a maximum of 5 cm wide have special significance to Ford as the RS is homologated with extension pieces as standard, so it is permitted to add 5 cm to the existing wings*

Rear of the prototype British-built Fiesta rally car with the unique double rear-window, fitted specially for the Monte Carlo Rally

Don Partington, the team's leading electrician, studying the engine compartment of Roger Clark's asphalt rally Fiesta

FACING PAGE *The man behind the power. Brian Hart poses with a BDA block and a complete Fiesta 1600 rally engine*

A 1600 Fiesta rally engine installed on a test bench

BDA aluminium rally engine block

BDA rally 4-valve cylinder head

through specialist outlets. Various specialist companies prepare engines for private customers, of which Terry Hoyle Limited is the best known.

Eventually the Escort will have to disappear, but even now there is no definite planning about a replacement rally car. Work with the Fiesta has been carried out through 1979, both with a group 2 version and, in British rallies, with a free-formula version using a 1700 cc BDA engine. To this end the fine result on the Monte Carlo Rally was a great encouragement. Nevertheless the Escort remains one of the the most remarkable rally cars of all time, successes following the skills and enthusiasm of the engineers, mechanics, managers and drivers alike. It will be an almost impossible order to produce another model which will be as successful.

THIS PAGE *Ford rally team personnel. Left to right Alan Wilkinson, Charles Reynolds and Mick Jones*

More Ford personnel! Peter Ashcroft, competitions manager, with Bjorn Waldegard (left) and Hannu Mikkola (centre)

FACING PAGE *Mick Jones driving one of the team's Transit service vans in a special slalom competition at Estoril in Portugal. Note the extra passenger space behind the front seats*

Norman Masters, left, and Mick Jones busy pressure-checking tyres at a service-point on the Acropolis Rally

At speed! Rallies are won by drivers, co-drivers and the backroom boys — seen at work on the Monte Carlo

MOTORSPORT

GTX

Motorcraft
MOTORSPO
Motorcraft

Lancia Stratos rallying record

Few cars in the nineteen-seventies have had as much influence on international rallying as the Lancia Stratos, a car which epitomized the concept of the 'special car' built just for rallying. Like the Ferrari 250GTO and Porsche 917, the Stratos was driven straight through the principles of homologation, that set of 'rules' which are designed to prevent such a vehicle from competing. It was as though the Lancia factory had beaten the rule-makers at their own game.

Lancia themselves believe that their Stratos was simply a furtherance of the precedent set by the lightweight Renault Alpine A110, which until the emergence of the Stratos into international competition was virtually all-powerful

Following after the list of chassis/registrations are details of the entries of the official Lancia team, first under Marlboro colours in 1974, then Alitalia from 1975 through to 1977 and then Pirelli in 1978. The records are limited to those cars entered by the factory, officially, and do not include any other similar entries.

Not included in these details of the entries are the rallies competed in by Bernard Darniche under Chardonnet colours and before that under Neyret/Aseptogyl colours. Darniche used three cars for Chardonnet (TON14328, TON14329 and TOR06880) all owned by the factory but on loan to him. In the early days, the cars were used with temporary registrations, or sometimes with none at all. Altogether some twenty-seven Stratos were used for official entries, including those lent to Darniche. The registration TOL64136 was carried on two chassis; the first being sold in April 1975 and the second being used after December 1975.

The two cars used by Graham Warner's Chequered Flag Team in Great Britain were TOL52902, the car which was ultimately destroyed in a fire in Wales (chassis number 1513), and TOL80932, which was purchased after being left in East Africa. A team of three cars was rallied by Andrzej Jaroszewicz during 1976 and 1977, but these were privately acquired and run separately from the factory cars. Jaroszewicz had WX-13-82 (chassis 1634), WX-30-93 (chassis 1864) and WX-30-96 (chassis 1560), of which the first was by far the most extensively used, being a practice car. 'Number 93' was the car which won in Bulgaria and Poland in 1976, but was then destroyed in an accident in the Spanish Rally later that year. Both other cars were destroyed at the Polish Rally the following year, the practice car first, before the event, and then 'Number 96' during the rally. One of the engines was then fitted into a Polonez for Polish circuit racing!

The chassis/registrations involved are as follows:

CHASSIS NUMBER		REGISTRATION NUMBER
1	never used on rallies	A6 14056
2		A6 14057
3		A6 14058
1512		A6 16044 and TOL52901
1513		A6 16043 and TOL52902
1524		TOL65176
1576	two chassis	A6 14112 and TOL64137
1577		A6 14113 and TOL64136
1578		A6 14114 and TOL64135
1579		TOL64134
1580		TON98792
1626		TOL80931
1637		TOL80932
1685		TON41648
1720		TON14328
1734		TOL87903
1751		TOL96266
1804		TOP50745
1806	not registered. Silhouette car	
1818		TOL96265 and TOL64136
1828		TOR06880
1832		TOL87904
1868		TON14329
1874		TOM26363 and TON12661
1914		TOP10315
1918		TOM54374
1989		TON36372

NOTE: The old chassis have either been sold or scrapped. 1626 was stolen from Salice Terme while being used by Tony Carello as a training car.

Official factory Lancia Stratos rally entries

1972	EVENT	NO.	CREW	RESULT	RALLY	TRAINING
3-5 Nov	Tour de Corse	3	Munari/Mannucci	rear suspension	A6 14057	
9-12 Dec	Costa del Sol	1	Munari/Mannucci	rear suspension	A6 14057	
1973						
9-11 Mar	Lyon-Charbonnières	11	Andruet/'Biche'	accident	A6 14058	
6-8 April	Firestone	2	Munari/Mannucci	1st	A6 14114	
13 May	Targa Florio	4	Munari/Andruet	2nd	A6 14057	A6 14114
26-27 May	Tour de l'Aisne	6	Andruet/'Biche'	1st	A6 14114	
24 June	Cevenole	1	Andruet	accident	A6 14114	
14-23 Sept	Tour de France	111	Munari/Mannucci	1st	A6 14113	
do.		118	Andruet/'Biche'	fuel tank	A6 14112	A6 14114
25-28 Oct	Giro d'Italia	528	Merzario/Sodano	engine	A6 14113	
do.		524	Andruet/'Biche'	accident	A6 14112	A6 14114
1974						
2-3 Feb	Chamonix	1	Munari/Andruet	2nd	TOL64136	TOL64135
16-17 Feb	Giraglia	91	Andruet/'Biche'	1st	TOL64136	
23-24 Feb	Neige et Glace	4	Andruet/'Biche'	1st	TOL64136	
1-3 Mar	Sicily	3	Ballestrieri/Maiga	1st	TOL64136	TOL64135
do.		1	Andruet/'Biche' (turbo)	engine	TOL64134	
12 May	Targa Florio	1	Ballestrieri/Larrousse	1st	TOL52902	TOL64137
do.		3	Munari/Andruet	engine	TOL52901	
12-19 May	Paris-St Raphael	1	Christine/'Biche'	1st	TOL64135	
31 May-2 June	Four Regions	1	Munari/Mannucci	1st	TOL64136	
do.		4	Ballestrieri/Maiga	2nd	TOL52902	TOL64135
29-30 June	Alpi Orientali	1	Ballestrieri/Maiga	suspension	TOL52902	TOL64135
13-21 Sept	Tour de France	136	Munari/Mannucci (turbo)	engine	TOL64134	TOL64136
do.		137	Andruet/'Biche'	3rd	TOL52901	
3-6 Oct	San Remo	2	Munari/Mannucci	1st	TOL65176	TOL64137
do.		4	Ballestrieri/Maiga	accident	TOL52902	TOL64135
16-20 Oct	Giro d'Italia	526	Andruet/'Biche' (turbo)	1st	TOL64134	
16-20 Oct	Rideau Lakes	103	Munari/Mannucci	1st	TOL65176	
31 Oct-4 Nov	Press-on-Regardless	64	Munari/Mannucci	rear suspension	TOL65176	
15-20 Nov	RAC	3	Munari/Sodano	3rd	TOL52901	
30 Nov-1 Dec	Tour de Corse	2	Andruet/'Biche'	1st	TOL80931	TOL64135
do.		6	Munari/Mannucci	engine	TOL65176	TOL64137
do.		9	Ballestrieri/Mannini	electrics	TOL52902	TOL64136
1975						
15-25 Jan	Monte Carlo	1	Andruet/Jouanny	accident	TOL80931	TOL87903
do.		14	Munari/Mannucci	1st	TOL65176	TOL87904
do.		17	Pinto/Bernacchini	accident	TOL52902	TOL52901
13-16 Mar	Swedish	4	Waldegard/Thorszelius	1st	TOL80931	TOL96265
22-23 Mar	Sicily	2	Pinto/Bernacchini	1st	TOL80931	TOL52901
27-31 Mar	Safari	3	Munari/Drews	2nd	TOL87904	
do.		8	Waldegard/Thorszelius	3rd	TOL87903	
27 May-2 June	Acropolis	1	Waldegard/Thorszelius	electrics	TOL87903	TOM26363
do.		4	Pinto/Bernacchini	engine	TOL80931	TOL52901

30-31 May	Four Regions	1	Munari/Mannucci	1st	TOL65176	
28-29 June	Alpi Orientali	1	Pinto/Bernacchini	4th	TOM26363	TOL87903
28-30 Aug	San Martino di C.	2	Pinto/Bernacchini	1st	TOL65176	TOL52901
20-21 Sept	Coppa Liburna	1	Pinto/Bernacchini	1st	TOL65176	
1-4 Oct	San Remo	1	Munari/Mannucci	puncture	TOL96265	TOL65176
						TOL87904
do.		7	Pinto/Bernacchini	engine	TOL80931	TOL87903
do.		11	Waldegard/Thorszelius	1st	TOM26363	TOL52901
12-17 Oct	Giro d'Italia	489	Facetti/Garzoglio	fire	TOL96266	
do.		514	Pinto/Bernacchini	clutch	TOM54374	TOL80931
						TOL64137
do.		519	Munari/Mannucci	6th	TOL64134	TOL87904
						TOL65176
8-9 Nov	Tour de Corse	1	Munari/Mannucci	accident	TOL96265	TOL87904
do.		4	Pinto/Bernacchini	suspension	TOL80931	TOL87903
21-26 Nov	RAC	2	Waldegard/Thorszelius	disqualified	TOM26363	
do.		8	Munari/Mannucci	4th	TOL96265	
6-7 Dec	Valli Piacentine	6	'Tony'/di Marco	2nd	TOL65176	

1976

16-24 Jan	Monte Carlo	6	Waldegard/Thorszelius	2nd	TON12661	TOL96265
do.		8	Pinto/Bernacchini	engine	TOL80931	TOL87903
do.		10	Munari/Maiga	1st	TOM54374	TOL87904
19-22 Feb	Swedish	1	Waldegard/Thorszelius	accident	TON12661	TOL65176
do.		3	Lampinen/Hertz	4th	TOL65176	
do.		8	Walfridsson/Nilsson	accident	TOL80931	
10-14 Mar	Portugal	1	Munari/Maiga	1st	TOM54374	
do.		4	Pinto/Bernacchini	4th	TOL64137	
27-28 Mar	Sicily	1	Pregliasco/Sodano	1st	TOL65176	
8-10 April	Elba	4	Pregliasco/Sodano	front suspension	TOM54374	TOL87903
15-20 April	Safari	1	Waldegard/Thorszelius	starter	TON12661	
do.		6	Munari/Maiga	engine	TOL96265	TOL87904
do.		17	Preston/Lyall	12th	TOL80931	
22-28 May	Acropolis	3	Waldegard/Thorszelius	oil pipe	TON12661	TOL96265
do.		7	Pinto/Bernacchini	driveshaft	TOL64137	TOL87903
do.		11	Pregliasco/Garzoglio	clutch	TOM54374	TOL65176
4-6 June	Four Regions	4	Pregliasco/Garzoglio	steering	TON36372	TOL65176
do.		6	Carello/Bernacchini	5th	TOM54374	
22-26 June	Morocco	3	Munari/Maiga	3rd	TOM54374	
22-25 July	Valli Piacentine	2	Pregliasco/Garzoglio	accident	TON36372	TOL65176
do.		6	Carello/Bernacchini	accident	TON12661	TOL96295
6-9 Oct	San Remo	1	Munari/Maiga	2nd	TON41648	
do.		4	Waldegard/Thorszelius	1st	TON12661	TOL96265
do.		6	Pinto/Bernacchini	3rd	TOL64137	TOL87903
17-20 Oct	Giro d'Italia	598	Facetti/Sodano	1st	*Prova* 2634	
do.		599	Pinto/Bernacchini	accident	TON98792	
6-7 Nov	Tour de Corse	1	Munari/Maiga	1st	TON41648	TON12661
20-21 Nov	Campagnolo	1	Carello/Bernacchini	2nd	TON12661	
26 Nov-1 Dec	RAC	7	Munari/Maiga	4th	TOL64137	
7-8 Dec	Ciocco	3	Carello/Bernacchini	1st	TON12661	

1977

22-29 Jan	Monte Carlo	1	Munari/Maiga	1st	TON41648	TON12661
do.		5	Pinto/Bernacchini	engine	TON98792	TOL87903
do.		8	Darniche/Mahe	road accident	TOL64137	TOL65176
11-12 Mar	Ciocco	1	Pinto/Bernacchini	suspension	TON98792	TOL87903

7-11 April	Safari	4	Lampinen/Andreasson	head gasket	TOP50745	TON12661
do.		6	Ulyate/Street	overheating	TOL80932	
do.		7	Munari/Sodano	3rd	TOP10315	TOM54374
21-23 April	Elba	7	Carello/Perissinot	accident	TOL64137	TOL96265
21-22 May	S Giacomo	2	Pregliasco/Reisoli	1st	TON41648	TOL65176
3-5 June	Four Regions	3	Pinto/Bernacchini	accident	TON93792	TOL37903
do.		5	Pregliasco/Reisoli	2nd	TON41648	TOL65176
do.		7	Carello/Perissinot	transmission	TOL64137	TOL96265
12-16 June	Giro d'Italia	539	Munari/Sodano (turbo)	turbine	*Prova* TO1533	TOP10315
18-19 June	Gargano	2	Pregliasco/Reisoli	3rd	TON41648	TOL65176
1-3 July	Campagnolo	3	Pregliasco/Reisoli	valve	TON41648	TOL65176
do.		122	Carello/Perissinot	1st	TOL64137	TOL96265
5-9 July	Total	4	Munari/Sodano	1st	TOP50745	
23-24 July	Valli Piacentine	3	Pregliasco/Reisoli	1st	TON41648	TOL65176
1-3 Sept	S Martino di C.	1	Munari/Sodano	1st	TOM54374	TOP10315
do.		5	Pregliasco/Reisoli	2nd	TON41648	TOL65176
16-17 Sept	Coppa Liburna	2	Pregliasco/Reisoli	1st	TON41648	
5-8 Oct	San Remo	2	Munari/Sodano	transmission	TOM54374	TOP10315
do.		4	Pinto/Bernacchini	accident	TON98792	TOM26363
						TON12661
do.		10	Pregliasco/Reisoli	4th	TON41648	TOL87903
do.		12	Carello/Perissinot	accident	TOL64137	TOL65176
21-23 Oct	RACE	1	Munari/Sodano	engine	TON98792	TOP10315
5-6 Nov	Tour de Corse	1	Munari/Sodano	accident	TOM54374	TON41648
do.		4	Pinto/Bernacchini	2nd	TON14328	
do.		19	Carello/Perissinot	4th	TOL64137	TOL65176
18-23 Nov	RAC	7	Munari/Sodano	25th	TON14328	TOP10315
3-4 Dec	Aosta	1	Munari/Perissinot	1st	TOM54374	TOP10315
do.		7	Bettega/Torghele	2nd	TON41648	TOM26363

1978

21-28 Jan	Monte Carlo	1	Munari/Sodano	engine	TOM54374	TOP10315
do.		5	Bacchelli/Bernacchini	10th	TON41648	TOL96265
10-12 Feb	Swedish	2	Blomqvist/Sylvan	4th	TOP50745	TON14328
17-19 Feb	Costa Brava	2	Carello/Perissinot	1st	TOL64137	TOL80931
24-26 Feb	Sachswinter	1	Rohrl/Geistdorfer	front suspension	TON98792	
18-19 Mar	Unterfranken	1	Rohrl/Geistdorfer	engine	TON98792	
24-26 Mar	Targa Florio	2	Carello/Perissinot	1st	TON64137	TOL80931
15-16 April	Saarland	1	Rohrl/Geistdorfer	1st	TOL64137	
4-5 May	Elba	3	Carello/Perissinot	clutch	TON41648	TOL80931
19-21 May	Four Regions	5	Carello/Perissinot	1st	TOL64137	TOL80931
16-18 June	Antibes	5	Carello/Perissinot	water pump belt	TOL64137	TOP10315
23-25 June	Ypres	4	Carello/Perissinot	3rd	TOL64137	TOP10315
24-25 June	Rheinhessen	1	Rohrl/Geistdorfer	1st	TOM54374	
1-3 July	Alpi Orientali	2	Carello/Perissinot	1st	TON41648	
8-9 July	Vorderpfalz	1	Rohrl/Geistdorfer	1st	TOM54374	
21-23 July	Hunsruck	1	Rohrl/Geistdorfer	1st	TOM54374	
11-13 Aug	Bayerwald	1	Rohrl/Geistdorfer	2nd	TOM54374	
9-11 Sept	Halkidikis	2	Carello/Perissinot	1st	TOL64137	
4-7 Oct	San Remo	4	Alen/Kivimaki	1st	TOM54374	TON14328
13-15 Oct	OASC	2	Carello/Perissinot	1st	TON64137	
14-19 Oct	Giro d'Italia	506	Alen/Kivimaki/Pianta	1st	TON12661	TON98792
20-22 Oct	RACE	2	Carello/Perissinot	1st	TOL41648	
19-23 Nov	RAC	3	Alen/Kivimaki	gearbox	TOL64137	TOL96265
do.		10	Munari/Sodano	engine	TOP50745	
7-8 Dec	Monza	1	Alen/Kivimaki	accident	TOM54374	

THIS PAGE *Lancia wins the 1974 World Championship for Makes at the final round in Corsica. Apart from the Safari, their only points in this series had been gained since October that year, when the Stratos was first eligible for these events. Here is Jean-Claude Andruet and 'Biche' on the first special stage in the north of the island. TOL80931 was new for this event, and was the only Stratos to finish.*

April 1973: Fourth outing and first victory. Sandro Munari and Mario Mannucci winning the Firestone Rally, a European Championship Rally in North Spain which in those days was not restricted to cars within groups 1 to 4. The car ran under 'tradeplates' A6 14114

February 1978: Stig Blomqvist drove an official Stratos for the first and only time on the Swedish Rally, making easily the greatest number of fastest times on the event, but was pushed back to fourth place. Few people expected this driver to be able to master this difficult machine so easily

FACING PAGE *November 1976: Sandro Munari winning Corsica, the third consecutive Stratos victory on that event with three separate drivers. In 1975 Bernard Darniche had been first with his Neyret/Aseptogyl/Chardonnet car, a private entry. Conditions in Corsica are notoriously unpleasant and often very changeable*

Sandro Munari and Mario Mannucci began the Lancia Stratos project running at the Tour de Corse in 1972, until rear suspension failure sidelined them

September 1976: The Tour de France has attracted many exciting cars in the past. Here Jean-Claude Andruet has an ex-works turbocharged Stratos, run by Bob Neyret with private sponsorship

End of the line for TOL52902, which apart from the two initial results had been an unlucky car for Turin. It was sold to Chequered Flag in England where its ill fortune persisted and eventually it crashed and was destroyed in Wales

Safari trim. Protective bars front and rear, additional support for the second spare wheel on the roof; at first sight it seemed the car needed the extra strength. In reality, the basic chassis had been over-engineered and was well up to the extra strain of the African roads, although they never won an event in Africa.

Morelli/Bertier

Moss/Howe

Thoughts of Walter Rohrl

I was first introduced to rallying by a skiing friend at the end of the sixties. Many times we would go together, either in my car or his, to the ski races. He used to compete in some navigation rallies in Germany and he kept saying I must do a rally with him. He promised to arrange everything, that he would get a car for the week-end; I should be free of working and then we do the rally. That was how it started. We retired after 500 km because the car broke down, but it was nice. Normally on the road you cannot go fast and it was good to be able to go really flat out. The next year the same rally came up, and then we had done two rallies more in that year. We always used cars from my colleagues at work and once we got one from a local dealer, but never used my own. In the third year we did four or five rallies like this, and for 1971 I got an offer from Ford Germany to drive a Capri in the German Championship. I accepted as it was possible to keep my normal job. I really started to go rallying in 1971 when I did ten or eleven rallies in our championship. At the end of 1971 I decided to give up because I had many problems at home. Every time when I was going to a rally there was big argument.

In 1965 my brother had a serious car accident. For my family it was terrible that I was interested in the motor sport. Every time it was a one-hour discussion before I left home; then if you have a one-hour big discussion, you cannot just go out and forget it. At the end of 1971 I was quite ready to give it all up. At that time I was working in the Bishop's office doing church administration. The church has a lot of land in our country and for eight years I was involved in this administration. During this time I trained to be a ski teacher, but it takes four years minimum to pass all examinations. So I concentrated on these. There was no sense to go rallying with all the problems at home.

Then after three months at home I felt very unhappy. Nobody could speak to me. I thought all the time about rallies rather than skiing. Finally I decided I had to do more rallies. I think today I will give it all up. Sometimes even now I still look and see what has happened with my cars. I cannot stand it when something is broken. I nearly gave up after Monte Carlo in 1979. I could have cancelled my contract I was so down. The problem is what would I do if I didn't make rallies! At the moment I am a little bit under pressure from my wife Monica that I should go into a family business, but after seven or eight years one does not feel able to change to being always at home. That is the problem. If I had another suitable occupation then I would stop driving rallies — it is better to be out and about and be happy rather than be at home and not happy. Maybe I could be a taxi driver!

Back with Ford again, the most important thing for us to do was the Olympia Rally, but really before going into this you need a bit of practice and so we went to Poland and then to the Baltic Rally. The Olympia Rally itself was good. I was practising for ten days making complete rally notes and one time checking them. Then, on the first stage, I did the best time! There were a lot of good people there like Hannu Mikkola, and even after ten or so stages I was still in first five. I was driving more by sight than with notes. Maybe this was the reason why I was still going well in this rally, driving on the stages which I had only seen once. Eventually I got to third and then second and then I had just overtaken Jean-Pierre Nicolas and I was fourteen seconds in front of him and near to my own home when there was a bang and we had to retire. This led to my association with Opel. There was discussion with Ford, but their programme for the next year was not so good and the Opel team Irmscher offered me the German Championship or maybe the European Championship, so I said OK to Opel. I had burned my boats with Ford.

Even though I am now with Fiat, I would go back to a German team if they had a good car which I could drive. I think it would be more easy for me. I would even drive for an Italian team like Carenini, who was my first mechanic. I can feel that these are really my friends. When you rally for friends I find everyone wants the best for me. But looking back now, it was the only decision which I could have made to go to Fiat. I have never once thought that it was wrong. I was asked by Waxenberger of Mercedes to go to Safari for him in October 1978. He asked me if I could do the Safari and I said yes, but when I signed a contract with Fiat it was no longer possible. So the only time I have driven for them was to make a test drive for a German magazine after the South American Rally in 1978. Now I am with Fiat things are very different. There is so much politics and activity behind the scenes I cannot feel this situation; the people I deal with are very nice. Sometimes you hear people say that Fiat should not have foreign drivers and use only Italian drivers, then you discover the journalist was fighting against Fiat not you. Especially in the team I cannot feel this. The mechanics are fantastic, they are so nice to me. It is even more so for Alen, as he is almost Italian himself.

Alen has been five years driving in this team, but I think that I am only accepted because I can drive fast. I don't think that somebody likes me for any other reason! In my group 5 racing I am working with Patrese, who is Italian, but then Patrese is number 1 and I am only a rally driver, so there is no conflict. Maybe if this situation occurred in rallies I would have some problems. If Sandro Munari was still driving in the team I would not stay, not any more. I would say to Fiat that if Sandro is driving one time more, don't call me: I would never go anywhere if Sandro was driving. All our situations are like this. Whenever a question arises, at first I have to have big discussions with the directors. It is incredible, but I think the problem is that I am the first pilot in this Fiat group who is not afraid of the management. Everybody else is afraid to go out and upset them and that makes the situation difficult. I know that they like to have good drivers, but only people who toe the line. We don't have any open fights, but I can feel it under ground.

The Group 5 Lancia Monte Carlo project arose when it was

This Ford Capri RS put Rohrl on the map of international rallying, when he gave a splendid performance on the Olympia Rally in 1972. The company which prepared the car for Rohrl was run by the brother of Jochi Kleint, now the Opel official driver

THIS PAGE *Winning the European championship in 1974 with this Opel Ascona gave Rohrl the taste for rallying abroad, which offered far more opportunities than his national series*

Winning the Acropolis Rally in 1975, the only time Opel had won a World Championship rally outright. As for the European title the year before, Jochen Berger was by his side

FACING PAGE *In the stifling heat of Ypres in 1976, Rohrl lead to the finish. The Opel Kadett GT/E's 16-valve engine caused endless trouble elsewhere*

agreed that this would not be a very active year. They had to give me something that maybe didn't stretch me. The programme was not enough and they said I could do some races as well. Patrese is always the number 1 driver, and things work well. Problems only start when the second driver is faster than the first, then it is more difficult to work together. Funnily enough the first time we raced, at Nürburgring, we made exactly the same time! It is a different sort of circuit. It is not important so much to brake very late or to fight with somebody, it demands a different style of driving. At Silverstone you must go like a computer and I don't think that I can do it even after 20 laps. These World Championship races, especially the six-hour races, are not so hard as the World Championship rallies, although of course you must be absolutely top fit for a six-hour race. I am more nervous before a start of a rally because I know I must be immediately in the lead, but for me in the races this is not so important. It is physically exhausting to drive in a group 5 car. Everything is heavy, especially the steering. Riccardo says that after two laps he is more worn out than after a whole Formula 1 race. At the Nürburgring he was completely exhausted after the first nine laps. I think that my experience as a rally driver helps in long-distance sports car races. Patrese has done one or two rallies. He did the Giro d'Italia and he said it was very good. He was fast in the ordinary rally stages in Ciocco. Two days before we raced at Nürburgring we did a small test in the forests with the Stratos and Riccardo was driving with me. Afterwards he admitted that he had thought about doing some more rallies, but not now! He said that the Stratos was a very nice car but it is very difficult to drive.

For me our rally programme in Germany was good experience. If you can drive a Stratos you can drive anything, even a Formula 1. I once drove a Copersucar Formula 1 car at Silverstone. Before I had thought Formula 1 would be completely different, but when I was sitting in the car going out of pits it was just like any other car. This is incredible, but I think that this impression comes from the Stratos. The Stratos is so nervous and the steering is so quick: a Formula 1 car is more easy to drive then the Stratos.

For me there is another thing. I am scared if I sit in a race car, especially where there are some very fast bends where you go at 250 kph. I feel more frightened at Nürburgring than at San Remo, despite the drops at the edge of the road there. A grand prix car is so perfect; if you brake or you turn the steering it is exact, but always with a rally car things are never so predictable. That is the difference. At Fiat I would think that we have the most sophisticated rally cars, but after Monte Carlo when we saw the Fords we were depressed. Now the only thing I say is that I think Fiat is stronger, even if it has 40 hp less. The cars for Markku and myself are prepared in the same way, except Markku is wanting his car to have braking more in the back and I don't like that, even though it is more safe to go sideways. For my feeling the Fiat goes too much sideways, especially on gravel, where you cannot put down the power. It is interesting competing against Markku. I think the only time where he will always beat me is on stages with snow walls. Without walls I can be faster than he is, but if there are snow walls he is faster. That is the only time that I think he is faster. You know for me touching a snow wall is accident. He can go deliberately too fast into these corners, like all Scandinavian drivers. You could see this by his time at Col du Lautaret on the Monte Carlo: it was the only stage which had snow from start to end, with big snow banks. I like the Monte Carlo Rally, but I also like the Acropolis, as it was in 1977.

This year I hear it was too rough. I think that one of the biggest mistakes for organizers is to start thinking we make very very rough rallies and if only five cars come to finish that makes a good rally. I drive rallies because I want to go fast, not to prove that my car is the strongest. That does not demand skill from the driver. If there was only one rally that I make each year, I think that I would go to Monte Carlo. Five years ago I would have said this was a bad rally, but it gets better all the time. They have good stages. You can go flat out, you don't have to be careful for your car and on ice or snow you have this feeling like on sand that you can go sideways. What is best is that all of the stages are drivers' stages. I have been unlucky twice running at Monte Carlo, but maybe more so in 1978 because I was thinking that we would win easily. In 1979 it was good, but at the beginning I think that I was a little bit sleepy. I was thinking this was a long rally so it was better to take safe tyres and so forth. Only on the last night I was thinking to fight back. We were going so well, but then on the last stage without any warning the engine went 'bang'. In the last night of this year's Monte Carlo I think I was going as well as I have ever done.

On the Safari I was thinking that I would be so clever, I would slow down and avoid problems with the car. I was lying fifth, then 4, 3 and 2 — then five hours from the finish it all went wrong. To make it worse, Markku was third on both the Monte and Safari. Everybody said that he is clever, but I think he is also lucky. It upsets me if you see somebody who always has good luck over three or four years and others who do not. You look at his results over the last three years. He is the sort of person who goes off the road and hits nothing. For sure if I do it there is a big stone in the way! Of course you can do nothing without luck. Markku is a very good driver, he is natural, but often he is completely crazy. Maybe he is so nervous, but I know he could never make his results on rallies without Kivimaki. 'Kikki' is very clever, he makes all the decisions. This is very important for Markku.

I think my best co-driver was Jochen Berger. Jochen was not afraid of me like Christian or Willi-Peter Pitz. Jochen was working with me before a stage, suggesting which tyre I should use, he was helping me and saying we use this one. With all my other co-drivers I have to decide what we do or how often we practice; everything I must decide. All three have been excellent at reading notes, as good as perfect. This makes all the difference in the world. I am often asked what is my favourite car; this must be an Escort for me, though I don't know why because I have only driven one once, which was Reinhard Hainbach's. It was very good and I think that it has to be a very good rally car because it is very well designed. The other favourite is the Porsche. It is more difficult to drive a Porsche than an Opel or a Fiat or Lancia. Even though the Lancia is very nervous you have some reaction. With the Porsche it is more heavy so if it locks up it does it for a long time. If it is understeering then it is always understeering or if it is going sideways you go sideways a hundred miles. You cannot change the situation, since all Porsche rally cars are private. Perhaps if the factory would prepare them then they would make them better. The engine has the best torque and the power is the most of any rally car I have driven. The Opels were so good, incredibly good. It is competitive simply if you put in a strong engine and four shock absorbers. That is the reason why they have never done more development on the Kadetts. The base where you start is so high. With Fiat and Ford it is necessary to do so much more to make them go well.

The old Ascona was an excellent car because it was

THIS PAGE *Happy anniversary! A year after joining Fiat, Rohrl and Geistdorfer won the Criterium Quebec, their second WCR victory in 1978*

FACING PAGE *German championship rallies in 1978 were not tackled consistently, and he could not beat Reinhard Hainbach who contested them exclusively. When Rohrl appeared and managed to finish he usually won, as here at the Hunsruck*

Riccardo Patrese and Walter Rohrl pose with their new group 5 Lancia Beta Monte Carlo 1.4-litre turbo at a Silverstone test session

unbelievably strong with good handling. It is more difficult to drive a Fiat than Opel, but if something is difficult then if you do it perfectly it is best of all. I think that a Ford is easier to drive than a Fiat, because the engine has a greater range of revolutions. It was incredible to see the Fords in Monte Carlo. You would think that they had automatic gearboxes. They never changed gears when we changed three times in our Fiat. We have a much better gearbox with Fiat than with Ford, but the Ford engine seems the most important factor. We tried to improve traction by putting the co-driver in the back, but that was a big mistake. I had never tested the car, but Georgio Pianta was testing a lot with weights in the back. It is a question of how you drove; Georgio drives very fast and braking hard, turning the car and accelerating like a racing driver. I drive more smoothly and that was the big problem with the weight in the back. It was also very deceptive. On the first day on the RAC we thought we were going better than we were.

In Monte Carlo I tried it again with Christian, but compared with Markku, who was also out testing, it became obvious this was a mistake. We only had Christian at the back at St Auban. We decided to go with studded racing tyres. The only place where there was a lot of snow is over six hairpins near the finish. I was sure that in this car it might be much faster here so we had seats front and back. I told Christian to stay in front until we came to the hairpins, then he had to move back. We did it like this and he was sitting at the back at the finish. I don't know whether it was better or not.

One of the fascinations about rallying is the complete diversity of people and their attitudes. I am sure that when Hannu and Markku are at home they relax from rallying — they only think you are on top when you make money. I never think about making money, I do it just for fun. In the days of Rauno and Timo in the mid-sixties they made a lot of money, an incredible amount. Then the money went down and now it seems that it is getting up again, but it is always Scandinavians who get the most. They are like a little Mafia: every factory thinks it must employ them. I have no problems with Markku. Even after staying four or five years in Opel when I was number 1 driver and now I have to share everything, which was something which I was not used to. If you were working in a big factory or in every profession you have to fight for what you can get, but there are absolutely no problems with Markku. Markku and I do not talk about our conditions, but then I don't know if you can find any driver who will tell you everything. The easiest team-mates I have had were Kullang and Nicolas: they are completely straight in their dealings and easy to work with. I think that if I were a team chief I would never take two leading drivers like are now in Ford with Hannu and Bjorn, and the same in Fiat. That is no good. I am sure that it is much better that you have one who is very fast and the second one who can go fast but who does not always want to beat the first one. At the end of every special stage we ask each other what were our times. When we beat Markku he is always angry. So many times we have been fighting each other, which cannot be best for the team. It was like this in Canada in 1978: we were fighting like anything. It was like this at Monte Carlo this year.

For the future I wish people would realize it is quite wrong to think that rallies must be very rough. A driver likes to go fast. It is no fun to concentrate on being careful with the car. In Brazil for example all I could do was hope from the first stage until the final afternoon that I would reach the last stage. I think that the new World Championship for Drivers is right as it makes rallying more interesting. It gives the world a person who everybody has heard about and who is a name. If you have nobody famous in the sport then you have no interest at all.

Rodenstock
PIRELLI
VS CORSE
LANCIA

aylor

DAILY EXPRESS
Lockheed
FERODO
Minolta
parmalat
Benetton
LANCIA
PIRELLI
VS
OLIO FIAT
LANCIA BETA MONTECARLO

Saab's turbo rally car

'You must not forget that the engine is only one part of the complete system of the rally car. Stig must have a car in which the engine and the chassis and the suspension, in fact everything, work well together as a system. We do not use the turbo simply as a method of increasing the horsepower.' So spoke Borje Jarl, the resident engineer at Saab's competition department at Trollhättan. For him the use of the turbo engine is a matter of gradual adaptation; Blomqvist has already proved that Saab have a winning turbo car, even with power outputs which are still similar to their old 16-valve 99. But things are different, very different, when you use a turbocharger on a car, and a rally car in particular. A turbocharger is in no way a modern sort of 'bolt-on goody' beloved of enthusiasts in the sixties.

The turbo era came to Saab competitions a long time ago, back in 1972, when the 96 V4 model needed more power in rallycross. For rallycross few of the extreme conditions in rallying are encountered, so it is possible to use less compromising engines. It is far nearer track racing, where turbo units are used more for their power outputs than anything else. It was the expiry of permission to use the 16-valve cars within FIA group 4 which bought the turbo into their rally cars, however. At that time the Saab engine development department at Sodertalje had produced an experimental engine giving about 200 bhp, and this was sent to the competitions department for comparative testing with the 16-valve unit, and immediately it was found to make the car almost as quick as the existing rally car. So it was decided, not that the list of alternatives was very long, that this was the way to proceed. As if to emphasize the original statement by Jarl, even now after a year of competition and development, the power output of the turbo in rally version has only increased some 50 bhp or so.

The problems which have arisen come not from the engine itself but from the many ancillary parts around it. The manifolds have produced the most. The exhaust manifold made from original ordinary steel would disappear at temperatures over 720°C, and with turbo design, temperatures of towards 1000°C are required for optimum performance, or rather that

Team engineer — Borje Jarl at work in his office in the competition department at Trollhattan

The actual turbine, which measures only 160 mm from end to end and 64 mm in diameter. This spins at 150,000 rpm, can withstand temperatures up to 1050°C, and is lubricated by floating on films of oil

is the limit for operation of the turbine. The antidote for this has been nimonic material, but this in turn led to cracking and redesigning. Then the inlet manifold has been subjected to expansions and contractions, which caused their own cracking, which redesigning the shape has eliminated. Then of course the very presence of this sort of heat demands all sorts of shielding, the engine plugs have permanent metal plates around them, all pipes which might be affected are relocated, and so forth. But in fact, this preparation is normal for all turbo cars, not just the competition cars.

The rally cars use a larger compressor and turbine, but this is simply to cater for the greater air flow from the competition engine, rather than as a method of increasing the power itself. When considering the design of the turbocharger the compressor is considered first, to find how to put the correct amount of air into the engine for the horsepower sought. The speed of the turbine on the exhaust side depends on the pressure and temperature drop across the turbine, and the size and shape of the turbine wheel are selected to let the compressor produce the required airflow into the engine, without overspeeding the turbine unit. The other important objection is to avoid knocking. Compression ratios on turbo cars are far lower than normally aspirated engines; at the moment the Saab rally cars use 6.5:1, which permits the entry of air/fuel mixture at 1.6 atmospheres. If it were possible to go down to 6.0:1, for example, then 2.0 atmospheres would be usable, but then for rallying this would lead at the moment to other troubles, including a turbine that was too big for acceptable throttle response. Compression ratios are compromises. Bigger fuel injection units are used on the rally cars, the same K-Jetronic units as fitted to the 8-cylinder normally aspirated Porsche 928 model, in fact.

Throttle lag is the most widely known problem concerning competition turbo cars, and with such a high proportion of part-throttle running on rally cars, this is far more critical than in racing. Various ways are available to reduce this problem, like changing ignition timing and moving the injection butterflies nearer to the cylinder head itself. By reducing the ignition timing from 42° to 30°, for instance, it is possible to put more energy into the exhaust, which creates a higher temperature difference over the turbine. This particularly increases the turbine speed at low revs, which in turn produces better throttle response. Then again, by altering the valve timing, it is possible, by raising the period of overlap when both valves are open, to let more fuel pass into the exhaust, and this helps to keep up the exhaust temperatures. Too long a period of overlap, because of the high pressure in the exhaust system, will cause a backflow into the cylinder which will reduce the torque and power. Keeping the boost pressure high at all times is one of the demands of the rally driver, Stig having to adjust his style accordingly. Saab have an advantage with their front-wheel-drive cars, since their Scandinavian drivers

A turbocharged Saab 99 engine dismantled on a test bed. Note the concave pistons which help decrease the compression ratio, which currently runs at about 6.5:1

Rally car cylinder head showing the twin valves per cylinder, in contrast to the four-valve type used until the end of 1977 on international rallies

are used to left-foot braking, during which the accelerator pedal is held down for longer periods. This means that the turbo pressure is kept up longer. Saab, with such a great knowledge of gravel-road rallying, admit to knowing less about the demands of asphalt-road rallies, and suspect that Stig was having consciously to accelerate out of corners on the Circuit of Ireland earlier than he would have wished.

In another respect Saab are fortunate with front-wheel drive, since front-wheel-drive cars demand a smoother power at the wheels than rear-wheel drive, and this is something the turbocharger will offer. The front wheels must steer as well as propel, and sudden power can disturb the steering work of the tyres. For Saab it also means that the front-wheel drive must dictate the turbo specification and that selected settings and objectives with the Saab 99 Turbo design will not necessarily apply to turbo engines for rear-wheel-drive designs. But front-wheel drive leads to a pressing tyre design problem. Not only must the front tyres perform this double duty, but Saab 99s are one of the heaviest rally cars in existence, and moreover current Saab suspension theories require the majority of the weight to be placed over the front wheels. The use of

An old Saab 96 V4 engine fitted with a turbocharger for rallycross, in which form the engine gave about 200 bhp against 160 bhp for the normally aspirated engine. This type was first used in this form in 1972

Later specification engine fitted with 'current' exhaust system, with the turbocharger clearly seen in the foreground Archives

The old 16-valves engine, banished by the FIA changes in regulations at the end of 1977 though used occasionally in national Swedish rallies afterwards

Borje Jarl (left) studies the final tuning of the 99 Turbo rally car being prepared in Trollhattan before being taken to the South Swedish Rally

really large-section front tyres, even if they were freely available, would lead to unacceptably high steering forces for the driver, and to reduce this, work on a power steering system, like Lancia used on the Beta Coupé, is in hand. Use of tyres of too narrow a section created the puncture troubles which destroyed Blomqvist's hopes of a high position on the Welsh Rally. The emphasis at the front is brought about for two reasons: firstly, to make a sliding car more controllable, achieved by reducing the inertia of the tail swinging wide, and secondly to control the rear of the car when jumping. The danger of the rear suddenly rising wildly is very serious, for this can easily cause a dangerous accident if it is out of control. The rear suspension is given serious thought, so that Blomqvist can force the rear of the car to slide when required, and to use the stabilizers to hold the slide if desired. The days of wildly sliding rally cars have long gone.

Wastegate design is subject to special consideration in rallying. Whereas this by-pass mechanism on production Saabs is controlled by excessive exhaust pressure, on rally cars the valve will operate when the inlet pressure exceeds a specific maximum pressure, about 1.6 atmospheres. On production cars the valve will therefore be closed at low revs and part load, which offers good low revs torque, but for rally use it is better to have a flat torque curve, with low torque at low revs and high torque at high revs. The valve is operated by a simple rubber pipe, which on the Swedish Rally was damaged through injection faults on Eklund's car. Without this pipe, the wastegate failed to operate, the pressure rose too high, the engine started to knock and a piston failed.

Already a lot of conclusions about turbo rallying are becoming evident. The most impressive is the smooth nature of the power, which means that parts which would fail with equivalent power on normal engines can be used. Back in the Saab 96 V4 days it was evident in rallycross that an extra 40 bhp from a turbo did not create the expected problems. Of course the 16-valve 99 rally car needed a lot of strengthening: the gearbox, the driveshafts in particular, needed redesign work, but these parts are used on the Turbo and should still be good when eventually the power increases still further. The Saab shares with the Triumph TR7 V8 the distinction of having probably more torque than other rally cars, but the torque on the Triumph must create far more trouble, more shocks down the transmission line. Compared with an Escort, for instance, the Saab power is that much smoother and there is nothing like so much wheelspin or its accompanying snatching. A new sintered clutch has had to be designed by AP, but this is working well. The reason for this smoothness is the built-in delay before the power becomes effective.

The engine itself must be more capable of taking the extra power that a turbocharger produces. High revolutions destroy more engines than any other abuse, and with the turbo Stig uses fewer revs than during the old 16-valve days. With

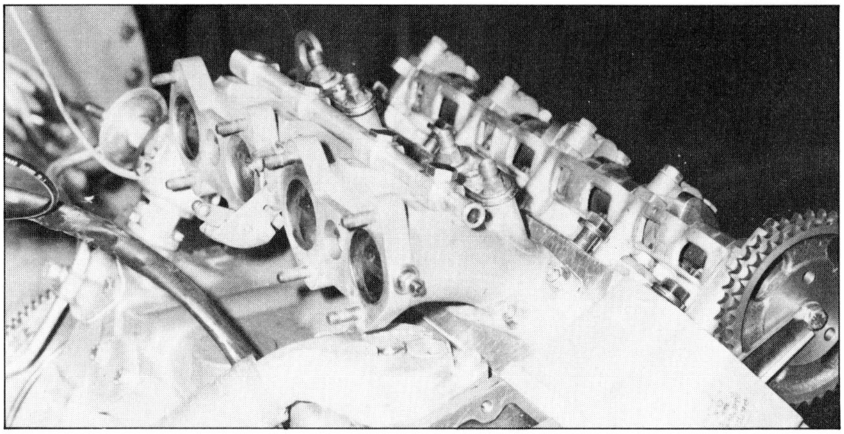

Rally car cylinderhead, showing the inlet manifold with the butterflies fitted as near as possible to the head itself, to help improve throttle response

Blomqvist on the 1978 RAC where, if nothing else the 99 Turbo showed a fine turn of speed being the fastest group 2 car. It retired with transmission problems

16 valves it was necessary to use 8500-9000 revs, with the turbo he only goes up to 8000, whilst the useful limit is only 7200 rpm. High revolutions damage valve gear and put intolerable loads on to the main bearings. Raising the boost level in itself creates nothing like the same trouble. Much more power is ultimately available with a turbocharger in a given engine than by any other system of modification. Getting more power is obviously the ultimate objective, but it is a very long job. At every step it is necessary to stop and consider whether the latest modification actually makes the car faster down the special stage, whether the driver still feels the car is as safe and therefore can drive with the same confidence, whether wheelspin is becoming intolerable and self-defeating and whether the extra power through the front wheels is destroying the cornering forces.

The exhaust manifold has gone through a series of changes in design, the latest shape being dictated as much through serviceability as anything. The old spaghetti system might have been better for power output, but the longer pipes gave more chance for the exhaust gases to cool, and anyway it caused too much trouble on actual rallies. That heat is needed to maintain low-speed horsepower and torque. Cold running is not a problem, for the turbine demands pressure, which depends on exhaust gas temperatures rather than the temperature of the manifold, and as soon as the fuel mixture is ignited it is hot. The quietness of the car has necessitated the fitment of an extra horn to warn spectators, but inside there is noise and vibration from the exhaust although even with the lack of carpeting creates no confusion in Blomqvist.

Only recently have Saab personnel realized just how lucky they had been back in the 96 days, when the car was competitive almost without effort. With the 99 they now have a competitive car once again, notwithstanding the change in the homologation rules at the end of 1977, which created the need for the competition turbo programme in the first place. But it has been a long, hard battle, far harder than any programme in the old 96 days. This might just be a reflection on the present professional state of rallying at the end of the seventies.

The 1979 rally cars

Here are details about the cars which are used by the official teams in international rallying. What constitutes an 'official' team is open to discussion, but we have included teams which are official in all except name — under which heading we include Alfa Romeo who compete through Autodelta and the Jolly Club, the dealer teams like DTV and DOT (Vauxhall and Opel respectively), and for comparative reasons Porsche and Lancia, even though their factories do not compete officially at the moment. Similarly we include Mercedes-Benz, whose degree of official participation is not clear. We have not included Lada/Vaz, whose cars represent their country rather than the manufacturer and are prepared outside the factory anyway, the smaller Eastern European cars or those companies which only compete nationally.

Several factors are arguable. We have selected normal power outputs for example, and since the track varies according to wheel sizes and off-sets we have taken standard measurements. The car's weight will also vary according to the standard of preparation, and is based on the standard rally car weighing system, that is with one spare wheel, full of oil, no occupants and no fuel. Furthermore the drivers' names are the usual team drivers and do not represent a complete record — nor indeed do they guarantee that the driver was still employed at the end of the season!

We are limited in the components we can usefully list because of the large variety of manufacturers and the likelihood of change from rally to rally. Various components are optional, for example, many cars have alternative ventilated rear disc brakes. Certain other features are also strictly limited, for instance the suspension — but then these are simply the same as those on standard production cars! We have not listed any group 1 cars as very few official group 1 (or group 3) cars are used in rallying, and anyway their specifications are not so interesting.

Alfa Romeo Alfetta GTV G2

TEAM

Driver *Pregliasco*
Address *Autodelta SpA, via Enrico Fermi 7, 20019 Settimo Milanese*
Chief Engineer *Marelli*
Team Manager, Chief Mechanic *Orofino*

ENGINE

No. cylinders *4 in line*
Cubic capacity cc *1962*
Bore×stroke mm *84×88.5*
Compression ratio *11.2:1*
Max. power bhp @ rpm *200 @ 7500*
Max. torque kgm @ rpm *22.3 @ 5000*
Carburation *2 Dell 'Orto 48*
No. of valves *8*
No. and position of cams *2 ohc*
Lubrication system *dry sump*

TRANSMISSION

Drive *rear*
Clutch type *1 plate*
No. forward gears *5*

BRAKES

Front, type and size *disc vented 255 mm*
Rear, type and size *disc 254 mm*

FRONT SUSPENSION

Type *wishbone, torsion bar*

REAR SUSPENSION

Type *De Dion*

STEERING

rack and pinion

SUPPLIERS

Oil *Agip*
Plugs *Champion*
Tyres *Pirelli*
Shock absorbers *Bilstein*
Ignition *Marelli*
Clutch *Fichtel and Sachs*
Brake friction material *Lockheed*

DIMENSIONS

Length mm *4153*
Width *1664*
Height *1334*
Wheelbase *2423*
Front track *1359*
Rear track *1367*
Weight kg *980*

DATE FIRST HOMOLOGATION AND NUMBER

1.2.76: 5622

DATE FIRST MAJOR RALLY

Corsica 1976

Audi 80 G4

TEAM

Drivers *Kottulinsky, Demuth*
Address *Ettinger Strasse, 8070 Ingolstadt, West Germany*
Chief Engineer *Stockmar*
Team Manager *Rode*
Chief Mechanic *Braun*

ENGINE

No. cylinders *4 in line*
Cubic capacity cc *1588*
Bore×stroke mm *79.5×80*
Compression ratio *11.2:1*
Max. power bhp @ rpm *160 @ 7600*
Max. torque kgm @ rpm *17.4 @ 6100*
Carburation *Bosch or Kugelfischer inj*
No. of valves *8*
No. and position of cams *1 ohc*
Lubrication system *dry sump*

TRANSMISSION

Drive *front*
Clutch type *1 plate*
No. forward gears *4*

BRAKES

Front, type and size *disc vented 241 mm*
Rear, type and size *drum 178 mm*

FRONT SUSPENSION

Type *McPherson*

REAR SUSPENSION

Type *dead, coil*

STEERING

rack and pinion

SUPPLIERS

Oil *Castrol*
Plugs *Bosch*
Tyres *Pirelli*
Shock absorbers *Boge*
Ignition *Bosch*
Clutch *Fichtel and Sachs*
Brake friction material *various*

DIMENSIONS

Length mm *4390*
Width *1760*
Height *1370*
Wheelbase *2541*
Front track *1430*
Rear track *1450*
Weight kg *930*

DATE FIRST HOMOLOGATION AND NUMBER

1.2.79: 659 (G4)

DATE FIRST MAJOR RALLY

Portugal 1979 (G4)

Chrysler Sunbeam G4

TEAM

Drivers *Pond, Nicolas*
Address *PO Box 25, Humber Road, Coventry, Warwicks, England*
Chief Engineer
Team Manager *O'Dell*
Chief Mechanic *Hughes*

ENGINE

No. cylinders *4 in line*
Cubic capacity cc *2174*
Bore×stroke mm *95.3×76.2*
Compression ratio *11.3:1*
Max. power bhp @ rpm *240 @ 7000*
Max. torque kgm @ rpm *25.6 @ 6000*
Carburation *2 Dell 'Orto 48*
No. of valves *16*
No. and position of cams *2 ohc*
Lubrication system *dry sump*

TRANSMISSION

Drive *rear*
Clutch type *1 plate*
No. forward gears *5*

BRAKES

Front, type and size *disc vented 268 mm*
Rear, type and size *disc 274 mm*

FRONT SUSPENSION

Type *McPherson*

REAR SUSPENSION

Type *live, coil*

STEERING

rack and pinion

SUPPLIERS

Oil *Shell*
Plugs *Champion*
Tyres *Dunlop*
Shock absorbers *Bilstein*
Ignition *Lucas*
Clutch *AP*
Brake friction material *various*

DIMENSIONS

Length mm *3830*
Width *1628*
Height *1395*
Wheelbase *2415*
Front track *1341*
Rear track *1328*
Weight kg *1015*

DATE FIRST HOMOLOGATION AND NUMBER

1.4.79: 662

DATE FIRST MAJOR RALLY

Mille Pistes 1978

Datsun 160J G2

TEAM

Drivers *Kallstrom, Salonen, Dawson*
Address *9 Denbigh Hall, Bletchley, Milton Keynes, Bucks, England*
Chief Engineer *Kudo*
Team Manager *Wakabyashi, Dawson*
Chief Mechanic *Blyth*

ENGINE

No. cylinders *4 in line*
Cubic capacity cc *1951*
Bore×stroke mm *75×76*
Compression ratio *11.2:1*
Max. power bhp @ rpm *195 @ 7200*
Max. torque kgm @ rpm *20 @ 5600*
Carburation *2 Solex 50*
No. of valves *8*
No. and position of cams *1 ohc*
Lubrication system *wet sump*

TRANSMISSION

Drive *rear*
Clutch type *1 plate*
No. forward gears *5*

BRAKES

Front, type and size *disc vented 254 mm*
Rear, type and size *drum 228 mm*

FRONT SUSPENSION

Type *McPherson*

REAR SUSPENSION

Type *live, coil*

STEERING

recirculating ball

SUPPLIERS

Oil *Castrol*
Plugs *NGK*
Tyres *Dunlop*
Shock absorbers *Tokico/Ampco*
Ignition *Nippondenso*
Clutch *Datsun*
Brake friction material *Ferodo*

DIMENSIONS

Length mm *4080*
Width *1600*
Height *547*
Wheelbase *2400*
Front track *1336*
Rear track *1331*
Weight kg *980*

DATE FIRST HOMOLOGATION AND NUMBER

1.1.78: 5684

DATE FIRST MAJOR RALLY

Safari 1978

Fiat Abarth 131 G4

TEAM

Drivers *Alen, Rohrl*
Address *Corso Marche 72, Torino, Italy*
Chief Engineer *Limone*
Team Manager *Audetto*
Chief Mechanic *Mowes*

ENGINE

No. cylinders *4 in line*
Cubic capacity cc *1995*
Bore×stroke mm *84×90*
Compression ratio *11:1*
Max. power bhp @ rpm *223 @ 7500*
Max. torque kgm @ rpm *23 @ 5750*
Carburation *Kugelfischer inj*
No. of valves *16*
No. and position of cams *2 ohc*
Lubrication system *dry sump*

TRANSMISSION

Drive *rear*
Clutch type *1 plate*
No. forward gears *5*

BRAKES

Front, type and size *disc vented 300 mm*
Rear, type and size *disc 252 mm*

FRONT SUSPENSION

Type *McPherson*

REAR SUSPENSION

Type *McPherson, wishbone*

STEERING

rack and pinion

SUPPLIERS

Oil *Olio Fiat*
Plugs *Champion*
Tyres *Pirelli*
Shock absorbers *Bilstein*
Ignition *Marelli*
Clutch *Valeo*
Brake friction material *Ferodo*

DIMENSIONS

Length mm *4158*
Width *1720*
Height *1385*
Wheelbase *2490*
Front track *1520*
Rear track *1490*
Weight kg *950-1020*

DATE FIRST HOMOLOGATION AND NUMBER

1.4.76: 647

DATE FIRST MAJOR RALLY

Elba 1976

Fiat Ritmo G2

TEAM

Driver *Bettega*
Address *Corso Marche 72, Torino, Italy*
Chief Engineer *Limone*
Team Manager *Audetto*
Chief Mechanic *Mowes*

ENGINE

No. cylinders *4 in line, transverse*
Cubic capacity cc *1498*
Bore×stroke mm *86.4×63.9*
Compression ratio *11:1*
Max. power bhp @ rpm *165 @ 7600*
Max. torque kgm @ rpm *17 @ 5600*
Carburation *Kugelfischer inj*
No. of valves *8*
No. and position of cams *1 ohc*
Lubrication system *wet sump*

TRANSMISSION

Drive *front*
Clutch type *1 plate*
No. forward gears *5*

BRAKES

Front, type and size *disc vented 243 mm*
Rear, type and size *disc 227 mm*

FRONT SUSPENSION

Type *McPherson*

REAR SUSPENSION

Type *McPherson, transverse leaf*

STEERING

rack and pinion

SUPPLIERS

Oil *Olio Fiat*
Plugs *Champion*
Tyres *Pirelli*
Shock absorbers *Bilstein*
Ignition *Marelli*
Clutch *Fichtel and Sachs*
Brake friction material *Ferodo*

DIMENSIONS

Length mm *3937*
Width *1747*
Height *1375*
Wheelbase *2450*
Front track *1400*
Rear track *1410*
Weight kg *800-840*

DATE FIRST HOMOLOGATION AND NUMBER

1.10.78: 5716

DATE FIRST MAJOR RALLY

Giro d'Italia 1978

Ford Escort RS G4

TEAM

Drivers *Waldegard, Mikkola, Vatanen*
Address *The Airfield, Boreham, Nr Chelmsford, Essex, England*
Chief Engineer *Wilkinson*
Team Manager *Ashcroft*
Chief Mechanic *Jones*

ENGINE

No. cylinders *4 in line*
Cubic capacity cc *1992*
Bore×stroke mm *90.4×77.6*
Compression ratio *11.6:1*
Max. power bhp @ rpm *260 @ 8400*
Max. torque kgm @ rpm *23.3 @ 7000*
Carburation *Kugelfischer inj or 2 Weber 48*
No. of valves *16*
No. and position of cams *2 ohc*
Lubrication system *dry sump*

TRANSMISSION

Drive *rear*
Clutch type *1 or 2 plate*
No. forward gears *5*

BRAKES

Front, type and size *disc vented 260 mm*
Rear, type and size *disc 260 mm*

FRONT SUSPENSION

Type *McPherson*

REAR SUSPENSION

Type *live, leaf*

STEERING

rack and pinion

SUPPLIERS

Oil *Shell/Castrol*
Plugs *Motorcraft*
Tyres *Dunlop*
Shock absorbers *Bilstein*
Ignition *Lucas*
Clutch *AP*
Brake friction material *various*

DIMENSIONS

Length mm *3978*
Width *1700*
Height *1300*
Wheelbase *2407*
Front track *1325*
Rear track *1340*
Weight kg *980*

DATE FIRST HOMOLOGATION AND NUMBER

1.4.77: 650

DATE FIRST MAJOR RALLY

1st rally as RS1800: Granite City 1975

Ford Fiesta 1600 G2

TEAM

Driver *Clark*
Address *The Airfield, Boreham, Nr Chelmsford, Essex, England*
Chief Engineer *Griffiths*
Team Manager *Ashcroft, Reynolds*
Chief Mechanic *Jones*

ENGINE

No. cylinders *4 in line, transverse*
Cubic capacity cc *1592*
Bore×stroke mm 80.9×77.6
Compression ratio *11.5:1*
Max. power bhp @ rpm *150 @ 7500*
Max. torque kgm @ rpm *172 @ 550*
Carburation *2 Weber 45*
No. of valves *8*
No. and position of cams *1 pushrod*
Lubrication system *dry sump*

TRANSMISSION

Drive *front*
Clutch type *1 plate*
No. forward gears *4*

BRAKES

Front, type and size *disc vented 266 mm*
Rear, type and size *disc 247 mm*

FRONT SUSPENSION

Type *McPherson*

REAR SUSPENSION

Type *dead, trailing arm, coil*

STEERING

rack and pinion

SUPPLIERS

Oil *Esso*
Plugs *Motorcraft*
Tyres *Dunlop*
Shock absorbers *Bilstein*
Ignition *Lucas*
Clutch *AP*
Brake friction material *various*

DIMENSIONS

Length mm *3750*
Width *1567*
Height *1360*
Wheelbase *2286*
Front track *1334*
Rear track *1321*
Weight kg *775-800*

DATE FIRST HOMOLOGATION AND NUMBER

1.5.77: 1686

DATE FIRST MAJOR RALLY

Monte Carlo 1979

Lancia Stratos G4

TEAM

Drivers
Address
Chief Engineer *No official factory entries*
Team Manager
Chief Mechanic

ENGINE

No. cylinders *V6 transverse*
Cubic capacity cc *2418*
Bore×stroke mm *92.5×60*
Compression ratio *9.5:1*
Max. power bhp @ rpm *260 @ 7800*
Max. torque kgm @ rpm *27.5 @ 6000*
Carburation *3 Weber 48 or Kugelfischer*
No. of valves *12*
No. and position of cams *2 ohc*
Lubrication system *dry sump*

TRANSMISSION

Drive *rear*
Clutch type *2 plate*
No. forward gears *5*

BRAKES

Front, type and size *disc vented 304 mm*
Rear, type and size *disc vented 304 mm*

FRONT SUSPENSION

Type *wishbone, coil*

REAR SUSPENSION

Type *McPherson*

STEERING

rack and pinion

SUPPLIERS

Oil
Plugs
Tyres
Shock absorbers *No official participation*
Ignition
Clutch
Brake friction material

DIMENSIONS

Length mm *3710*
Width *1750*
Height *1110*
Wheelbase *2180*
Front track *1430*
Rear track *1460*
Weight kg *960*

DATE FIRST HOMOLOGATION AND NUMBER

1.10.74: 640

DATE FIRST MAJOR RALLY

San Remo 1974

Mercedes-Benz 280E G2

TEAM

Drivers
Address
Chief Engineer *No official factory entries*
Team Manager
Chief Mechanic

ENGINE

No. cylinders *6 in line*
Cubic capacity cc *2746*
Bore×stroke mm *86×78.8*
Compression ratio *9:1*
Max. power bhp @ rpm *200 @ 6000*
Max. torque kgm @ rpm *25.5 @ 5000*
Carburation *Bosch inj*
No. of valves *12*
No. and position of cams *2 ohc*
Lubrication system *wet sump*

TRANSMISSION

Drive *rear*
Clutch type *1 plate*
No. forward gears *4*

BRAKES

Front, type and size *disc vented 278 mm*
Rear, type and size *disc vented 279 mm*

FRONT SUSPENSION

Type *wishbone, coil*

REAR SUSPENSION

Type *independent, semi-trailing, coil*

STEERING

power-assisted recirculating ball

SUPPLIERS

Oil
Plugs *Bosch*
Tyres *Dunlop*
Shock absorbers *Bilstein*
Ignition *Bosch*
Clutch *Fichtel and Sachs*
Brake friction material *various*

DIMENSIONS

Length mm *4725*
Width *1780*
Height *1438*
Wheelbase *2795*
Front track *1446*
Rear track *1445*
Weight kg *1395*

DATE FIRST HOMOLOGATION AND NUMBER

1.7.76: 5633

DATE FIRST MAJOR RALLY

London to Sydney 1977

Mercedes-Benz 450SLC 5.0 G4

TEAM

Drivers
Address
Chief Engineer *No official factory entries*
Team Manager
Chief Mechanic

ENGINE

No. cylinders *V8*
Cubic capacity cc *5025*
Bore×stroke mm *97×85*
Compression ratio *8.8:1*
Max. power bhp @ rpm *c. 300 @ 5400*
Max. torque kgm @ rpm *43 @ 4000*
Carburation *Bosch inj*
No. of valves *16*
No. and position of cams *2 ohc*
Lubrication system *wet sump*

TRANSMISSION

Drive *rear*
Clutch type *automatic hydraulic torque converter*
No. forward gears *3*

BRAKES

Front, type and size *disc vented 278 mm*
Rear, type and size *disc vented 279 mm*

FRONT SUSPENSION

Type *wishbone, coil*

REAR SUSPENSION

Type *independent, semi-trailing, coil*

STEERING

power assisted recirculating ball

SUPPLIERS

Oil
Plugs *Bosch*
Tyres *Dunlop*
Shock absorbers *Bilstein*
Ignition *Bosch*
Clutch —
Brake friction material *various*

DIMENSIONS

Length mm *4750*
Width *1750*
Height *1331*
Wheelbase *2815*
Front track *1452*
Rear track *1440*
Weight kg *1430*

DATE FIRST HOMOLOGATION AND NUMBER

1.4.79: 661

DATE FIRST MAJOR RALLY

Safari 1979

Opel Ascona G2

TEAM

Driver *Kleint*
Address *Elisabethstrasse, 6090 Russelsheim, West Germany*
Chief Engineer *Koch*
Team Manager *Fall*
Chief Mechanic *Meuer*

ENGINE

No. cylinders *4 in line*
Cubic capacity cc *1996*
Bore×stroke mm *95.4×69.8*
Compression ratio *11.5:1*
Max. power bhp @ rpm *185 @ 7100*
Max. torque kgm @ rpm *21 @ 5500*
Carburation *2 Weber 48*
No. of valves *8*
No. and position of cams *1 ohc*
Lubrication system *wet sump*

TRANSMISSION

Drive *rear*
Clutch type *1 plate*
No. forward gears *5*

BRAKES

Front, type and size *disc vented 256 mm*
Rear, type and size *disc 253 mm*

FRONT SUSPENSION

Type *wishbone, coil*

REAR SUSPENSION

Type *live, coil*

STEERING

rack and pinion

SUPPLIERS

Oil *Mobil*
Plugs *Bosch*
Tyres *Pirelli*
Shock absorbers *Bilstein*
Ignition *Bosch*
Clutch *Fichtel and Sachs*
Brake friction material *Ferodo*

DIMENSIONS

Length mm *4321*
Width *1659*
Height *1380*
Wheelbase *2518*
Front track *1375*
Rear track *1375*
Weight kg *1000*

DATE FIRST HOMOLOGATION AND NUMBER

1.1.76: 5612

DATE FIRST MAJOR RALLY

Boucles de Spa 1979

Opel Kadett GT/E — G2

TEAM

Driver *Kleint*
Address *Elisabethstrasse, 6090 Russelsheim, West Germany*
Chief Engineer *Koch*
Team Manager *Fall*
Chief Mechanic *Meuer*

ENGINE

No. cylinders *4 in line*
Cubic capacity cc *1996*
Bore×stroke mm *95.4×69.8*
Compression ratio *11.5:1*
Max. power bhp @ rpm *185 @ 7100*
Max. torque kgm @ rpm *21 @ 5500*
Carburation *2 Weber 48*
No. of valves *8*
No. and position of cams *1 ohc*
Lubrication system *wet sump*

TRANSMISSION

Drive *rear*
Clutch type *1 plate*
No. forward gears *5*

BRAKES

Front, type and size *disc vented 245 mm*
Rear, type and size *drum 230 mm*

FRONT SUSPENSION

Type *wishbone, coil*

REAR SUSPENSION

Type *live, coil*

STEERING

rack and pinion

SUPPLIERS

Oil *Mobil*
Plugs *Bosch*
Tyres *Pirelli*
Shock absorbers *Bilstein*
Ignition *Bosch*
Clutch *Fichtel and Sachs*
Brake friction material *Ferodo*

DIMENSIONS

Length mm *4124*
Width *1590*
Height *1335*
Wheelbase *2395*
Front track *1318*
Rear track *1314*
Weight kg *950*

DATE FIRST HOMOLOGATION AND NUMBER

1.2.76: 5624

DATE FIRST MAJOR RALLY

San Remo 1975 (G4)

Peugeot 104ZS — G2

TEAM

Drivers *Lefebvre*
Address *CES Essais-Rallye, Belchamp BP50, 25200 Montbeliard, France*
Chief Engineer *Calviac*
Team Manager *Charavay*
Chief Mechanic *Meynet*

ENGINE

No. cylinders *4 in line, transverse*
Cubic capacity cc *1124*
Bore×stroke mm *72×69*
Compression ratio *11.0:1*
Max. power bhp @ rpm *106 @ 7500*
Max. torque kgm @ rpm *11.5 @ 6000*
Carburation *2 Weber 40*
No. of valves *8*
No. and position of cams *1 ohc*
Lubrication system *wet sump*

TRANSMISSION

Drive *front*
Clutch type *1 plate*
No. forward gears *4*

BRAKES

Front, type and size *disc 241 mm*
Rear, type and size *drum 180 mm*

FRONT SUSPENSION

Type *McPherson*

REAR SUSPENSION

Type *independent trailing arm, coil*

STEERING

rack and pinion

SUPPLIERS

Oil *Esso*
Plugs *Champion*
Tyres *Michelin*
Shock absorbers *Peugeot*
Ignition *Ducellier*
Clutch *Verto*
Brake friction material *Ferodo*

DIMENSIONS

Length mm *2360*
Width *1520*
Height *1340*
Wheelbase *2230*
Front track *1290*
Rear track *1240*
Weight kg *740*

DATE FIRST HOMOLOGATION AND NUMBER

1.6.75: 5613

DATE FIRST MAJOR RALLY

Tour de Corse 1976

Peugeot 504 V6 Coupé — G4

TEAM

Drivers *Nicholas, Makinen, Lampinen*
Address *CES Essais-Rallye, Belchamp BP50, 25200 Montbeliard, France*
Chief Engineer *Calviac*
Team Manager *Charavay*
Chief Mechanic *Meynet*

ENGINE

No. cylinders *V6*
Cubic capacity cc *2664*
Bore×stroke mm *88×73*
Compression ratio *9.8:1*
Max. power bhp @ rpm *225 @ 7200*
Max. torque kgm @ rpm *24.5 @ 3500*
Carburation *3 Weber 48*
No. of valves *8*
No. and position of cams *1 ohc*
Lubrication system *wet sump*

TRANSMISSION

Drive *rear*
Clutch type *1 plate*
No. forward gears *4 or 5*

BRAKES

Front, type and size *disc vented 273 mm*
Rear, type and size *disc 273 mm*

FRONT SUSPENSION

Type *McPherson*

REAR SUSPENSION

Type *McPherson*

STEERING

rack and pinion

SUPPLIERS

Oil *Esso*
Plugs *Champion*
Tyres *Michelin*
Shock absorbers *Peugeot*
Ignition *Bosch*
Clutch *Verto*
Brake friction material *Ferodo*

DIMENSIONS

Length mm *4360*
Width *1700*
Height *1350*
Wheelbase *2530*
Front track *1490*
Rear track *1430*
Weight kg *1350*

DATE FIRST HOMOLOGATION AND NUMBER

1.7.75: 3069

DATE FIRST MAJOR RALLY

Safari 1976

Polski Fiat Polonez G4

TEAM

Drivers *Jaroszewicz, Groblewski, Stawowiak*
Address *Al Waszyngtona 50, 03-910 Warszawa, Poland*
Chief Engineer *Rogalski*
Team Manager *Bartos*
Chief Mechanic *Ryzel*

ENGINE

No. cylinders *4 in line*
Cubic capacity cc *1995*
Bore×stroke mm *84×90*
Compression ratio *10.5:1*
Max. power bhp @ rpm *170 @ 7100*
Max. torque kgm @ rpm *24.3 @ 5000*
Carburation *2 Weber 45*
No. of valves *8*
No. and position of cams *2 ohc*
Lubrication system *wet sump*

TRANSMISSION

Drive *rear*
Clutch type *1 plate*
No. forward gears *5*

BRAKES

Front, type and size *disc vented 270 mm*
Rear, type and size *disc 227 mm*

FRONT SUSPENSION

Type *wishbone, coil*

REAR SUSPENSION

Type *live, leaf*

STEERING

worm and peg

SUPPLIERS

Oil *Castrol*
Plugs *Champion*
Tyres *Michelin*
Shock absorbers *Bilstein*
Ignition *Marelli*
Clutch *Polski-Fiat*
Brake friction material *Textar*

DIMENSIONS

Length mm *4272*
Width *1651*
Height *1367*
Wheelbase *2509*
Front track *1314*
Rear track *1292*
Weight kg *1140*

DATE FIRST HOMOLOGATION AND NUMBER

1.1.79: 657

DATE FIRST MAJOR RALLY

Monte Carlo 1979

Porsche 911 G4

TEAM

Drivers
Address
Chief Engineer *No official factory entries*
Team Manager
Chief Mechanic

ENGINE

No. cylinders *flat 6, rear*
Cubic capacity cc *2994*
Bore×stroke mm *95×70.4*
Compression ratio *10.8:1*
Max. power bhp @ rpm *260 @ 6800*
Max. torque kgm @ rpm *32 @ 5000*
Carburation *Bosch inj*
No. of valves *12*
No. and position of cams *1 ohc per bank*
Lubrication system *dry sump*

TRANSMISSION

Drive *rear*
Clutch type *1 plate*
No. forward gears *5*

BRAKES

Front, type and size *disc vented 300 mm*
Rear, type and size *disc vented 300 mm*

FRONT SUSPENSION

Type *McPherson*

REAR SUSPENSION

Type *semi-trailing arm, torsion bar*

STEERING

rack and pinion

SUPPLIERS

Oil
Plugs
Tyres
Shock absorbers *No official participation*
Ignition
Clutch
Brake friction material

DIMENSIONS

Length mm *4235*
Width *1778*
Height *1300*
Wheelbase *2271*
Front track *1437*
Rear track *1462*
Weight kg *960*

DATE FIRST HOMOLOGATION AND NUMBER

1.3.73: 3053

DATE FIRST MAJOR RALLY

Corsica 1972 (G5)

Renault 5 Alpine G2

TEAM

Drivers *Frequelin, Ragnotti*
Address *34 Quai du Point du Jour, 92109 Boulogne Billancourt, France*
Chief Engineer *Tetu*
Team Manager *Larrousse*
Chief Mechanic *Santoni*

ENGINE

No. cylinders *4 in line*
Cubic capacity cc *1397*
Bore×stroke mm *76:77*
Compression ratio *11.3:1*
Max. power bhp @ rpm *137 @ 7000*
Max. torque kgm @ rpm *15.8 @ 4500*
Carburation *2 Weber 45*
No. of valves *8*
No. and position of cams *1 pushrod*
Lubrication system *wet sump*

TRANSMISSION

Drive *front*
Clutch type *1 plate*
No. forward gears *5*

BRAKES

Front, type and size *disc vented 228 mm*
Rear, type and size *disc 228 mm*

FRONT SUSPENSION

Type *wishbone, torsion bar*

REAR SUSPENSION

Type *trailing arm, torsion bar*

STEERING

rack and pinion

SUPPLIERS

Oil *Elf*
Plugs *Champion*
Tyres *Michelin*
Shock absorbers *Bilstein or De Carbon*
Ignition *Marelli*
Clutch *Borg and Beck*
Brake friction material *Ferodo*

DIMENSIONS

Length mm *3550*
Width *1620*
Height *1340*
Wheelbase *2410R/2440L*
Front track *1320*
Rear track *1290*
Weight kg *800*

DATE FIRST HOMOLOGATION AND NUMBER

1.8.76: 5650

DATE FIRST MAJOR RALLY

Mille Pistes 1977

Saab 99 Turbo G2

TEAM

Drivers *Blomqvist*
Address *46180 Trollhattan, Sweden*
Chief Engineer *Jarl*
Team Manager *Swaner*
Chief Mechanic

ENGINE

No. cylinders *4 in line, turbo*
Cubic capacity cc *1985/2780*
Bore×stroke mm *90.0×78.0*
Compression ratio *6.5:1*
Max. power bhp @ rpm *250 @ 6000 (0.6 boost)*
Max. torque kgm @ rpm *34.0 @ 5000*
Carburation *Bosch inj*
No. of valves *8*
No. and position of cams *1 ohc*
Lubrication system *wet sump*

TRANSMISSION

Drive *front*
Clutch type *1 plate*
No. forward gears *4*

BRAKES

Front, type and size *disc 279 mm*
Rear, type and size *disc 266 mm*

FRONT SUSPENSION

Type *wishbone, coil*

REAR SUSPENSION

Type *dead, coil*

STEERING

rack and pinion

SUPPLIERS

Oil *Castrol*
Plugs *Bosch*
Tyres *Dunlop*
Shock absorbers *Bilstein*
Ignition *Bosch*
Clutch *AP*
Brake friction material *various*

DIMENSIONS

Length mm *4385*
Width *1690*
Height *1435*
Wheelbase *2475*
Front track *1410*
Rear track *1440*
Weight kg *1100 (G2), 1080 (G4)*

DATE FIRST HOMOLOGATION AND NUMBER

1.2.79: 658

DATE FIRST MAJOR RALLY

RAC 1978 (3 door model)

Skoda 130RS G2

TEAM

Drivers *Kvaizar, Blahna, Sedivy*
Address *AZNP Mlada Boleslav, Czechoslovakia*
Chief Engineer *Hnatevic*
Team Manager *Vlebny*
Chief Mechanic *Budin*

ENGINE

No. cylinders *4 in line, rear*
Cubic capacity cc *1288*
Bore×stroke mm *75.5×72*
Compression ratio *10.5:1*
Max. power bhp @ rpm *125 @ 7500*
Max. torque kgm @ rpm *11.5 @ 6000*
Carburation *2 Weber 40*
No. of valves *8*
No. and position of cams *pushrod*
Lubrication system *dry sump*

TRANSMISSION

Drive *rear*
Clutch type *1 plate*
No. forward gears *4*

BRAKES

Front, type and size *disc 247 mm*
Rear, type and size *drum 230 mm*

FRONT SUSPENSION

Type *wishbone*

REAR SUSPENSION

Type *wishbone*

STEERING

worm and peg

SUPPLIERS

Oil *Castrol*
Plugs *Champion*
Tyres *Barum*
Shock absorbers *Bilstein*
Ignition *Bosch*
Clutch *Ferodo*
Brake friction material *Ferodo*

DIMENSIONS

Length mm *4255*
Width *1710*
Height *1340*
Wheelbase *2400*
Front track *1415*
Rear track *1368*
Weight kg *850*

DATE FIRST HOMOLOGATION AND NUMBER

1.6.76: 1676

DATE FIRST MAJOR RALLY

Skoda 1976

Toyota Celica RA40 G2

TEAM

Drivers *Andersson, Warmbold, Therier*
Address *Bachemer Landstrasse, 5000 Koln 40, West Germany*
Chief Engineer
Team Manager *Andersson*
Chief Mechanic *Wessman*

ENGINE

No. cylinders *4 in line*
Cubic capacity cc *1998*
Bore×stroke mm *89×80*
Compression ratio *11.5:1*
Max. power bhp @ rpm *180 @ 7300*
Max. torque kgm @ rpm *21.5 @ 5500*
Carburation *Nippondenso inj*
No. of valves *8*
No. and position of cams *2 ohc*
Lubrication system *dry sump*

TRANSMISSION

Drive *rear*
Clutch type *1 plate*
No. forward gears *5*

BRAKES

Front, type and size *discs vented 266 mm*
Rear, type and size *disc 254 mm*

FRONT SUSPENSION

Type *McPherson*

REAR SUSPENSION

Type *live, coil*

STEERING

recirculating ball

SUPPLIERS

Oil *Castrol*
Plugs *Nippondenso*
Tyres *Pirelli*
Shock absorbers *Bilstein*
Ignition *Nippondenso*
Clutch *Fichtel and Sachs*
Brake friction material *Ferodo*

DIMENSIONS

Length mm *4330*
Width *1635*
Height *1320*
Wheelbase *2500*
Front track *1350*
Rear track *1365*
Weight kg *1000*

DATE FIRST HOMOLOGATION AND NUMBER

1.5.79: 5702

DATE FIRST MAJOR RALLY

1000 Lakes 1978

Triumph TR7V8 (TR8) G4

TEAM

Drivers *Elsmore, Eklund, Lampinen*
Address *Abingdon-on-Thames, Oxon, England*
Chief Engineer *Wood*
Team Manager *Davenport*
Chief Mechanic *Price*

ENGINE

No. cylinders *V8*
Cubic capacity cc *3492*
Bore×stroke mm *88.2×71.1*
Compression ratio *10.7:1*
Max. power bhp @ rpm *285 @ 7500*
Max. torque kgm @ rpm *34.0 @ 5500*
Carburation *2 Weber 45*
No. of valves *16*
No. and position of cams *1 pushrod*
Lubrication system *dry sump*

TRANSMISSION

Drive *rear*
Clutch type *1 plate*
No. forward gears *5*

BRAKES

Front, type and size *disc vented 266 mm*
Rear, type and size *disc 266 mm*

FRONT SUSPENSION

Type *McPherson*

REAR SUSPENSION

Type *live, coil*

STEERING

rack and pinion

SUPPLIERS

Oil *Castrol*
Plugs *Champion*
Tyres *Dunlop*
Shock absorbers *Bilstein*
Ignition *Lucas*
Clutch *AP*
Brake friction material *various*

DIMENSIONS

Length mm *4060*
Width *1680*
Height *1270*
Wheelbase *2150*
Front track *1409*
Rear track *1404*
Weight kg *1070*

DATE FIRST HOMOLOGATION AND NUMBER

1.4.78: 654

DATE FIRST MAJOR RALLY

Granite City 1978

Vauxhall Chevette 2300HS G4

TEAM

Drivers *Airikkala, McRae*
Address *Station Works, Shepreth, Nr Royston, Herts, England*
Chief Engineer
Team Manager *Johnstone*
Chief Mechanic *Hall*

ENGINE

No. cylinders *4 in line*
Cubic capacity cc *2279*
Bore×stroke mm *97.5×76.2*
Compression ratio *11.5:1*
Max. power bhp @ rpm *240 @ 7200*
Max. torque kgm @ rpm *25.6 @ 6000*
Carburation *2 Dell 'Orto 48*
No. of valves *16*
No. and position of cams *2 ohc*
Lubrication system *dry sump*

TRANSMISSION

Drive *rear*
Clutch type *1 plate*
No. forward gears *5*

BRAKES

Front, type and size *disc vented 257 mm*
Rear, type and size *disc 263 mm*

FRONT SUSPENSION

Type *wishbone, coil*

REAR SUSPENSION

Type *trailing arm, coil*

STEERING

rack and pinion

SUPPLIERS

Oil *Castrol*
Plugs *Champion*
Tyres *Dunlop*
Shock absorbers *Bilstein*
Ignition *Lucas*
Clutch *AP*
Brake friction material *Mintex or Ferodo*

DIMENSIONS

Length mm *3940*
Width *1571*
Height *1371*
Wheelbase *2395*
Front track *1340*
Rear track *1346*
Weight kg *1000*

DATE FIRST HOMOLOGATION AND NUMBER

1.11.76: 649

DATE FIRST MAJOR RALLY

RAC 1976

VW Golf GTi G2

TEAM

Driver *Bohne*
Address *1 Karusallee 34, 3000 Hannover 1, West Germany*
Chief Engineer *Hansch*
Team Manager
Chief Mechanic *Burckhardt*

ENGINE

No. cylinders *4 in line, transverse*
Cubic capacity cc *1598*
Bore×stroke mm *79.5×80*
Compression ratio *11.0:1*
Max. power bhp @ rpm *168 @ 7200*
Max. torque kgm @ rpm *18.1 @ 6000*
Carburation *Zenith inj*
No. of valves *8*
No. and position of cams *1 ohc*
Lubrication system *wet sump*

TRANSMISSION

Drive *front*
Clutch type *1 plate*
No. forward gears *4*

BRAKES

Front, type and size *disc vented 239 mm*
Rear, type and size *disc 239 mm*

FRONT SUSPENSION

Type *McPherson*

REAR SUSPENSION

Type *trailing arm, coil*

STEERING

rack and pinion

SUPPLIERS

Oil *Castrol*
Plugs *Bosch*
Tyres *Pirelli*
Shock absorbers *Bilstein*
Ignition *Bosch*
Clutch *Fichtel and Sachs*
Brake friction material *various*

DIMENSIONS

Length mm *3710*
Width *1630*
Height *1390*
Wheelbase *2400*
Front track *1404*
Rear track *1372*
Weight kg *785*

DATE FIRST HOMOLOGATION AND NUMBER

1.1.75: 5731

DATE FIRST MAJOR RALLY

Sachs Winter 1975

World-class drivers

In 1979 the system for Priority A and Priority B seeding remained the same, the requirements for Priority A qualification being results obtained in World Championship rallies, or in the European Championship itself, and for Priority B being according to selection by the national motor sport authorities. In the case of A-priority drivers the qualification starts from the moment when the result is announced through to the end of the following (or the end of the third following) season. Priority continues until a subsequent FIA list is published in which a name no longer appears, which explains the presence here of Andersson, Danielsson, Lampinen, 'Tony', Vatanen and Zanini, whose priority should have expired in December 1978. Their names were mistakenly included in the official list at the start of the 1979 season though Andersson and Vatanen soon earned their status through good WCR results. More countries selected drivers for 1979, twenty-nine instead of twenty the year before. Increasingly this recognition serves to help the drivers in their reception by organizers of foreign rallies, over and above the initial assurance of priority in the starting order of the event. This year, Great Britain nominated Tony Pond, who previously had been on the A list, Andrew Cowan (in recognition of his incredible success in long-distance events) and John Taylor, who has entered overseas events on occasions and who was overall winner of the 1978 Tarmac Championship of rallies in Britain and Ireland.

We have included all drivers officially on the Priority A list at the end of July 1979, or who have earned their inclusion by results at that date. We have only listed results obtained by the end of the 1978 season although we have updated the 'Date of expiry of Priority' according to results achieved in the first part of 1979.

This year we have listed drivers' results according to the status of the events. Although the World Championship only began officially in 1973, in the section 'Results WCR' we have included the European Manufacturers' series of 1968 and 1969 together with the International Manufacturers' series of 1970, 1971 and 1972.

Priority A drivers

Aaltonen, Airikkala, Alen, Andersson, Andruet, Bacchelli, Blomqvist, Brookes, Carello, Clark, Danielsson, Darniche, Eklund, Frequelin, Hamalainen, Kallstrom, Kullang, Lampinen, Makinen, Mehta, Mikkola, Mouton, Munari, Nicolas, Preston, Ragnotti, Robson, Rohrl, Salonen, Singh, Staepelaere, 'Tony' (Fassina), Vatanen, Verini, Vincent, Waldegard, Wittmann, Zanini

Priority B drivers (in country and driver alphabetical order)

Australia AUS Colin Bond, Greg Carr, Ross Dunkerton
Austria A Georg Fischer, Josef Haider, †Wolfgang Sulc
Belgium B Guy Colsoul, 'Didi', Jean-Louis Dumont
Brazil BR Carlos Farina, Mario Figueiredo, Christian Nygaard
Bulgaria BG Stefan Kolev, Radoslav Petkov, Ilia Tchubrikov
Canada CDN Andy Flakiewicz, Taisto Heinonen, Jean-Paul Perusse
Cyprus CY Alkis Kirmitsis, Kypros Kyprianou, Lefteris Makrides
Denmark DK Jens-Ole Kristiansen, Jan Mortensen, Ole Pallesen
Finland SF Erkki Pitkanen, Markku Saaristo, Henri Toivonen
France F Jean-Louis Clarr, Jean-Claude Lefebvre, Jean-Luc Therier
Great Britain GB Andy Cowan, Tony Pond, John Taylor
Greece GR Evangelo Gallo, 'Iaveris', 'Siroco'
Holland NL Andre Jetten, Henk van der Lee, Jan van der Marel
Hungary H Attila Ferjancz, Gyula Simor, Janos Toth
Ireland IRL James Doherty, Donal Keating, Mike O'Connell
Italy I Attilio Bettega, Mauro Pregliasco, Adartico Vudafieri
Ivory Coast CI Alain Ambrosino, Samir Assef, Jean-Francois Vincens
Kenya EAK Robert Collinge, John Hellier, Bert Shankland
Luxembourg L Alain Beauchef, Nico Demuth, Aly Kridel
New Zealand NZ Alan Carter, Jim Donald
Norway N Rolf-Jakob Andersen, John Haugland, Jens Sogaard
Poland PL Blazej Krupa, Maciej Stawowiak, Sobieslaw Zasada
Portugal P 'Meqepe', Giovanni Salvi, Carlos Torres
South Africa ZA Roelof Fekken, Sarel van der Merwe, Geoff Mortimer
Spain E Jorge de Bagration, Beny Fernandez, Salvador Servia
Sweden S Leif Asterhag, Bjorn Johansson, Ola Stromberg
Switzerland CH Philippe Carron, Eric Chapuis, Andre Savary
United States of America USA Hendrik Blok, John Buffum, Eric Jones
West Germany D Holger Bohne, Jochi Kleint, Achim Warmbold

Rauno Aaltonen (SF)

Born 7 January 1938 in Turku
First rally car Saab 96 in 1956
Date of expiry of Priority December 197

RESULTS WCR

1971 5th Monte Carlo *Datsun 240Z*
1972 3rd Monte Carlo
6th Safari *Datsun 240Z*
1973 2nd Acropolis *Fiat Abarth 124*
1974 6th Safari *Datsun 180B SSS*
1975 4th Portugal *Opel Ascona*
1977 2nd Safari *Datsun Violet*
1978 3rd Safari *Datsun 160J*

RESULTS ECR

1961 1st 1000 Lakes *Mercedes-Benz 220 SE*
1962 5th RAC *BMC Mini Cooper*
1963 3rd Monte Carlo *BMC Mini Cooper*
2nd Alpine
3rd 1000 Lakes *BMC Mini Cooper S*
1964 4th Alpine
3rd 1000 Lakes *BMC Mini Cooper S*
1st Spa-Sofia-Liège *Austin-Healey 3000*
1965 1st Geneva
1st Czech
1st Polish
2nd 1000 Lakes
1st Munich-Vienna-Budapest
1st RAC *BMC Mini Cooper S*
1966 1st Tulip
1st Czech
3rd 1000 Lakes
3rd Alpine
4th RAC *BMC Mini Cooper S*
1967 1st Monte Carlo
3rd Swedish
3rd Tulip *BMC Mini Cooper S*
1968 3rd Monte Carlo
5th Acropolis *BLMC Mini Cooper S*
1969 2nd San Remo *Lancia Fulvia*

OTHER RESULTS

1965 European Champion
1968 5th London-Sydney *BLMC 1800*
1970 3rd World Cup *Ford Escort*
1977 1st Southern Cross *Datsun Violet*

Pentti Airikkala (SF)

Born 4 September 1945 in Helsinki
First rally car Volvo 544 in 1965
Date of expiry of Priority December 1980

RESULTS WCR

1976 2nd 1000 Lakes *Ford Escort RS1800*
1978 3rd 1000 Lakes *Vauxhall Chevette 2300HS*

RESULTS ECR

1973 3rd Arctic *Renault 12 Gordini*
1975 5th Arctic
6th Hanki *Vauxhall Magnum Coupé*
1976 2nd Welsh
4th Scottish *Ford Escort RS1600*
1977 1st Welsh
1st Manx *Vauxhall Chevette 2300HS*
1978 1st Hanki
1st Circuit of Ireland
1st Scottish *Vauxhall Chevette 2300HS*

OTHER RESULTS

1978 1st Mintex *Vauxhall Chevette 2300HS*

Markku Alen (SF)

Born 15 February 1951 in Helsinki
First rally car Renault Gordini R8 in 1969
Date of expiry of Priority December 1981

RESULTS WCR

1973 2nd 1000 Lakes *Volvo 142*
3rd RAC *Ford Escort RS1600*
1974 3rd TAP
3rd 1000 Lakes
2nd POR *Fiat Abarth 124*
1975 3rd Monte Carlo
6th Swedish
1st Portugal *Fiat Abarth 124*
1976 6th Monte Carlo *Fiat Abarth 124*
1st 1000 Lakes *Fiat Abarth 131*
1977 3rd South Pacific
1st Portugal *Fiat Abarth 131*
1978 1st Portugal
3rd Swedish
2nd Acropolis
1st 1000 Lakes
2nd Quebec *Fiat Abarth 131*
1st San Remo *Lancia Stratos*

RESULTS ECR

1971 3rd 1000 Lakes *Volvo 142*
1972 3rd 1000 Lakes *Volvo 142*
1973 2nd Arctic *Volvo 142*
1974 1st Welsh *Ford Escort RS1600*
1975 2nd YU *Fiat Abarth 124*
1976 1st Elba
4th Tulip *Fiat Abarth 131*
1978 3rd Arctic
2nd Hanki
3rd Circuit of Ireland
3rd Welsh *Fiat Abarth 131*

OTHER RESULTS

1970 Finnish Ice Racing Champion
1978 1st Giro d'Italia *Lancia Stratos*
1978 FIA Cup Champion
Finnish Rally Champion

Rauno Aaltonen

Pentti Airikkala

Markku Alen

Ove Andersson

Ove Andersson (S)

Born 3 January 1938 in Uppsala
First rally car Saab 96 in 1961
Date of expiry of Priority December 1980

RESULTS WCR

1968	3rd Flowers
	2nd Tulip. *Ford Escort TC*
1970	3rd Acropolis *Ford Escort TC*
1971	1st Monte Carlo
	1st Italia
	1st Austrian Alpine
	1st Acropolis *Renault Alpine A110*
1973	2nd Monte Carlo
	3rd Safari *Peugeot 504*
1974	4th TAP *Toyota Corolla*
1975	1st Safari *Peugeot 504*
	3rd Portugal *Toyota Corolla*
1976	2nd Portugal
	5th RAC *Toyota Corolla*
1977	3rd Portugal *Toyota Celica*
1978	4th Portugal *Toyota Celica*

RESULTS ECR

1965	6th Swedish
	4th Acropolis
	6th Polish *Saab 96*
1966	3rd Monte Carlo *Lancia Flavia*
	3rd Flowers
	4th Acropolis *Lancia Fulvia*
1967	2nd Monte Carlo
	3rd Flowers
	2nd Acropolis
	1st Spanish *Lancia Fulvia*
1968	6th Monte Carlo *Lancia Fulvia*
1969	4th RAC *Ford Escort TC*
1975	1st Maritim Nordland *Toyota Corolla*
1977	3rd Circuit of Ireland *Toyota Celica*

OTHER RESULTS

1974	3rd Wiesbaden *Toyota Corolla*
	1st Total *Toyota Celica*

Jean-Claude Andruet (F)

Born 13 August 1942 in Montreuil
First rally car Renault Gordini R8 in 1966
Date of expiry of Priority December 1979

RESULTS WCR

1971	1st Monte Carlo *Renault Alpine A110*
1973	1st Monte Carlo *Renault Alpine A110*
1974	1st Tour de Corse *Lancia Stratos*
1975	3rd Tour de Corse *Alfa Romeo Alfetta GT*
1977	2nd Monte Carlo
	1st San Remo
	4th Portugal *Fiat Abarth 131*
1978	6th Monte Carlo
	2nd Tour de Corse *Fiat Abarth 131*

RESULTS ECR

1967	5th Alpine *Renault Alpine A110*
1969	2nd Alpine *Renault Alpine A110*
1970	1st Lyon-Charbonnières
	1st Lorraine
	1st Geneva
	1st Polish
	1st Munich-Vienna-Budapest *Renault Alpine A110*
1972	1st Lyon-Charbonnières *Renault Alpine A110*
	1st Tour de France *Ferrari 365GTB*
	1st Tour de Corse *Renault Alpine A110*
1975	4th Elba *Alfa Romeo Alfetta GT*
1977	1st Antibes *Fiat Abarth 131*
1978	2nd Lorraine *Fiat Abarth 131*

OTHER RESULTS

1970	**European Champion**
1974	3rd Tour de France *Lancia Stratos*
1978	1st Limousine *Fiat Abarth 131*

Fulvio Bacchelli (I)

Born 27 February 1951 in Trieste
First rally car Porsche 911 in 1971
Date of expiry of Priority December 1980

RESULTS WCR

1974	6th Tour de Corse *Fiat Abarth 124*
1975	4th Monte Carlo *Fiat Abarth 124*
1977	1st South Pacific
	3rd Tour de Corse *Fiat Abarth 131*
1978	10th Monte Carlo *Lancia Stratos*

RESULTS ECR

1974	1st San Martino *Fiat Abarth 124*
1975	2nd Lyon-Charbonnières
	1st Zlatni Piassatzi
	3rd Polish
	3rd San Martino *Fiat Abarth 124*
1976	2nd Elba *Fiat Abarth 131*

Jean-Claude Andruet

Fulvio Bacchelli

Stig Blomqvist (S)

Born 29 January 1946 in Orebro
First rally car Saab 96 in 1964
Date of expiry of Priority December 1982

RESULTS WCR

1970 2nd Swedish *Saab 96 V4*
1971 1st Swedish
1st RAC *Saab 96 V4*
1972 1st Swedish
2nd RAC *Saab 96 V4*
1973 1st Swedish *Saab 96 V4*
1974 4th 1000 Lakes
2nd RAC *Saab 96 V4*
1975 2nd Swedish *Saab 96 V4*
1976 2nd Swedish *Saab 96 V4*
2nd RAC *Saab 99EMS*
1977 1st Swedish *Saab 99EMS*
1978 4th Swedish *Lancia Stratos*

RESULTS ECR

1971 1st 1000 Lakes *Saab 96 V4*
1973 1st Cyprus *Saab 96 V4*
1974 2nd Arctic
2nd JAMT *Saab 96 V4*
1975 1st Polar
2nd Arctic
5th Hessen *Saab 96 V4*
1976 1st Boucles de Spa *Saab 99EMS*
1977 1st Hanki *Saab 99EMS*

OTHER RESULTS

1971, 1973, 1975 and 1976 Swedish Group 2 Champion
1978 1st Smaaland
Swedish Rally Champion (special class) *Saab 99EMS*

Russell Brookes (GB)

Born 16 August 1948 in Birmingham
First rally car BMC Mini in 1968
Date of expiry of Priority December 1979

RESULTS WCR

1977 3rd RAC *Ford Escort RS1800*
1978 3rd RAC *Ford Escort RS*

RESULTS ECR

1976 1st Scottish
2nd Circuit of Ireland *Ford Escort RS1800*
1977 1st Circuit of Ireland
3rd Tulip
3rd Scottish *Ford Escort RS1800*
1978 1st Circuit of Ireland
1st Tulip
5th Welsh
7th Scottish *Ford Escort RS*

OTHER RESULTS

1976 2nd Mintex *Ford Escort RS1800*
1977 British Rally Champion
1978 2nd Mintex
1st Motogard *Ford Escort RS*

Tony Carello (I)

Born 10 March 1951 in Torino
First rally car Fiat 125 in 1972
Date of expiry of Priority December 1981

RESULTS WCR

1977 4th Tour de Corse *Lancia Stratos*

RESULTS ECR

1977 1st Campagnolo *Lancia Stratos*
1978 1st Costa Brava
1st Sicily
1st 4 Regions
1st Halkidikis
1st OASC
1st RACE *Lancia Stratos*

OTHER RESULTS

1972 6th San Martino
1975 4th Saluzzo
1976 1st Ciocco *Lancia Stratos*
1977 2nd Romagna di S Giacomo *Lancia Stratos*
1978 European Champion

Roger Clark (GB)

Born 5 August 1939 in Narborough
First rally car Ford Thames van in 1956
Date of expiry of Priority December 1979

RESULTS WCR

1968 1st Tulip *Ford Escort TC*
1969 2nd Acropolis *Ford Escort TC*
1970 5th Monte Carlo *Ford Escort TC*
1972 1st RAC *Ford Escort RS1600*
1973 2nd RAC *Ford Escort RS1600*
1975 2nd RAC *Ford Escort RS1800*
1976 5th Monte Carlo
1st RAC *Ford Escort RS1800*
1977 2nd Acropolis
3rd Quebec
4th RAC *Ford Escort RS1800*

RESULTS ECR

1965 6th Monte Carlo *Rover 2000*
1966 2nd Acropolis
4th Polish
2nd Alpine *Ford Cortina Lotus*
1968 1st Acropolis *Ford Escort TC*
1969 6th RAC *Ford Escort TC*
1970 1st Circuit of Ireland *Ford Escort RS1600*
1972 2nd Scottish *Ford Escort RS1600*
1973 1st Welsh
1st Scottish *Ford Escort RS1600*
1975 1st Welsh
1st Scottish *Ford Escort RS1800*
1976 3rd Welsh
2nd Scottish *Ford Escort RS1800*
1977 1st Galway *Ford Escort RS1800*
1978 4th Circuit of Ireland
2nd Welsh
3rd Scottish
4th Manx
1st Cyprus *Ford Escort RS*

OTHER RESULTS

1974 1st Tour of Britain *Ford Escort RS2000*
1975 1st Total *Ford Escort RS1800*
1978 4th European Championship

Stig Blomqvist

Russell Brookes

Tony Carello *BELOW: Roger Clark*

Bror Danielsson

Bernard Darniche

Per Eklund BELOW: *Guy Frequelin*

Bror Danielsson (S)

Born 28 September 1948 in Arjang
First rally car Volvo Amazon in 1967
Date of expiry of Priority December 1978

RESULTS WCR

1976 10th RAC *Opel Kadett GT/E*
1977 2nd Swedish
10th RAC *Opel Kadett GT/E*
1978 7th Swedish
10th RAC *Opel Kadett GT/E*

RESULTS ECR

1978 2nd Tulip
2nd South Swedish *Opel Kadett GT/E*

Bernard Darniche (F)

Born 28 March 1942 in Cenon
First rally car NSU 1000 in 1967
Date of expiry of Priority December 1982

RESULTS WCR

1970 5th Austrian Alpine *Renault Alpine A110*
1971 4th Italia *Renault Alpine A110*
1973 1st Maroc
1st Austrian Alpine *Renault Alpine A110*
1974 6th POR *Renault Gordini 17*
1975 1st Tour de Corse *Lancia Stratos*
1976 3rd Monte Carlo
2nd Tour de Corse *Lancia Stratos*
1977 1st Tour de Corse *Fiat Abarth 131*
1978 5th Monte Carlo
1st Tour de Corse *Fiat Abarth 131*

RESULTS ECR

1970 3rd Spanish
1st Tour de Corse *Renault Alpine A110*
1971 2nd Belgian *Renault Alpine A110*
1972 1st Neige et Glace
2nd Lyon-Charbonnières
2nd TAP *Renault Alpine A110*
1976 1st Lyon-Charbonnières
1st Four Regions
1st Antibes
1st San Martino
1st Sachs Baltic
2nd Spanish *Lancia Stratos*
1977 1st Sicily
1st Elba
1st Firestone
1st Alpin
1st Lucien Bianchi
1st Four Regions
1st Ypres
1st Polish
1st Tour de France *Lancia Stratos*
1978 1st Alpin
1st Lorraine
1st Antibes
1st Chataigne *Lancia Stratos*

OTHER RESULTS

1972, 76-78 Champion of France
1974 2nd Tour de France *Ligier JS2*
1975 1st Tour de France *Lancia Stratos*
1976-77 European Champion
1978 1st Lyon-Charbonnières
1st Jean Behra
1st Touraine
1st Cevenole *Lancia Stratos*

Per Eklund (S)

Born 26 June 1946 in Arvika
First rally car Volvo PV 544 in 1964
Date of expiry of Priority December 1979

RESULTS WCR

1972 3rd Austrian Alpine *Saab 96 V4*
1973 2nd Swedish
3rd Austrian Alpine *Saab 96 V4*
1975 4th Swedish
4th 1000 Lakes *Saab 96 V4*
1976 1st Swedish *Saab 96 V4*
1977 9th RAC *Saab 96 V4*
1978 4th 1000 Lakes *Porsche 911*

RESULTS ECR

1974 1st JAMT *Saab 96 V4*
1975 3rd Polar *Saab 96 V4*
1977 5th Tulip *Saab 99EMS*
1978 7th Hanki *Saab 99EMS*

OTHER RESULTS

1976 2nd Three Cities *Saab 96 V4*

Guy Frequelin (F)

Born 2 April 1945 in Langres
First rally car Renault Gordini R8 in 1967
Date of expiry of Priority December 1979

RESULTS WCR

1974 9th Tour de Corse *Alfa Romeo Alfetta GT*
1975 8th Monte Carlo *Alfa Romeo 2000GTV*
1976 7th Monte Carlo *Porsche 911*
1978 3rd Monte Carlo
5th Bandama *Renault 5 Alpine*

RESULTS ECR

1975 6th Lyon-Charbonnières *Alfa Romeo 2000GTV*
1977 1st Chataigne *Renault Alpine A310 V6*
1st Warsaw *Renault 5 Alpine*

OTHER RESULTS

1975 French Group 1 Champion
1977 French Rally Champion

Kyosti Hamalainen (SF)

Born 16 September 1945 in Helsinki
First rally car VW 1600 in 1969
Date of expiry of Priority December 1980

RESULTS WCR

1977 5th Swedish *Ford Escort RS2000*
1st 1000 Lakes
6th RAC *Ford Escort RS1800*
1978 8th 1000 Lakes *Ford Escort RS*

RESULTS ECR

1977 5th Arctic
4th Hanki *Ford Escort RS2000*
1978 5th Hanki
6th Welsh
5th Ypres *Ford Escort RS*

Harry Kallstrom (S)

Born 30 June 1939 in Sudertalje
First rally car VW 1200 in 1957
Date of expiry of Priority December 1980

RESULTS WCR

1970 2nd Flowers
1st RAC
2nd Czech
1st San Martino *Lancia Fulvia*
1971 3rd Swedish *Lancia Fulvia*
1972 3rd Swedish
4th RAC *Lancia Fulvia*
1973 4th Swedish *Lancia Fulvia*
2nd Safari *Datsun 1800 SSS*
1974 5th TAP
4th Safari *Datsun 260Z*
1976 1st Acropolis *Datsun Violet*
1977 3rd Acropolis *Datsun Violet*
1978 4th Acropolis *Datsun 160J*

RESULTS ECR

1963 2nd RAC *Volkswagen 1500S*
1964 2nd Midnight Sun *BMC Mini Cooper S*
1966 2nd RAC *BMC Mini Cooper S*
1967 4th Alpine *Renault Gordini R8*
1968 6th Acropolis
4th Flowers *Lancia Fulvia*
1969 6th Swedish
1st San Remo
2nd Austrian Alpine
2nd Czech
3rd Polish
1st Spanish
1st RAC *Lancia Fulvia*
1972 3rd Elba *Lancia Fulvia*

OTHER RESULTS

1969 2nd Monte Carlo
5th Alpine *Lancia Fulvia*
European Champion
1977 2nd Southern Cross *Datsun Violet*
1978 1st Qatar *Datsun 160J*

Anders Kullang (S)

Born 28 September 1943 in Karlstad
First rally car Volvo PV544 in 1962
Date of expiry of Priority December 1979

RESULTS WCR

1972 4th Swedish
3rd RAC *Opel Ascona*
1975 5th 1000 Lakes *Opel Ascona*
1976 3rd Swedish
7th RAC *Opel Kadett GT/E*
1977 3rd Swedish *Opel Kadett GT/E*
1978 9th Monte Carlo
6th Portugal
7th 1000 Lakes
3rd Quebec
5th RAC *Opel Kadett GT/E*

RESULTS ECR

1972 2nd Olympia *Opel Ascona*

Simo Lampinen (SF)

Born 22 June 1943 in Porvoo
First rally car Saab 96 in 1961
Date of expiry of Priority December 1978

RESULTS WCR

1968 1st RAC
2nd Czech *Saab 96 V4*
1969 2nd 1000 Lakes *Saab 96 V4*
1971 6th Monte Carlo
3rd Acropolis
6th RAC *Lancia Fulvia*
1972 4th Monte Carlo
1st Maroc
2nd Acropolis
5th RAC *Lancia Fulvia*
1973 4th 1000 Lakes *Saab 96 V4*
1974 5th 1000 Lakes *Saab 96 V4*
2nd Rideau Lakes
4th POR *Lancia Beta Coupé*
1975 3rd Swedish *Lancia Beta Coupé*
2nd 1000 Lakes *Saab 96 V4*
1976 4th Swedish *Lancia Stratos*
5th Safari
2nd Maroc *Peugeot 504*
1977 4th Swedish
4th South Pacific
4th Acropolis
2nd Quebec
7th RAC *Fiat Abarth 131*
1978 6th Swedish *Fiat Abarth 131*
5th Safari *Peugeot 504 V6 Coupé*
5th 1000 Lakes *Fiat Abarth 131*
4th Bandama *Peugeot 504 V6 Coupé*

RESULTS ECR

1964 1st 1000 Lakes *Saab 96*
1965 4th 1000 Lakes *Saab 96*
1966 2nd Swedish
5th 1000 Lakes *Saab 96*
1967 2nd Swedish
2nd 1000 Lakes *Saab 96 V4*
1968 2nd 1000 Lakes *Saab 96 V4*
1969 2nd Swedish
4th Austrian Alpine
4th Czech *Saab 96 V4*
1970 3rd 1000 Lakes
1st TAP
1st 1000 Minutes *Lancia Fulvia*
1971 2nd TAP *Lancia Fulvia*
1972 1st 1000 Lakes *Saab 96 V4*
1973 2nd Zlatni Piassatzı *Lancia Fulvia*
1975 1st Arctic
1st Hanki *Saab 96 V4*

OTHER RESULTS

1963 1st 1000 Lakes *Saab 96*

Kyosti Hamalainen

Harry Kallstrom

Anders Kullang

Simo Lampinen

Timo Makinen

Shekhar Mehta

Timo Makinen (SF)

Born 18 March 1938 in Helsinki
First rally car Triumph TR3 in 1959
Date of expiry of Priority December 1979

RESULTS WCR

1969 4th 1000 Lakes *Saab 96 V4*
1971 5th RAC *Ford Escort RS1600*
1973 1st 1000 Lakes
1st RAC *Ford Escort RS1600*
1974 2nd 1000 Lakes
1st RAC *Ford Escort RS1600*
1975 5th Maroc *Peugeot 504*
3rd 1000 Lakes
1st RAC *Ford Escort RS1800*
1976 4th 1000 Lakes *Ford Escort RS1800*
1978 7th Portugal *Peugeot 104ZS*
2nd Bandama *Peugeot 504 V6 Coupé*

RESULTS ECR

1963 5th RAC *Austin Healey 3000*
1964 4th Monte Carlo
1st Tulip
4th 1000 Lakes *BMC Mini Cooper S*
2nd RAC *Austin Healey 3000*
1965 1st Monte Carlo
2nd Alpine
1st 1000 Lakes *BMC Mini Cooper S*
2nd RAC *Austin Healey 3000*
1966 2nd Polish
1st 1000 Lakes
3rd Czech
1st Munich-Vienna-Budapest *BMC Mini Cooper S*
1967 2nd Tulip
1st 1000 Lakes *BMC Mini Cooper S*
1970 2nd 1000 Lakes *Ford Escort TC*
1972 2nd Arctic
2nd 1000 Lakes *Ford Escort RS1600*
1973 1st Arctic *Ford Escort RS1600*
1974 3rd Arctic *Ford Escort RS1600*
1975 5th Scottish *Ford Escort RS1800*
1976 2nd Firestone *Ford Escort RS1800*

OTHER RESULTS

1970 5th World Cup *Ford Escort*
1974 1st Bandama *Peugeot 504*
1976 1st Bandama *Peugeot 504 V6 Coupé*

Hannu Mikkola

Shekhar Mehta (GB)

Born 20 June 1945 in Kampala
First rally car BMW 1800 in 1966
Date of expiry of Priority December 1982

RESULTS WCR

1971 2nd Safari *Datsun 240Z*
1972 6th Acropolis *Datsun 240Z*
1973 1st Safari *Datsun 240Z*
1974 4th San Remo *Lancia Beta Coupé*
1975 5th Maroc *Datsun Violet*
1976 3rd Acropolis *Datsun Violet*
1978 3rd Acropolis *Datsun 160J*

RESULTS ECR

1976 1st Cyprus *Datsun Violet*
1977 6th Tulip *Datsun Violet*

OTHER RESULTS

1976 3rd Southern Cross *Datsun Violet*
1977 6th Southern Cross *Datsun 120Y*

Hannu Mikkola (SF)

Born 24 May 1942 in Joensuu
First rally car Volvo PV544 in 1963
Date of expiry of Priority December 1982

RESULTS WCR

1968 2nd Austrian Alpine *Lancia Fulvia*
1969 1st 1000 Lakes *Ford Escort TC*
1971 4th RAC *Ford Escort RS1600*
1972 1st Safari *Ford Escort RS1600*
1973 4th Monte Carlo *Ford Escort RS1600*
1974 1st 1000 Lakes *Ford Escort RS1600*
1975 2nd Monte Carlo
2nd Portugal *Fiat Abarth 124*
1st 1000 Lakes *Toyota Corolla*
1st Maroc *Peugeot 504*
1976 3rd 1000 Lakes *Toyota Celica*
1977 2nd RAC *Toyota Celica*
1978 2nd Swedish
2nd Portugal
1st RAC *Ford Escort RS*

RESULTS ECR

1967 3rd 1000 Lakes *Volvo 122S*
1968 1st 1000 Lakes *Ford Escort TC*
1969 1st Austrian Alpine *Ford Escort TC*
1970 1st 1000 Lakes *Ford Escort TC*
1972 1st Scottish *Ford Escort RS1600*
1973 2nd Scottish *Ford Escort RS1600*
1977 4th Arctic *Toyota Corolla*
3rd Welsh *Toyota Celica*
1978 1st Welsh
1st Scottish *Ford Escort RS*

OTHER RESULTS

1970 1st World Cup *Ford Escort*
1978 1st Burmah *Ford Escort RS*
3rd FIA Cup
British Open Rally Champion

Michele Mouton (F)

Born 23 June 1951 in Grasse
First rally car Renault Alpine A110 in 1973
Date of expiry of Priority December 1979

RESULTS WCR

1977	8th Tour de Corse	*Fiat Abarth 131*
1978	7th Monte Carlo	*Lancia Stratos*
	1st Tour de France	
	5th Tour de Corse	*Fiat Abarth 131*

RESULTS ECR

1976	2nd Alpin	*Renault Alpine A310*
1977	4th Alpin	
	2nd Antibes	
	2nd Tour de France	
	1st RACE	*Porsche 911*
1978	3rd Alpin	
	4th Lorraine	
	3rd Antibes	*Fiat Abarth 131*

OTHER RESULTS

1978	4th Giro d'Italia	*Fiat Abarth 131*
	5th European Championship	

Sandro Munari (I)

Born 27 March 1940 in Cavarzere
First rally car Lancia Fulvia in 1965
Date of expiry of Priority December 1980

RESULTS WCR

1972	1st Monte Carlo	*Lancia Fulvia*
1974	3rd Safari	*Lancia Fulvia*
	1st San Remo	
	1st Rideau Lakes	
	3rd RAC	*Lancia Stratos*
1975	1st Monte Carlo	
	2nd Safari	*Lancia Stratos*
1976	1st Monte Carlo	
	1st Portugal	
	3rd Maroc	
	1st Tour de Corse	
	2nd San Remo	
	4th RAC	*Lancia Stratos*
1977	1st Monte Carlo	
	3rd Safari	*Lancia Stratos*
1978	3rd Tour de Corse	*Fiat Abarth 131*

RESULTS ECR

1967	5th Monte Carlo	
	2nd Geneva	
	2nd Spanish	*Lancia Fulvia*
1970	2nd TAP	*Lancia Fulvia*
1971	1st Semperit	
	1st 1000 Minutes	*Lancia Fulvia*
1972	1st San Martino	*Lancia Fulvia*
1973	1st Costa Brava	*Lancia Fulvia*
	1st Firestone	*Lancia Stratos*
	2nd Czech	
	3rd Danube	
	1st San Martino	*Lancia Fulvia*
	1st Tour de France	*Lancia Stratos*
1975	1st Four Regions	*Lancia Stratos*
1977	1st San Martino	*Lancia Stratos*

OTHER RESULTS

1971	Mitropa Cup	
1973	**European Champion**	
1977	1st Total	*Lancia Stratos*
	FIA Cup Champion	

Jean-Pierre Nicolas (F)

Born 22 January 1945 in Marseilles
First rally car Renault Gordini R8 in 1965
Date of expiry of Priority December 1981

RESULTS WCR

1970	3rd Monte Carlo	*Renault Alpine A110*
1971	6th San Remo	
	2nd Acropolis	*Renault Alpine A110*
1973	3rd Monte Carlo	
	2nd TAP	
	5th Maroc	
	3rd Acropolis	
	4th Austrian Alpine	
	3rd San Remo	
	1st Tour de Corse	
	5th RAC	*Renault Alpine A110*
1974	3rd POR	
	2nd Tour de Corse	*Renault Alpine A110*
1975	2nd Tour de Corse	*Renault Alpine A110*
1976	1st Maroc	*Peugeot 504*
1978	1st Monte Carlo	*Porsche 911*
	1st Safari	*Peugeot 504 V6 Coupé*
	3rd Portugal	*Ford Escort RS*
	1st Bandama	*Peugeot 504 V6 Coupé*
	7th Tour de Corse	*Opel Kadett GT/E*

RESULTS ECR

1970	2nd Geneva	
	2nd Munich-Vienna-Budapest	
	1st Spanish	*Renault Alpine A110*
1971	1st Lyon-Charbonnières	
	1st Geneva	
	1st TAP	
	1st Spanish	*Renault Alpine A110*
1972	2nd Neige et Glace	
	1st Firestone	
	1st Olympia	*Renault Alpine A110*
1974	1st Antibes	*Renault Alpine A110*
1975	1st Alpin	
	1st Antibes	*Renault Alpine A110*
1978	2nd Alpin	*Ford Escort RS*

OTHER RESULTS

1969	5th Monte Carlo	
	6th Alpine	*Renault Alpine A110*
1974	1st Tour de France	*Ligier JS2*
1976	2nd Bandama	*Peugeot 504*
1977	1st Chamonix	*Peugeot 104ZS*
1978	**2nd FIA Cup**	

Michele Mouton

Sandro Munari

Jean-Pierre Nicolas

Vic Preston

Jean Ragnotti

Vic Preston (EAK)

Born 20 November 1950 in Nairobi
First rally car Ford Capri 1600 in 1968
Date of expiry of Priority December 1979

RESULTS WCR

1971 3rd Safari *Ford Escort TC*
1972 6th Safari *Ford Escort TC*
1973 9th Safari *Ford Escort RS1600*
1978 2nd Safari *Porsche 911*

OTHER RESULTS

1972, 1973, 1975, 1977 East African Champion

Jean Ragnotti (F)

Born 29 August 1945 in Carpentras
First rally car Renault Gordini R8 in 1967
Date of expiry of Priority December 1979

RESULTS WCR

1977 7th San Remo *Renault 5 Alpine*
1978 2nd Monte Carlo
3rd Bandama *Renault 5 Alpine*

RESULTS ECR

1970 2nd Tulip *Opel Kadett*
1972 3rd Olympia *Opel Ascona*

OTHER RESULTS

1970 1st G1 Monte Carlo *Opel Kadett*
1971 1st G2 Monte Carlo *Opel Kadett*
1972 1st G1 Monte Carlo *Opel Ascona*
1975 1st New Caledonia *Datsun Violet*
1st Reunion *Renault Alpine A110*
1977 French rallycross Champion *Renault Alpine A310 V6*
1978 1st New Caledonia *Datsun 710*

Blair Robson (NZ)

Born 15 May 1935 in Auckland
First rally car BLMC Mini Cooper in 1969
Date of expiry of Priority December 1980

OTHER RESULTS

1966-68 NZ Trials Champion
1974 Unofficial NZ rally champion *Ford Escort RS1600*
1975 2nd NZ Rally Championship *Ford Escort RS1600*
1976 2nd Heatway Rally *Ford Escort RS1800*
1978 NZ Rally Champion *Ford Escort RS*

Walter Rohrl (D)

Born 7 March 1947 in Regensburg
First rally car Fiat 850 Coupé in 1968
Date of expiry of Priority December 1981

RESULTS WCR

1974 5th RAC *Opel Ascona*
1975 1st Acropolis *Opel Ascona*
1976 4th Monte Carlo *Opel Kadett GT/E*
1978 4th Monte Carlo
1st Acropolis
1st Quebec
6th RAC *Fiat Abarth 131*

RESULTS ECR

1971 1st Wiesbaden *Ford Capri 2600RS*
1972 2nd Polish
1st Baltic *Ford Capri 2600RS*
1973 2nd Semperit
1st Czech
1st Danube
1st Munich-Vienna-Budapest *Opel Ascona*
1974 1st Firestone
1st Wiesbaden
1st Czech
1st Danube
1st Lugano *Opel Ascona*
1975 4th Costa Brava *Opel Ascona*
1976 2nd Hessen
1st Ypres
5th San Martino *Opel Kadett GT/E*
1977 4th Welsh *Opel Kadett GT/E*
1978 1st Saarland
1st Hunsruck *Lancia Stratos*

OTHER RESULTS

1974 European Champion
1978 1st Rheinhessen
1st Vorderpfalz *Lancia Stratos*

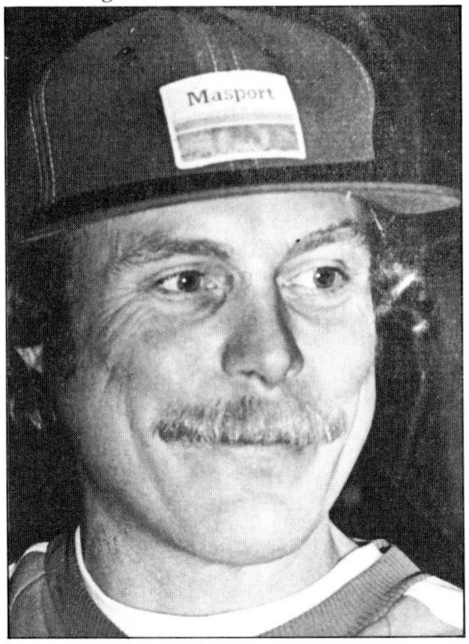

Blair Robson

Walter Rohrl

Timo Salonen (SF)

Born 8 October 1951 in Helsinki
First rally car Datsun 1600 SSS in 1970
Date of expiry of Priority December 1980

RESULTS WCR

1975 6th 1000 Lakes *Datsun Violet*
1976 6th 1000 Lakes *Datsun Violet*
1977 2nd 1000 Lakes
1st Quebec *Fiat Abarth 131*
1978 2nd 1000 Lakes *Fiat Abarth 131*

RESULTS ECR

1976 5th Hanki *Datsun Violet*
1977 2nd Hanki *Fiat Abarth 131*
1978 3rd Hanki *Fiat Abarth 131*

Joginder Singh (EAK)

Born 9 February 1932 in Kericho
First rally car Morris Minor 1000 in 1958
Date of expiry of priority December 1979

RESULTS WCR

1970 2nd Safari *Datsun 1600 SSS*
1974 1st Safari *Mitsubishi Colt Lancer*
1976 1st Safari *Mitsubishi Colt Lancer*
1977 2nd Bandama *Mitsubishi Colt Lancer*

OTHER RESULTS

1965 1st Safari *Volvo PV544*
1965 East African Rally Champion
1966 3rd Safari *Volvo 132*
1969 2nd Safari *Volvo 142S*
1970 East African Rally Champion
1973 4th Southern Cross *Mitsubishi Colt Lancer*
1975 2nd Southern Cross *Mitsubishi Colt Lancer*
1975 East African Rally Champion

Gilbert Staepelaere (B)

Born 5 June 1937 in Antwerp
First rally car Ford Anglia in 1960
Date of expiry of Priority December 1979

RESULTS ECR

1965 6th Tulip
9th Geneva *Ford Cortina GT*
1966 1st Geneva
9th Munich-Vienna-Budapest
5th Coupes des Alpes *Ford Cortina Lotus*
1968 3rd Czech
3rd Spanish
4th Geneva *Ford Escort TC*
1969 1st Tulip
1st Czech
2nd Polish
2nd Spanish *Ford Escort TC*
6th Austrian Alpine *Ford Taunus 20 MRS*
1970 1st Czech
3rd Munich-Vienna-Budapest
6th Spanish
1st Tour de Belgique *Ford Escort TC*
3rd Polish *Ford Cortina Lotus*
1972 1st Tour de Belgique *Ford Escort RS1600*
1974 1st 12 hours of Ypres *Ford Escort RS1600*
1975 2nd Lucien Bianchi
7th Touraine
4th 24 hours of Ypres
1st Taurus *Ford Escort RS1600*
1976 3rd Tulip
1st Lucien Bianchi
1st Taurus *Ford Escort RS1800*
1977 1st Tulip
2nd Lucien Bianchi
1st OASC *Ford Escort RS1800*
1978 4th Galway
1st Lucien Bianchi
3rd Tulip
1st Omloop van Haspengouw
2nd 24 hours of Ypres
1st Warsaw
5th Spanish
1st Bosphorus Winter Rally *Ford Escort RS*

OTHER RESULTS

1962, 1963, 1964 Golden cup in the Liège-Sofia-Liège *Ford Anglia and Cortina GT*
1965 2nd Marathon de la Route Nürburgring *Ford Mustang*
1966 1st Marathon de la route Nürburgring *Ford Cortina Lotus*
2nd ECR Group 1
1969 2nd European Championship
1970 5th London-Mexico *Ford Escort*
2nd European Championship
1976 1st West Euro Cup
1977 1st West Euro Cup
1978 1st Benelux Championship
1st overall Belgian Motorsport Champion
3rd European Championship
1st Luxembourg
1st Kempen
1st Circuit des Ardennes *Ford Escort RS*

Timo Salonen

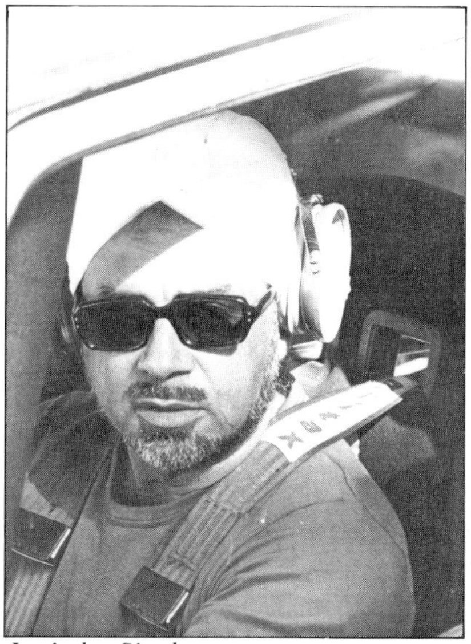
Joginder Singh

Gilbert Staepelaere

'Tony' (Fassina)

Ari Vatanen

'Tony' (Fassina) (I)

Born 26 July 1945 in Treviso
First rally car Renault Gordini R8 in 1970
Date of expiry of Priority December 1978

RESULTS WCR
1976 4th San Remo *Lancia Stratos*
1977 3rd San Remo *Fiat Abarth 131*

RESULTS ECR
1976 3rd San Martino *Lancia Stratos*
1977 2nd Giro di Sicilia *Fiat Abarth 131*

OTHER RESULTS
1976 1st Piacenza *Lancia Stratos*
1976 Italian International Champion

Ari Vatanen (SF)

Born 27 April 1952 in Joensuu
First rally car Opel Ascona 1970
Date of expiry of Priority December 1980

RESULTS WCR
1977 2nd South Pacific *Ford Escort RS1800*
1978 5th Swedish *Ford Escort RS*

RESULTS ECR
1976 1st Welsh
1st Manx *Ford Escort RS1800*
1977 1st Arctic
2nd Welsh
1st Scottish
4th Hunsruck *Ford Escort RS1800*
1978 1st Arctic
1st Donegal *Ford Escort RS*

OTHER RESULTS
1976 1st Tour of Britain *Ford Escort RS2000*
1978 1st Madeira
1st Cork *Ford Escort RS*

Maurizio Verini (I)

Born 9 July 1943 in Riola Terme
First rally car Fiat 124 Coupé in 1969
Date of expiry of Priority December 1979

RESULTS WCR
1973 2nd San Remo *Fiat Abarth 124*
1975 2nd San Remo *Fiat Abarth 124*
1977 5th Portugal
2nd San Remo
7th Tour de Corse *Fiat Abarth 131*
1978 8th Monte Carlo
2nd San Remo *Fiat Abarth 131*

RESULTS ECR
1974 2nd San Marino
2nd San Martino *Fiat Abarth 124*
1975 1st Costa Brava
1st Lyon-Charbonnières
1st Firestone
1st YU
4th Alpine
1st Polish
2nd San Martino *Fiat Abarth 124*
1976 2nd Tulip
4th San Martino *Fiat Abarth 131*
1977 2nd Elba
4th Alpi Orientali
3rd San Martino *Fiat Abarth 131*
1978 2nd Elba
2nd Alpi Orientali
5th Manx *Fiat Abarth 131*

OTHER RESULTS
1975 European Champion
1978 1st Costa Smeralda
1st Gargano *Fiat Abarth 131*

Francis Vincent (F)

Born 27 September 1949 in Paris
First rally car Renault Gordini R8 in 1968
Date of expiry of Priority December 1979

RESULTS WCR
1978 3rd San Remo *Porsche 911*

RESULTS ECR
1978 4th Antibes
4th Ypres *Porsche 911*

OTHER RESULTS
1978 1st Var *Porsche 911*

Maurizio Verini

Francis Vincent

Bjorn Waldegard (S)

Born 12 November 1943 in Ro
First rally car VW 1200 in 1962
Date of expiry of Priority December 1982

RESULTS WCR

1968 1st Swedish *Porsche 911*
1970 1st Monte Carlo
1st Swedish
1st Austrian Alpine
3rd TAP *Porsche 911*
1971 3rd Monte Carlo *Porsche 914/6*
4th Swedish
2nd RAC *Porsche 911*
1972 2nd Swedish *Porsche 911*
1973 6th Swedish *Volkswagen 1500S*
6th Maroc *Fiat Abarth 124*
3rd Austrian Alpine *BMW 2002tii*
1974 2nd Safari *Porsche 911*
4th RAC *Toyota Corolla*
1975 1st Swedish
3rd Safari
1st San Remo *Lancia Stratos*
1976 2nd Monte Carlo
1st San Remo *Lancia Stratos*
3rd RAC *Ford Escort RS1800*
1977 2nd Portugal
1st Safari
1st Acropolis
1st RAC
5th San Remo
3rd 1000 Lakes *Ford Escort RS1800*
1978 1st Swedish *Ford Escort RS*
4th Safari *Porsche 911*
2nd RAC *Ford Escort RS*

RESULTS ECR

1965 3rd Swedish *Volkswagen 1500S*
1967 4th Tulip *Porsche 911*
1969 1st Swedish *Porsche 911*
1970 3rd TAP *Porsche 911*
1972 3rd TAP *Citroën SM*
1978 1st South Swedish *Ford Escort RS*

OTHER RESULTS

1969 1st Monte Carlo *Porsche 911*

Franz Wittmann (A)

Born 7 April 1950 in Ramsau
First rally car VW 1500 in 1971
Date of expiry of Priority December 1979

RESULTS WCR

1977 7th Portugal
7th 1000 Lakes *Opel Kadett GT/E*

RESULTS ECR

1974 1st Taurus
1st OASC *BMW 2002ti*
1975 4th YU
1st Janner *BMW 2002ti*
1976 3rd Boucles de Spa *BMW 2002ti*
1st Janner *Opel Kadett GT/E*
1977 1st Janner
3rd Campagnolo *Opel Kadett GT/E*
1978 3rd Janner
4th Costa Brava
1st ARBO Rallye
3rd Elba
1st Zlatni Piassatzi
2nd Polish
1st Danube
3rd Halkidikis *Opel Kadett GT/E*

OTHER RESULTS

1976-1978 Austrian Champion
1976-1977 Mitropa Cup Winner
1978 2nd European Championship

Antonio Zanini (E)

Born 9 February 1948 in Barcelona
First rally car Simca 1000 in 1970
Date of expiry of Priority December 1978

RESULTS WCR

1977 3rd Monte Carlo *SEAT 124 Especial*

RESULTS ECR

1974 1st Spanish *SEAT 1430*
1975 3rd Costa Brava
1st Spanish *SEAT 1430/1800*
1976 1st Costa Brava
1st Firestone
4th Ypres
2nd Polish
2nd Cyprus
3rd RACE *SEAT 1430/1800*
1977 5th Ypres
2nd Polish *SEAT 124 Especial*
1978 2nd Costa Brava
1st Polish *Fiat Abarth 131*

OTHER RESULTS

1978 1st Montseny/Guillerias
1st Maspalomas
1st Luis de Baviera
1st Cataluna *Fiat Abarth 131*
Spanish Champion

Bjorn Waldegard

Franz Wittmann

Antonio Zanini

Rallye Monte Carlo

To many people, it seemed Darniche knew all along that this time he would win the greatest rally in his native France. After a long snowy spell, which persisted until the day before the start, a heavy thaw cleared away the snow and denied the chances of teams like Fiat and Renault, who had openly declared their cars were prepared with heavy snow in mind. Darniche noted with enthusiasm the effect of the warming sun as he drove through the concentration run from his starting point in Paris. On the approach to the converging control at Vals les Bains, journalists who knew him well could tell by the bounce in his behaviour that things would go well for him this time. It was the one big French event he had never won before. Victory would not come easily, however. Carburettor trouble and problems with tyres on the *parcours commun* would all cost him time. With a surprisingly effortless domination by the Ford Escorts (prepared in the hopes of clear conditions), the chances of a fourth Stratos victory did not initially seem so

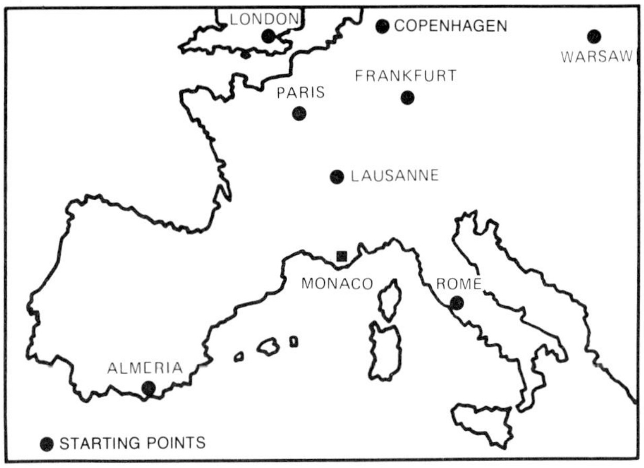

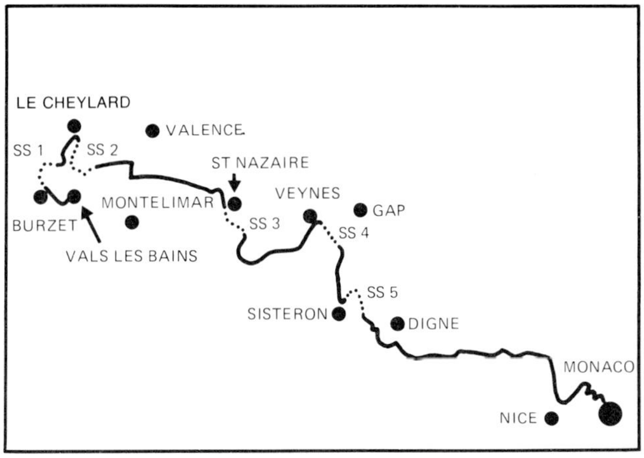

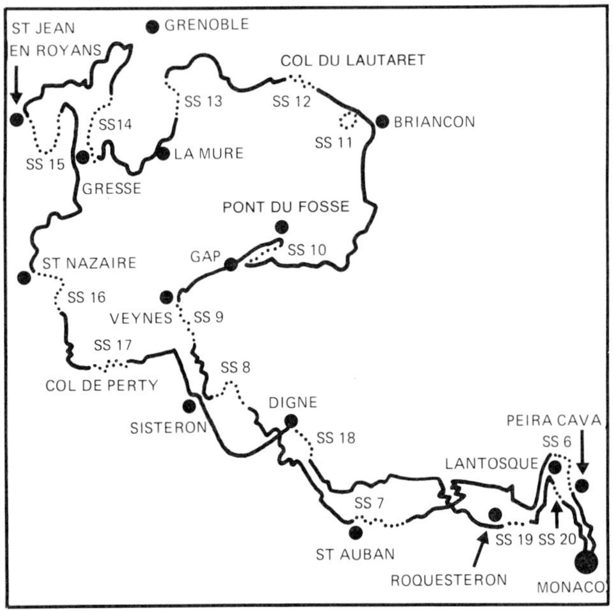

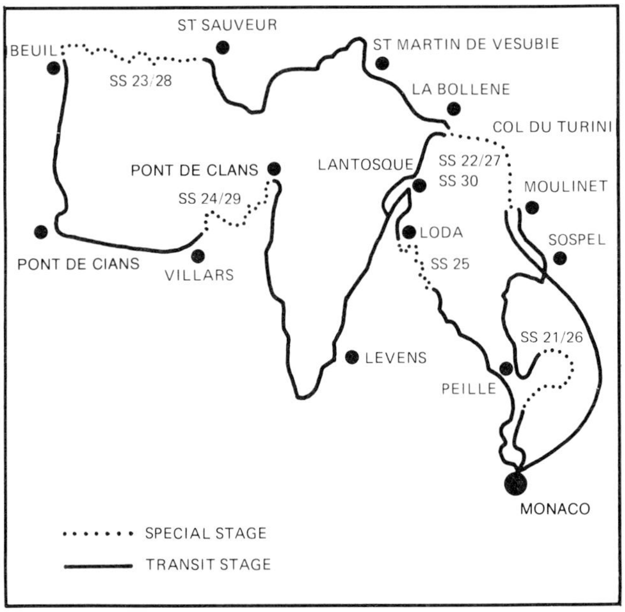

good. But Fords were not as good on the later clear tarmac stages as on the stages with rutted ice patches. Using A2 and old-style SP44 tyres, coupled with the benefit of many detailed improvements, the Escorts began by walking away from the opposition.

The events of the final night will be remembered for a long time. Problems that had afflicted Darniche up to that stage were now at an end; he began a 'grand attack' with victory his objective. With only 175 stage kilometres to go the Lancia Superman started the last night 6 minutes 27 seconds behind Bjorn Waldegard. He had almost settled for second place, when on the penultimate stage Waldegard had to stop for a half-minute to move some rocks lying on the road. Eventually the Lancia won by a mere six seconds.

The rally started with great promise, with no fewer than sixteen drivers on the A-seeded list taking part. This promise continued for a considerable distance through the event in view of a remarkable small retirement rate — which made the performances of the Escorts of Waldegard and Mikkola all the more impressive. Of the Escorts, Mikkola was quicker, but he was twice delayed,

once through a puncture and then through a five-minute penalty incurred as a result of a police report that he had overtaken dangerously. This penalty was almost the final straw of bad luck for Ford, for in no other WCR rally would such a penalty have stood — unless as in Scandinavia there had been a proper control at which a rally official had been in attendance. Achim Warmbold, fighting for the lead with a Citroën CX2500 in the Diesel category, also suffered — once for which a five-minute penalty was imposed and then a second time which led to his expulsion. Coupled with a variety of random penalties imposed on private drivers for offences within control zones, this matter caused a lot of disappointment and no little distrust of the attitude of the organizers generally.

The initial speed of the Escorts was

Bernard Darniche on his first passage through the Turini pass during his amazing chase of Bjorn Waldegard whom he overtook on the final stage

47 Rallye Monte Carlo

20-26 January 1979 Monte Carlo

Overall results

POSITION	DRIVER/NAVIGATOR	NATIONALITY	COMP NO.	CAR	GROUP	TOTAL STAGE TIME
1st	Bernard Darniche/Alain Mahe	F	4	Lancia Stratos	G4	8h.13m.38s
2nd	Bjorn Waldegard/Hans Thorszelius	S	2	Ford Escort RS	G4	8h.13m.44s
3rd	Markku Alen/Ilkka Kivimaki	SF	3	Fiat Abarth 131	G4	8h.17m.47s
4th	Jean-Claude Andruet/Chantal Lienard	F	9	Fiat Abarth 131	G4	8h.19m.20s
5th	Hannu Mikkola/Arne Hertz	SF/S	5	Ford Escort RS	G4	8h.23m.07s
6th	Jean-Pierre Nicolas/Jean Todt	F	1	Porsche 911	G4	8h.26m.37s
7th	Michele Mouton/Francoise Conconi	F	12	Fiat Abarth 131	G4	8h.34m.46s*
8th	Guy Frequelin/Jacques Delaval	F	16	Renault 5 Alpine	G2	8h.44m.27s
9th	Jacques Almeras/Maurice Gelin	F	36	Porsche 911	G4	8h.49m.56s
10th	Ari Vatanen/David Richards	SF/GB	17	Ford Fiesta 1600	G2	8h.50m.15s
12th	Jean-Louis Clarr/Dominique Mahuteaux	F	26	Opel Kadett GT/E	G1	8h.59m.45s
17th	Gerard Swaton/Martine Cordesse	F	38	Porsche 911	G3	9h.17m.44s
50th	Dany Snobeck/Christian Delferrier	F	42	Volkswagen Golf D	Diesel	9h.51m.45s

233 starters. 154 finishers. 84 finished *parcours final*. *Ladies winner. 16 A-priority drivers.

World Championship positions after Round 1
Lancia 18 points, Ford 16, Fiat 14, Renault 11, Porsche 8.

World Championship for Drivers positions after Round 1
Darniche 20 points, Waldegard 15, Alen 12, Andruet 10, Mikkola 8, Nicolas 6, Mouton 4, Frequelin 3, Almeras 2, Vatanen 1.

Leading retirements

DRIVER/NAVIGATOR	NATION-ALITY	COMP NO.	CAR	GROUP	CAUSE	STAGES COMPLETED
Anders Kullang/Bob de Jong	S/NL	10	Opel Kadett GT/E	G2	punctures	1
Attilio Bettega/Maurizio Perissinot	I	20	Fiat Ritmo	G2	engine	7
Achim Warmbold/Phillipe Alessandrini	F	21	Citroën CX2500D	Diesel	disqualified (Police)	19
Jean-Luc Therier/Michel Vial	F	19	VW Golf GTi	G2	broken throttle cable	20
Fulvio Bacchelli/Bruno Scabini	I	6	Lancia Stratos	G4	accident	25
Per Eklund/Hans Sylvan	S	7	Fiat Ritmo	G2	engine	25
Walter Rohrl/Christian Geistdorfer	D	14	Fiat Abarth 131	G4	engine	29
Tony Carello/Renato Meiohas	I	8	Ford Escort RS	G4	lost wheel	29

Rally leaders
Mikkola stage 1, Waldegard 2-4, Mikkola 5-11, Waldegard 12, (13 cancelled), Mikkola 14-18, Waldegard 19-29, Darniche 30.

Leading special stage positions

	1ST	2ND	3RD	4TH	5TH	6TH		1ST	2ND	3RD	4TH	5TH	6TH		1ST	2ND	3RD	4TH	5TH	6TH
Darniche	13	2	2	1	3	4	Rohrl	3	7	5	8	2	1	Nicolas	—	4	2	2	4	1
Mikkola	8	4	3	2	4	3	Alen	3	—	8	4	6	6	Bacchelli	—	1	—	—	1	1
Waldegard	3	7	8	1	1	6	Andruet	1	2	3	5	6	5	Vatanen	—	—	1	1	—	1

The route

		SPECIAL STAGES	TOTAL DISTANCE
'Concentration'	9 starting cities — Vals le Bains Saturday until Sunday evening	—	Average 1700 km
'Classement'	Vals le Bains (0300 Monday) — Monaco (1500 Monday)	5 — 106 km	584 km
'Commun'	Monaco (0800 Tuesday) — Gap — Digne — Monaco (1600 Wednesday) (1 stage cancelled because of delays)	14 — 294 km (reduced from 15 — 313)	About 1300 km
'Final'	Monaco (1800 Tuesday) — Monaco (0800 Friday) (only the best 100 cars in general classification)	10 — 175 km	645 km
		29 stages — 575 km	About 4200 km

All stages asphalt, mostly covered by wet ice or snow in places. 14 stages daylight. Most stages in clear weather.

Previous winners

1969 Bjorn Waldegard Porsche 911
1970 Bjorn Waldegard Porsche 911
1971 Ove Andersson Renault Alpine A110
1972 Sandro Munari Lancia Fulvia
1973 Jean-Claude Andruet Renault Alpine A110
1974 Rally cancelled
1975 Sandro Munari Lancia Stratos
1976 Sandro Munari Lancia Stratos
1977 Sandro Munari Lancia Stratos
1978 Jean-Pierre Nicolas Porsche 911

One of the unsolved mysteries of the year — why did Bjorn Waldegard in this factory Ford Escort RS ease up on the last special stage, to let Darniche through to win? Seen here at the Col de Corobin, one of the few stages clear of ice and snow this year

The end of the line for Fiat? Third place was a disappointment. The end of development of their Abarth 131 was indicated by their inability to match the speed of the Lancia and the official Fords

not the only surprise that Ford sprang: the performance of the Fiesta 1600, making its rally debut, was another. Vatanen had delays on road sections which cost him victory in group 2, which through reliability rather than performance went to the 1400 cc Renault 5 Alpine of Guy Frequelin. But even quicker than the Fiesta was the French-prepared Volkswagen Golf GTi of Jean-Luc Therier, which used Zenith fuel injection. The Fiat Ritmo also went well, but both eventually retired with engine troubles. The Monte Carlo Rally offered a very interesting comparison between the various front-wheel-drive group 2 cars — with Fiat, Ford, VW and Renault all represented. Only Audi, Peugeot and the bigger Saab Turbo were absent.

For the second year running, Fiats were defeated. Like Ford they entered two different types of car, a complication which often leads to confusion. In the case of Ford the division of effort between the Escort and the Fiesta could have been the reason why Dunlop, their tyre suppliers, did not bring studded racing tyres for the Escorts to use — the prime cause of their ultimate defeat at the hands of the French Lancia team. For Fiat, the main chance of success was to have been snow: on the three snowy stages on the rally the Abarth 131 cars were quickest. The Ritmo was contesting its third rally, the first WCR outing, using two drivers (Eklund and Bettega) who were new to the official team.

The one unanswered question is whether the Abarth 131 would have been defeated so conclusively by the Fords if their cars had been prepared for

THIS PAGE *Jean-Claude Andruet started an unhappy year well, with fourth place in this French team Fiat Abarth 131, with a new co-driver (another girl, Chantal Lienard), although both Alen and Rohrl with factory cars were faster*

Spectacular as ever but far less successful this year were the Renault 5 Alpines. This is Guy Frequelin who eventually won the group 2 category, partnered by Jacques Delaval

Ari Vatanen drove well after a lucky incident earlier when a broken driveshaft occured within full view of the mechanics. This car was built by the German team while the other Fiesta, built at Boreham, did well in the hands of Roger Clark

Technically the great interest was in the front-wheel drive battle in group 2. The fastest car was this Golf GTi, prepared in France and driven by Jean-Luc Therier. A throttle problem caused retirement on the final night

FACING PAGE *One of the best private performances came from Jurgen Barth who finished in 20th place with this Porsche 924. Originally the car was to be a Turbo, but when homologation was delayed this pre-production model had to be converted back to an ordinary 924*

Fiat entered with two car models, the Abarth 131 and the new Ritmo. Here is the Ritmo of Eklund having its gearbox changed in the Monte Carlo service area

A new model to appear on international rallies this year was the Mazda RX7. Here is Nakagawa's car, which finished 73rd and won its class

clear conditions. One suspects that the result would have been the same, though a little closer perhaps. It looked like the beginning of the eclipse of the design, of the inevitable end of the successes which often have been achieved more through driving skills and organization than design advantage.

The Monte Carlo Rally claimed one important record: it was the first ever rally to count for the new World Championship for Rally Drivers. Already it seems that this series might well assume an importance at the expense of the manufacturer's series. Drivers signed up for manufacturers for certain WCR rounds were anxiously seeking contracts to drive for other teams — something which will strengthen the position of the leading drivers but edge out the others. The Monte Carlo Rally is the oldest round in the WCR, it is usually the most heavily subscribed and it is never short of interest. It would be just perfect if the organizations reacted like their colleagues on other events.

Swedish Rally

Stig Blomqvist's win with the Saab 99 Turbo made the first important breakthrough in international rallying for many years: the first world victory by a turbocharged car. It will take time to understand just how important this victory will have been, but immediately nobody could be happier than Saab themselves, since it provided just the momentum their international sales force needed for the Turbo models. It was a victory gained at the expense, once again, of the Ford team, who had last year completely dominated this event. Of the three official Escort drivers, the two leaders, Waldegard and Mikkola, both left the road, and only Vatanen had a clear run. His objective of proving himself against these master rally drivers expired when the engine failed. He had been leading the event outright, pulling ahead of Blomqvist. Eventually Waldegard recovered from lying virtually last on the first stage to second, whilst Mikkola was able to finish fifth — the same positions they had achieved in Monte Carlo.

After the remarkable level of competition at Monte Carlo, the Swedish and its specialist demands of driving skills seemed less exciting, there were ten seeded drivers entered (out of a possible sixteen from Scandinavia), but with the exception of the Frenchman Jean-Luc Therier there were no drivers of any consequence from outside northern Europe on the list at all. Factory cars were entered by Saab, Ford, Fiat, Opel, Datsun, Toyota, Lada/Vaz and Vauxhall, though only Ford came in strength. Fiat were represented by Alen under a system in which the local dealers rented the car and mechanics from Italy. The greatest interest lay with Saab, however, since the car used by Blomqvist was a new type, in group 4. It was in fact an old 99EMS two-door carburettor car fitted with a turbo engine, rather than the actual estate-type three-door production car, which was used in group 2 and an example of which was driven by

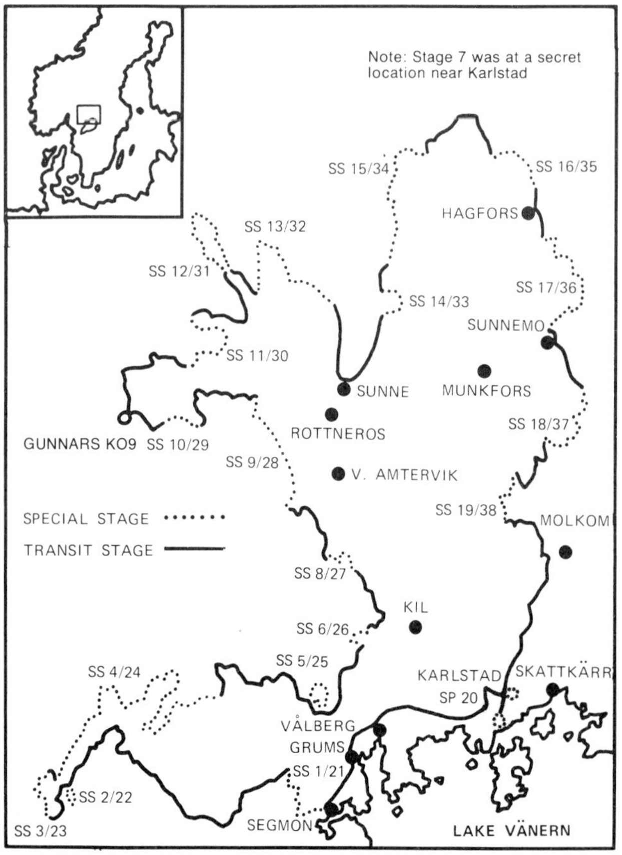

Eklund as well. In addition, Opel created great interest, since their two cars were fitted with much more powerful engines than those used by Eurohandler cars; large valves were the special feature, and even though carburettors were still used, some 197 bhp was quoted for the cars driven by Kullang and Danielsson. These engines were built in Sweden by Jan Carneborn. Fords came with Escorts only, which in view of the difficulties at Monte Carlo and the impending chaos here must have been a wise decision.

The trouble in Sweden was brought about by the weather; or rather the lack of it! For an event known as the only winter rally in the World series, the concept of drivers having to travel along stretches of gravel was bizarre. In fact, the winter concept still remained, the temperatures were still as low as usual — often below −20°C — but the roads never had the usual protective layer of ice between the gravel and the packed snow. The problem was heightened by the short training period (one week) in which decisions about tyres had to be made — and stocks obtained — in addition to the normal tasks of learning the roads to be used. A club rally one week before the Swedish had used some of the same stages, and the effect was soon noticed by the drivers on the International. But there were many unsolved problems, like whether there were special problems with these stages or whether the same effect would afflict all the others (in fact these stages cut up much more than others) and of course whether there would be snowfalls between then and the event itself. Every stage, with two exceptions, was used twice, once on the first night and once on the second, and many teams sent out crews after the first run to see what changes the stages had suffered.

LEFT *Stig Blomqvist scored the first international championship rally win for a turbocharged car on the Swedish, partnered by a new co-driver Bjorn Cederberg, formerly the co-driver of Eklund. See how narrow are the front tyres, especially for such a heavy car*

BELOW *Pentti Airikkala drove to third place, the best non-Swedish driver. This avenged the memory of retirement the year before due to a minor engine fault*

The basis of the rally was the convenience and pleasure of the competitors themselves. With the duplication of the stages, training was cut down, whilst the stages themselves were held nearer to the headquarters at Karlstad than previously. If ever there is a pity about the Swedish, it is that the event is so specialized. It would be so nice if foreign drivers could fully enjoy the event, but the demands are so special that this can never really happen. Quite apart from the problems of the cold and the driving, even the snow itself is unlike that anywhere else in Europe. It is so dry.

Markku Alen enjoyed a very brief moment of glory; he made best time on the very first stage! From then onwards

29 Swedish Rally

16-18 February 1979 Sweden

Overall results

POSITION	DRIVER/NAVIGATOR	NATIONALITY	COMP NO.	CAR	GROUP	TOTAL STAGE TIME
1st	Stig Blomqvist/Bjorn Cederberg	S	3	Saab 99 Turbo (Sedan)	G4	6h.34m.49s
2nd	Bjorn Waldegard/Hans Thorszelius	S	1	Ford Escort RS	G4	6h.36m.09s
3rd	Pentti Airikkala/Risto Virtanen	SF	5	Vauxhall Chevette 2300HS	G4	6h.39m.31s
4th	Markku Alen/Ilkka Kivimaki	SF	2	Fiat Abarth 131	G4	6h.40m.42s
5th	Hannu Mikkola/Arne Hertz	SF/S	4	Ford Escort RS	G4	6h.45m.19s
6th	Bjorn Johansson/Ragnar Spjut	S	14	Opel Kadett Rallye E	G2	6h.56m.07s
7th	Ola Stromberg/Hans-Joran Ericson	S	15	Saab 99EMS	G2	7h.05m.55s
8th	Lars Carlsson/Mats Nordstrom	S	37	Ford Escort RS	G1	7h.10m.27s
9th	John Haugland/Martin Holmes	N/GB	12	Datsun 160J	G2	7h.11m.25s
10th	Sven-Inge Neby/Lars Backman	S	19	Volvo 142	G2	7h.12m.37s
28th	Tom Trana/Lars Billengren	S	51	Peugeot 504D	Diesel	8h.26m.49s

113 starters, 39 finishers. No lady crews. No separate group 3 class. 10 A-priority drivers.
(Note: A total of 145 crews started the event, the extra 32 were competing in a national event using the same route except for the last 9 stages. (Official results gave results in seconds taken, i.e. Blomqvist incurred 23689 penalties.)

World Championship positions after Round 2
Ford 32 points, Fiat 26, Lancia and Saab 18, Vauxhall 14, Opel 13, Renault 11, Porsche and Datsun 8, Volvo 6.

Leading positions in World Championship for Drivers after Round 2
Waldegard 30 points, Alen 22, Darniche and Blomqvist 20, Mikkola 16, Airikkala 12, Andruet 10, Nicolas and Johansson 6, Mouton and Stromberg 4.

Leading retirements

DRIVER/NAVIGATOR	NATIONALITY	COMP NO.	CAR	GROUP	CAUSE	STAGES COMPLETED
Harry Kallstrom/Claes Billstam	S	9	Datsun 160J	G2	engine	0
Jens Sogaard/Ojvind Sogaard	N	16	Opel Kadett GT/E	G2	accident	0
Anders Tunemar/Raymond Eriksson	S	18	Saab 99	G2	accident	3
Leif Asterhag/Anders Gullberg	S	11	Toyota Celica	G2	head gasket	10
Jean-Luc Therier/Michel Vial	F	13	Toyota Celica	G2	accident	11
Ari Vatanen/David Richards	SF/GB	6	Ford Escort RS	G4	head gasket	15
Per Eklund/Hans Sylvan	S	8	Saab 99 Turbo (Combi)	G2	engine	23
Anders Kullang/Bruno Berglund	S	7	Opel Kadett GT/E	G2	crankshaft pulley	23
Bror Danielsson/Ulf Sundberg	S	10	Opel Kadett GT/E	G2	wheel studs	36

Rally leaders
Alen stage 1, Mikkola 2-3, Kullang 4-9, Vatanen 10-15, Blomqvist 16-end.

Leading special stage positions

	1ST	2ND	3RD	4TH	5TH	6TH		1ST	2ND	3RD	4TH	5TH	6TH		1ST	2ND	3RD	4TH	5TH	6TH
Waldegard	19	9	2	4	2	—	Airikkala	3	4	3	7	5	3	Kullang	2	1	4	3	6	3
Blomqvist	7	8	10	6	4	1	Mikkola	2	12	6	3	4	3	Danielsson	—	2	—	1	5	15
Vatanen	5	4	1	1	1	—	Alen	2	2	8	7	7	3	Eklund	—	—	1	6	3	1

The route

		SPECIAL STAGES	TOTAL DISTANCE
Etape 1	Karlstad (Friday 1300) — Gunnarskog — Karlstad (Saturday 0500)	19 — 319 km	752 km
Etape 2	Karlstad (Saturday 1200) — Gunnarskog — Karlstad (Sunday 0325)	19 — 314 km	696 km
		38 stages — 633 km	1448 km

All stages gravel, mostly snow or ice covered. 9 stages in daylight. All stages in clear weather.

Previous winners

1969 Bjorn Waldegard Porsche 911
1970 Bjorn Waldegard Porsche 911
1971 Stig Blomqvist Saab 96 V4
1972 Stig Blomqvist Saab 96 V4
1973 Stig Blomqvist Saab 96 V4
1974 Rally not held
1975 Bjorn Waldegard Lancia Stratos
1976 Per Eklund Saab 96 V4
1977 Stig Blomqvist Saab 99EMS
1978 Bjorn Waldegard Ford Escort RS

Surely the best drive of the rally came from the local driver Bjorn Johansson with this Opel Kadett Rallye 2.0E, a 'cheap' version of the Kadett GT/E. Ultimately he won group 2 after the Kadett GT/Es of Kullang and Danielsson both retired

he had a rally of misery, and did well to finish fourth. Hannu Mikkola took over the lead, but then he had a series of troubles, not the least being two excursions off the road and the conviction that the car was not working well. Then on the fourth stage, the longest of the rally, Kullang with his group 2 Opel Kadett GT/E pulled ahead. Already one Datsun had failed (Kallstrom had his engine overheat and seize) and Eklund had damaged the engine in his Saab Turbo. The remarkable fact was that not only was one Kadett leading but Danielsson in the other one was third! What was more, Therier in his Toyota group 2 was fourth. These positions were not fully indicative, however, for Vatanen was a strong second and Blomqvist was temporarily down at fifth.

Vatanen began his battle with Blomqvist, gradually pulling into the lead after ten stages, Blomqvist overtaking Kullang after twelve. On stage fifteen Vatanen scored a remarkable fastest time, thirty-six seconds better than the next fastest, Blomqvist — and promptly the engine failed. From then on Blomqvist was alone. Waldegard was up to sixth place at the end of the first leg; on the second leg Kullang, whilst still second, had his crankshaft pulley fail, Waldegard eventually reached second place after the long stage was run again and Airikkala came to an excellent third place despite valve trouble with his Vauxhall Chevette. Group 4 cars scored the top five places, group 2 went to the young Swede Bjorn Johansson, who drove an Opel Kadett Rallye E instead of the more expensive GT/E model, whilst Danielsson fell to fifth before retiring one stage before the finish.

THIS PAGE *Markku Alen, borrowed this Fiat Abarth 131 with some friendly mechanics and drove privately with the help of the local importers. His fourth place put him temporarily into second place on the Drivers World Championship, the successor to the FIA Cup which he won in 1978*

Anders Kullang actually led the rally outright on the first leg with this Opel Kadett GT/E. For this rally locally built engines with big valve heads were fitted, and they gave greater power than Irmscher engines had done in the past

Amazingly agile was this old model Volvo 142, driven by Sven-Inge Neby, prepared with the help of the rallycross expert Per-Inge Walfridsson

FACING PAGE *First important winter rally for the live-axle Datsun 160J resulted in ninth place for the Norwegian John Haugland. Note the Dunlop stickers, although locally made tyres are essential for winter rallies*

With the excitement of the Turbo victory, Vatanen was forgotten. He had been leading when his engine failed

DAD
OK motorhotell
UDDEHOLM
12
DATSUN
DUNLOP
MARTIN HOLMES
DUNLOP
DUNLOP
DUNLOP

ROTHMANS ESCORT ROTHMANS
ROTHMANS
ROTHMANS
ROTHMANS
6
FORD
WTW 567S
DUNLOP

Vinho do Porto Rallye de Portugal

Not every rally can be as exciting as the 1978 Portuguese Port Wine Rally, and a quick glance at the entry list for the 1979 event showed that there was clearly to be an anti-climax. Only one team, Ford, were taking the event seriously; the number of A-priority drivers was down to six. Without Fiat any rally seems dull, and Ford eventually claimed their first victory of the season and strengthened their position at the head of the World Championship. Victory went to Mikkola, although Waldegard had been marginally faster through the rally: for Waldegard this was the fourth consecutive second place on a WCR event, but as on the RAC he had more troubles with his car than his team-mate. It was the first time a British car had won this event, but despite the best endeavours of the Ford drivers, the early stages of the rally were commanded by Bernard Darniche with his Chardonnet Lancia Stratos. Electrical trouble forced him to retire at the start of the eighth stage, and from then on Fords had no rivals.

Hannu Mikkola started this year showing signs of the bad luck which had often hung over his career. The RAC Rally, indeed the whole Sedan Products series, last year made it seem that Mikkola was now getting the results that his skills deserved, but then little things started to afflict him again. Now things were on the up for this Finn once more. His only problem, and one which could easily have put him out of the whole rally, was an axle fault on the third section, which caused great anxiety. Waldegard also had to change his axle unexpectedly. Otherwise the two Ford machines were able to finish without serious trouble, well ahead of the opposition. Their third car, the Rothman's-sponsored car of Ari Vatanen, retired on the first day due to the driver's back trouble, a convenient situation which eased the service plans and the tyre supply.

Apart from Ford's activities, the 1979 Portuguese Rally mattered little. There was a handful of other group 4 entries, the Chevette 2300HS of 'Meqepe' which never went well, a few Porsches

Bjorn Waldegard scored his fourth successive second place on a World Championship Rally when Mikkola beat him on this event. It was another two events before he would win again

and two Audi 80 two-door models, which are expected to be accepted into group 2 when production justifies. For Audi this event was an important step in their programme of giving their models exposure in leading rallying activities. Last year the team ventured abroad to Romania, the 1000 Lakes in Finland and then the RAC, but this time the poor entry enabled a lot of attention to be focused on this well-presented team, which made their ultimate finishing very important. This they achieved, in sixth and seventh places, the first time the official team had gained WCR points. Apart from these cars the top group in international rallying ended. Group 2, on the other hand, attracted much more activity.

Hannu Mikkola led the Portuguese Rally after the first night retirement of Bernard Darniche. This picture was taken at Fafe

Opel and Toyota are currently the leaders in international group 2. Opel have found a new turn of speed this year, and the initial pace of Anders Kullang in the semi-official Dutch Opel

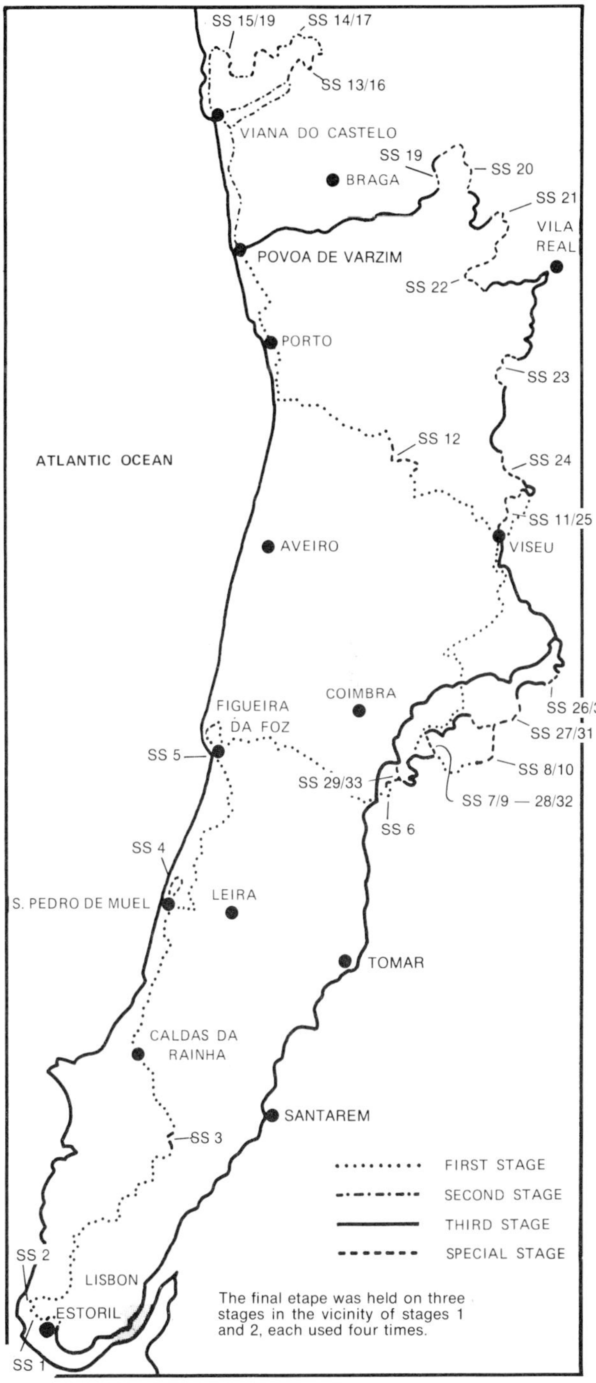

12 Vinho do Porto Rallye de Portugal

6-11 March 1979 Portugal

Overall results

POSITION	DRIVER/NAVIGATOR	NATIONALITY	COMP NO.	CAR	GROUP	TOTAL STAGE TIME
1st	Hannu Mikkola/Arne Hertz	SF/S	1	Ford Escort RS	G4	9h.13m.52s
2nd	Bjorn Waldegard/Hans Thorszelius	S	3	Ford Escort RS	G4	9h.16m.36s
3rd	Ove Andersson/Henry Liddon	S/GB	4	Toyota Celica	G2	9h.35m.00s
4th	Andy Dawson/Martin Holmes	GB	11	Datsun 160J	G2	10h.01m.37s
5th	Carlos Torres/Pedro de Almeida	P	10	Ford Escort RS	G1	10h.05m.49s
6th	Harald Demuth/Arwed Fischer	D	16	Audi 80	G4	10h.06m.37s
7th	Freddy Kottulinsky/Michael Schwagerl	S/D	24	Audi 80	G4	10h.52m.38s
8th	Joaquim Santos/Albino Tristao	P	21	Opel Kadett GT/E	G2	11h.32m.10s
9th	Jorge Ortigao/Joaquim Bessa	P	22	Opel 1904SR	G2	11h.44m.58s
10th	Marques Baptista/Isabel Baptista	P	90	Opel 1904SR	G1	11h.58m.12s
16th	Natacha Milon/Berthe Lubert	F	106	VW Golf GTi	G1	15h.28m.33s*

88 starters. 16 finishers. *Ladies winner. No group 3 finishers. No diesel cars. 6 A-priority drivers.
(Note: Opel 1904SR is local name for Ascona)

World Championship positions after Round 3
Ford 50, Fiat 26, Datsun and Opel 22, Lancia and Saab 18, Toyota 16, Vauxhall 14, Renault and Audi 11, Porsche 8, Volvo 6.

Leading positions in World Championship for Drivers after Round 3
Waldegard 45, Mikkola 36, Alen 22, Darniche and Blomqvist 20, Airikkala and Andersson 12, Andruet and Dawson 10, Nicolas, Johansson and Torres 8.

Leading retirements

DRIVER/NAVIGATOR	NATION-ALITY	COMP NO.	CAR	GROUP	CAUSE	STAGES COMPLETED
Jean-Paul Luc/Bernard Martin-Dondoz	F	15	Citroën CX2400	G2	head gasket	3
Ari Vatanen/Peter Bryant	SF/GB	5	Ford Escort RS	G4	driver illness	4
Bernard Darniche/Alain Mahe	F	2	Lancia Stratos	G4	electrics	7
Anders Kullang/Bob de Jong	S/NL	6	Opel Kadett GT/E	G2	rear axle	9
Giovanni Salvi/Jorge Cirne	P	12	Ford Escort RS	G2	halfshaft	9
'Meqepe'/Miguel Vilar	P	8	Vauxhall Chevette 2300HS	G4	electrics	10
Carlos Peres/Jose Peres	P	17	Opel Kadett GT/E	G2	accident	12
Jean-Luc Therier/Michel Vial	F	7	Toyota Celica	G2	engine	17
Americo Nunes/Antonio Morais	P	18	Porsche 911	G4	disqualified (short-cut)	18

Rally leaders
Darniche stage 1-7, Mikkola 8-end.

Leading special stage positions

	1st	2nd	3rd	4th	5th	6th		1st	2nd	3rd	4th	5th	6th		1st	2nd	3rd	4th	5th	6th
Waldegard	21	17	4	1	1	1	Therier	1	1	2	10	1	1	Kullang	—	1	2	1	2	—
Mikkola	19	20	2	3	1	—	Andersson	—	6	24	4	5	3	Dawson	—	—	1	11	11	9
Darniche	6	—	1	—	—	—	Torres	—	1	4	11	5	7	Demuth	—	—	1	2	12	12

The route

		SPECIAL STAGES	TOTAL DISTANCE
Etape 1	Estoril (Wednesday 1000) — Figueira da Foz — Povoa de Varzim (Thursday 0730)	4 asphalt — 26 km 8 gravel — 184 km	884 km
Etape 2	Povoa de Varzim (Thursday 1630) — Povoa de Varzim (Friday 0045)	6 gravel — 121 km	410 km
Etape 3	Povoa de Varzim (Friday 1000) — Viseu — Tomar — Estoril (Saturday 1200)	15 gravel — 316 km	1085 km
Etape 4	Estoril (Saturday 2200) — Estoril (Sunday 0515)	12 asphalt — 88 km	287 km
		45 stages — 735 km	2666 km

All but one stage was dry. 12 stages in daylight.

Previous winners

1969 Fernando Romaozinho Citroën DS21
1970 Simo Lampinen Lancia Fulvia
1971 Jean-Pierre Nicolas Renault Alpine A110
1972 Achim Warmbold BMW 2002tii
1973 Jean-Luc Therier Renault Alpine A110
1974 Raffaele Pinto Fiat Abarth 124
1975 Markku Alen Fiat Abarth 124
1976 Sandro Munari Lancia Stratos
1977 Markku Alen Fiat Abarth 131
1978 Markku Alen Fiat Abarth 131

*Ove **Andersson**, Portugal Rally specialist, tackles one of the Sintra stages on the final night. Note the formidable tyres fitted for this all-asphalt stage, as some protection against the debris thrown on the roads by the spectators*

team showed that his Swedish performance was no fluke. Certainly the engines built in Sweden are far more powerful than those prepared previously in Germany. Toyota themselves have now turned from Germany to Sweden for their engines, although this move has not yet given them any greater reliability than before. Kullang retired when his rear axle failed through lack of oil, while Therier, the faster of the two drivers, failed to finish when a connecting rod broke. From these teams only the car of Ove Andersson reached the finish. Team Datsun Europe started with one car, and this finished second in the group behind Andersson with team manager Andy Dawson driving. Other positions were gained by private Portuguese drivers. In group 1 there was no opposition to Carlos Torres's Ford Escort RS, which despite a cylinder head gasket failure finished almost two hours ahead of the second driver!

The Port Wine Rally has one claim which even the poorest of entries can never deny, that is the almost perfect organization. Perhaps a country like Portugal does not present the traffic problems of countries nearer the centre of Europe, but equally the poorer facilities of Portugal cannot make the organization easy. The organization even coped with the amazing crowds, which were greater in places than any on the RAC — and which were far more excitable. If there is any criticism due, it must be that the rally is so popular. At the finish, at 0530 hours on Sunday morning, the main grandstand of the Estoril racetrack was almost full! Drivers at Sintra stated that they could only follow the special stage by aiming their cars down the gaps in the spectators. Luckily few drivers were travelling fast, and there were no incidents.

With the first quarter of the championship over, Ford have no real group 4 opposition, in view of the official Fiat team's absence from most events. Possibly their only real opposition will come from one of the group 2 teams. Of these, Datsun have the biggest programme, but their cars are the least powerful. Already the Ford drivers Waldegard and Mikkola have started to pull well ahead in the Drivers' series, leaving behind their unlucky team-mate Vatanen. One of the most important aspects of Ford's championship campaign is the reliability of their cars. In over half a year there has been only one retirement due to mechanical failure, Vatanen's engine trouble in Sweden. For success in any World series, reliability is the first requirement, and this is something Ford possesses in good measure.

ABOVE *Andy Dawson jumps over the humps at Ponte de Lima, on the northern loop. His fourth place was lucky as a broken valve very nearly caused retirement*

FACING PAGE *Carlos Torres, the reigning Portuguese rally champion, finished fifth and best in group 1, despite engine troubles*

Some idea of Portuguese enthusiasm! These people crowded the Estoril stadium for a slalom test that was optional for the drivers

Darniche was unlucky to retire with electrical trouble. He was leading and pulling away when he had to give up. Here is the Lancia at Montejunto, the first gravel stage of the event

Two anonymous brothers: left is 'Meqepe' who this year competed with an ex-DTV Vauxhall Chevette 2300HS (one of the cars banned the year before) and right is 'Peqepe' who competes with an Opel Kadett GT/E

How the mighty are fallen! This monument of a spectator's appreciation for Tony Fall in years gone by, now lies in the gutter beside the track at the Freita special stage (SS 12). Andy Dawson pays tribute, in a pause during training

UHM 738S
Herculano
ALFAIAS AGRICOLAS
Castrol
Firestone
10

FORD ESCORT
1

CHARDONNET
MICHELIN
CIBIE
LANCIA

James
OPEL
OPEL

Safari Rally

On several occasions one thought that the might of Mercedes would smash the Safari traditions, but in the end it seemed that money alone could not win through. The best drivers, the most powerful cars, the greatest numbers of mechanics — they were not enough, no substitute for the wisdom of experience. Their problems came to a head when things did not go to plan, when there were breakdowns they had not expected, and they did not know how to adapt themselves in the moment of crisis. So it was that Datsun came through to win, a team which used drivers known more for their experience than their speed, with cars that the drivers complained had quite the wrong sort of engine, with just a handful of supporting service crews. They had a team which used cars that were simple in specification and were the most reliable. Four major teams entered the event: in addition to Mercedes and Datsun there were Fiat and Peugeot, all of which combined to make this a Safari to remember.

The Safari is a rally which exasperates the losers and gratifies, like no others, those who win. Mercedes made what most people considered to be a fundamental error in using two types of car, something which probably cost Ford their Monte Carlo victory, but then Peugeot had one type of car (the 504 Coupé V6), and their three leading runners retired with identical problems! Fiat entered three Abarth 131s, nearly withdrew through problems with their cars before the rally and poured endless energy into the efforts of their Safari specialists Munari and Rohrl, only to obtain third place with their other driver Alen, who had never rallied in Kenya before! But even with the activity of all the other teams, the one intriguing question was whether Mercedes could buy

their way to success. If they could, the exasperation of the other teams would be complete.

Mercedes came with the 280E cars, a proven rallying model, and the 450SLC 5.0, using a proven chassis and a new engine specification. There were three of each type on the entry list, Mikkola, Waldegard and the local driver Preston with the big cars, and Singh, Cowan and Zasada with the saloons. The new cars were homologated for the moment in group 4, pending full-scale production, and were fitted with automatic gear boxes. These were modified to provide quicker gearshifts, and although the drivers were non-committal about their advantages, they were expected to offer advantages if the going got muddy. The Peugeots were cars developed since the Bandama, with more powerful engines and some lightening. This lightening was to prove their downfall, since in the predominantly dry conditions their undershielding was insufficient. Makinen, Nicolas, Lampinen, and Lefebvre were the drivers, the last-named with an older, heavier car which alone was able to finish. The Fiats were normal European-type cars modified for the rigours of Africa and a lot heavier than usual, whilst Datsun also came with heavyweight 160J cars, prepared in Japan. There was another first-time competitor, though not strictly official. This was the Porsche 924 Turbo, two of which were entered by a private team run by Porsche engineer and racing driver Jurgen Barth.

Pre-rally forecasts had led to expectations of a wet Safari, but for the front-runners at least the rally was drier than anticipated. The starting order therefore was expected to be more important than ever, since only the first driver on the road will have a route clear of dust. Even despite the dangers of being the first to drive through the open roads used on this event, it is better to be in front. Rauno Aaltonen was drawn to be number one with his Datsun and kept this advantage until he suffered a broken axle towards the end of the first of the three legs, when Makinen forced his way through. Mercedes lost one of their 450SLCs when Preston had an axle locating bolt fail and he was stranded, whilst Nicolas and Lampinen both retired with engine troubles. This was a mystery to Peugeot, for whereas Lampinen admitted that his engine failed after a heavy landing, the reason was not so apparent to Nicolas. Still, Makinen had managed to take the lead, after the first night when Mehta was delayed repairing suspension damage and after Waldegard was stopped with a similar problem to Preston. Makinen was forced to relinquish his lead on the road when he stopped to change his engine sump, and this let secondplace-man Mikkola into the head of the rally.

On the second leg Makinen had more

Shekhar Mehta played a waiting game with his underpowered Datsun, and eventually fought through to win. The bent wing is evidence of a skirmish with Timo Makinen, which led to damaged suspension and delay

Bookmakers at the rally headquarters at the Kenyatta Centre in Nairobi do a brisk trade, updating their odds as the rally progresses. At this moment, Munari was favourite

DUNLOP
DATSUN
9

Guptas
TEL 25431 - 26354
(E. AFRICA'S OLDEST BOOKMAKERS)
12th to 16th BETTING ON SAFARI 27th RALLY
ODDS DRIVERS MAKE CAR No
8 AALTONEN DREWS DATSUN 160 1
7 JOGINDER DOIG BENZ 280 2
6 MARKKU ALEN - KIVIMAKI FIAT 131 3
OUT LAMPINEN AHO PEUGE 504 4
20 KALLSTROM BILLSTAM DATSUN 160 5
OUT VIC PRESTON LYALL BENZ 450
MUNARI MAIGA FIAT 131
MAKINEN TODT PEUG 504
S MEHTA DOUGHTY DATSUN 160
WALDEGAARD THORSZEL BENZ 450
W ROHRL GEISTDORFER FIAT 131
NICHOLAS LIDDON PEUG. 504
MIKKOLA HERTZ BENZ 450
R ULYATE STREET FIAT 131
COWAN SYER BENZ 280
HELLIER SHAH DATSUN 160
LEFEBVRE DELFERRIER PEUG 504
ZASADA KRUPA
BARTH KUSSMAUL PORSCHE
WE LAY
OUTRIGHT WINNER
FORECASTS CORRECT/REVERSE
TRICASTS limit £ 2000 X1
CARS JUST TO FINISH
TOP TEN
NO. OF CARS TO FINISH

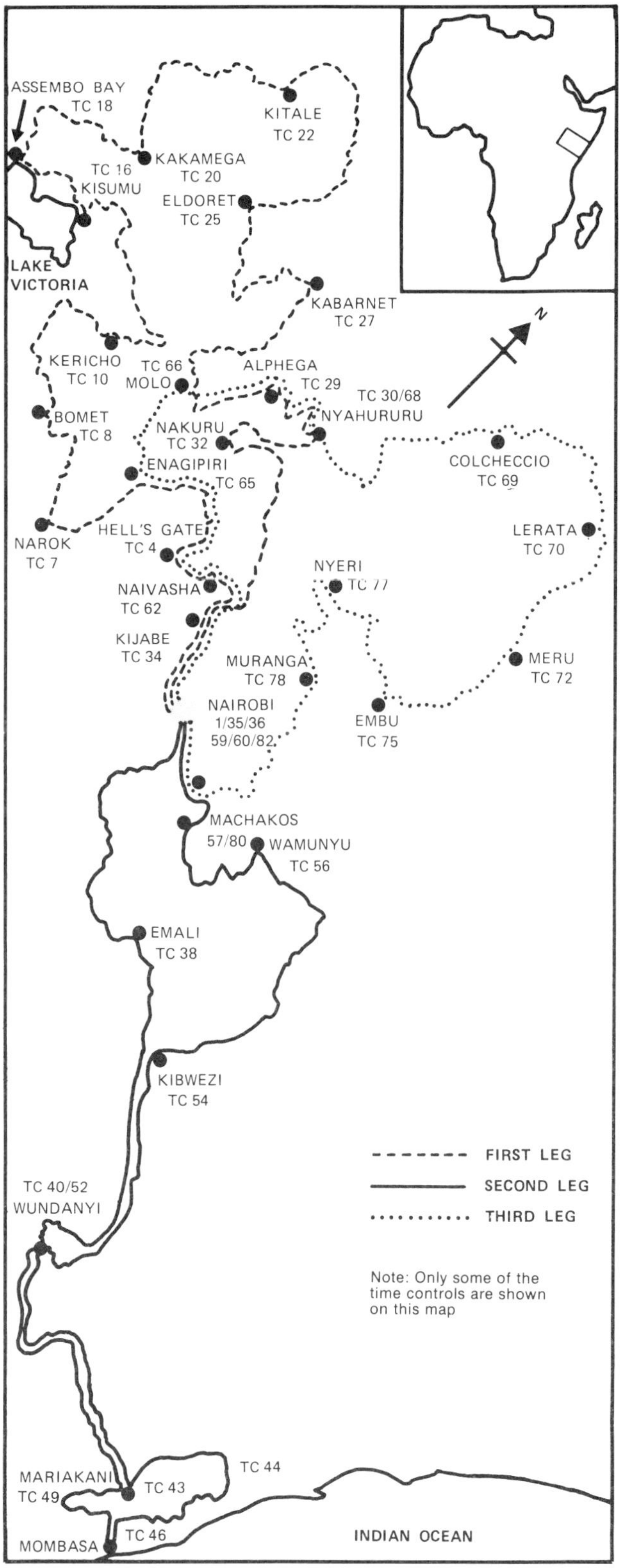
ASSEMBO BAY
TC 18
KITALE
TC 22
KAKAMEGA
TC 20
TC 16
KISUMU
ELDORET
TC 25
LAKE
VICTORIA
KABARNET
TC 27
N
KERICHO
TC 10
TC 66
MOLO
ALPHEGA
TC 29
TC 30/68
NYAHURURU
BOMET
TC 8
NAKURU
TC 32
ENAGIPIRI
TC 65
COLCHECCIO
TC 69
NAROK
TC 7
HELL'S GATE
TC 4
LERATA
TC 70
NYERI
TC 77
NAIVASHA
TC 62
KIJABE
TC 34
MURANGA
TC 78
MERU
TC 72
NAIROBI
1/35/36
59/60/82
EMBU
TC 75
MACHAKOS
57/80
WAMUNYU
TC 56
EMALI
TC 38
KIBWEZI
TC 54
FIRST LEG
SECOND LEG
THIRD LEG
TC 40/52
WUNDANYI
Note: Only some of the time controls are shown on this map
TC 44
MARIAKANI
TC 49
TC 43
TC 46
MOMBASA
INDIAN OCEAN

27 Safari Rally

12-16 April 1979 Kenya, East Africa

Overall results

POSITION	DRIVER/NAVIGATOR	NATIONALITY	COMP NO.	CAR	GROUP	TOTAL PENALTY
1st	Shekhar Mehta/Mike Doughty	EAK	9	Datsun 160J	G2	6h.27m.
2nd	Hannu Mikkola/Arne Hertz	SF/S	14	Mercedes-Benz 450SLC 5.0	G4	7h.15m.
3rd	Markku Alen/Ilkka Kivimaki	SF	3	Fiat Abarth 131	G4	7h.20m.
4th	Andrew Cowan/Johnstone Syer	GB	16	Mercedes-Benz 280E	G2	7h.36m.
5th	Rauno Aaltonen/Lofty Drews	SF/EAK	1	Datsun 160J	G2	8h.06m.
6th	Bjorn Waldegard/Hans Thorszelius	S	10	Mercedes-Benz 450SLC 5.0	G4	9h.20m.
7th	Mike Kirkland/Dave Haworth	EAK	22	Datsun Violet	G2	9h.34m.
8th	Walter Rohrl/Christian Geistdorfer	D	11	Fiat Abarth 131	G4	10h.25m.
9th	Harry Kallstrom/Claes Billstam	S	5	Datsun 160J	G2	10h.43m.
10th	Sandro Munari/Silvio Maiga	I	7	Fiat Abarth 131	G4	11h.33m.

66 starters. 21 finishers. No group 3 or ladies starters. No group 1 finishers. No diesel cars. 13 A-priority drivers.

World Championship positions after Round 4
Ford 50 points, Fiat 41, Datsun 40, Opel 22, Lancia and Saab 18, Toyota and Mercedes-Benz 16, Vauxhall 14, Renault and Audi 11, Porsche 8, Volvo 6.

Leading positions in World Championship for Drivers after Round 4
Waldegard and Mikkola 51 points, Alen 34, Darniche, Blomqvist and Mehta 20, Airikkala and Andersson 12, Andruet, Dawson and Cowan 10.

Leading Retirements

DRIVER/NAVIGATOR	NATIONALITY	COMP NO.	GROUP	CAUSE	CAUSE	CONTROLS VISITED
Jean-Pierre Nicolas/Henry Liddon	F/GB	12	Peugeot 504 V6 Coupé	G4	engine	22
Vic Preston Jnr/John Lyall	EAK	6	Mercedes-Benz 450SLC 5.0	G4	rear axle location	23
Simo Lampinen/Atso Aho	SF	4	Peugeot 504 V6 Coupé	G4	engine	29
Timo Makinen/Jean Todt	SF/F	8	Peugeot 504 V6 Coupé	G4	engine	49
Sobieslaw Zasada/Blazej Krupa	PL	19	Mercedes-Benz 280E	G2	accident	52
Jurgen Barth/Roland Kussmaul	D	20	Porsche 924 Turbo	G4	transmission	70

Rally Leaders
Start —
Control-2 many cars without penalty, 3-4 Munari, Makinen, Mehta and Waldegard without penalty, 5-8 Waldegard, 9 Mehta, 10-21 Waldegard, 22-24 Mehta, 25 Waldegard and Makinen, 26-29 Waldegard, 30-39 Makinen, 40-68 Mikkola, 69-end Mehta.

This grill on the Escort driver's window can be a sensible precaution against rocks thrown by spectators. Munari had his side window smashed by a rock, which he subsequently found in the back of the car

Inexperience was the main reason why Mercedes-Benz, with all their resources, did not win. Hannu Mikkola lost the lead when a problem with his radiator threw the service network into confusion. Mechanically, the automatic V8 5-litre cars were amazingly well suited to the event

The route

		CONTROLS	TOTAL DISTANCE
Etape 1	Nairobi (Friday 1400) — Kisumu — Eldoret — Nakuru — Nairobi (Saturday 1727)	Start — 35	1961 km
Etape 2	Nairobi (Sunday 0700) — Mombasa Nairobi (Monday 0243)	36 — 59	1697 km
Etape 3	Nairobi (Monday 1600) — Nyahururu — Nyeri — Nairobi (Tuesday 1200)	60 — 82	1373 km
		82 controls	5031 km

800 km approximately asphalt, the rest gravel. Total scheduled time 47h.35m., winner's time 54h. 02m. Total of 82 sections of which only 44 not attainable by the leading crews within the time allowance. No special stages. Rally held in mostly dry conditions.

Previous winners
1969 Robin Hillyar Ford Taunus 20M
1970 Edgar Herrman Datsun 1600 SSS
1971 Edgar Herrman Datsun 240Z
1972 Hannu Mikkola Ford Escort RS1600
1973 Shekhar Mehta Datsun 240Z
1974 Joginder Singh Mitsubishi Colt Lancer
1975 Ove Andersson Peugeot 504
1976 Joginder Singh Mitsubishi Colt Lancer
1977 Bjorn Waldegard Ford Escort RS1800
1978 Jean-Pierre Nicolas Peugeot 504 V6 Coupé

Alitalia
3

AMIGO HOTEL
MARIAKANI Bata STOCKIST
Alitalia
MAGNETI MARELLI

FACING PAGE *Marathon man Andrew Cowan enjoys the challenge of the Safari, coming fourth with the smaller model Mercedes-Benz 280E, the best non-seeded driver. He had previously also finished fourth in 1977 and in 1975, both times with Mitsubishi Colt Lancers Markku Alen came to the Safari the only member of the Fiat-Alitalia team not to have competed there before, and came home the best finisher. All five Fiat Abarth 131s to start reached the finish Walter Rohrl had many diversions, the most spectacular being a collision with a minibus which caused extensive damage to the fibreglass bodywork of his Fiat Abarth 131*

ABOVE *Rear axle problems were the result of having disc brakes fitted there for the first time. Harry Kallstrom waits for help without attempting to aid the repair by dismantling the axle*

troubles, his fanbelt broke, and this delay put Mikkola ahead on penalties as well as the road, and later the Peugeot retired with yet another engine failure. Mehta was meanwhile holding his station behind the Mercedes and had become the leading Datsun (Kallstrom was delayed with a similar trouble to Aaltonen, and so all the Datsuns changed their axles as a precaution), whilst Fiat were concerned when Rohrl hit a minibus to the detriment of his car, though he continued. Mercedes lost Zasada, who left the road and the rally was almost brought to a stop by sudden floods. The floods caused penalties on that section to be discounted. Cowan, the canny Scot, brought his 280E Mercedes to fourth place behind Munari.

The third leg started wet and brought the muddiest sections and more troubles for Mercedes. Mikkola had to stop when his radiator was punctured by a fan, and there were delays through service problems, which lost him his lead to Mehta. Mehta then got stuck twice, but continued, while Fiat started to have their hopes disintegrate. Rohrl was stopped with broken steering and Munari had transmission trouble, which dropped both cars many hours behind Alen, who had overtaken Cowan when the 280E had power steering failure. Singh continued, delayed by broken engine mountings, eventually finishing eleventh. Mehta's position was eased when Mikkola had shock absorber troubles, which was unknown to Alen, who had speeded up in the later sections and who unknowingly had almost caught his fellow Finn. Aaltonen and Waldegard continued well to finish fifth and sixth, at speeds which would have given them positions in the top three but for their earlier troubles.

The new Mercedes as a car had proved itself, which was more than could be said for the troublesome Porsche 924 Turbos, neither of which finished, but the reasons for the Mercedes' failure was something that even the perfection of Stuttgart cannot immediately overcome. By everyone else's account, second place was still pretty good.

Acropolis Rally

Tyre troubles once again caused Ford considerable anxiety, and a rally which they should have won with ease was only finally secure on the last morning of the four-day event. Bjorn Waldegard gained an early lead, after his two team-mates Hannu Mikkola and Roger Clark had retired, of almost ten minutes over his rivals. Slowly this was wasted until on the final night (like at Monte Carlo) his lead was lost to the Chardonnet-Lancia of Bernard Darniche. He had started very badly, delayed mostly with tyre troubles as well, but as the rally progressed his chase of the leaders developed. After three hours of stages, at the end of the first afternoon, he was ninth. By the second morning he was third, though still some fourteen minutes behind. At midway he was still third, but now he was only eight minutes behind. By the midnight halt on the third day he was second, only sixty-six seconds behind. With ten stages to go he took the lead — but after only two more sections he was out with rear suspension failure. Waldegard had, at last, gained his revenge for Monte Carlo. He gained a handsome lead as well in the driver's series, whilst Ford had increased their grip on the manufacturers' series too.

The Acropolis was made tougher than ever for 1979, with longer stages and tighter road sections. Despite pleas from the leading teams before the event, the fast road sections were retained, although the overall time limits were extended. The reason for these new changes was difficult to comprehend, since the previous style Acropolis has always been an event popular with private drivers and teams alike. It had been felt that private drivers were at a disadvantage, although none who entered this event had ever been deceived by its challenge. These changes only harmed

the respect held for the organizers, and by good fortune they did not cause the accidents which drivers had feared. Notwithstanding these faults the rally was eagerly anticipated. Full works teams were entered by Ford, Datsun, Toyota, Audi, Lada, Skoda and Polonez; Opel entered through their Dutch team; Renault sent a single car, and only an unavailability of mechanics and insufficient development prevented Mercedes-Benz and Peugeot from entering. Add to this mixture the private Lancia teams of Chardonnet and the Greek privateer 'Siroco' clearly few likely contenders for victory in this style of event were absent.

Group 2 cars were quite the strongest numerically on the entry list, with the competitive group 4 teams being severely limited. With the Safari this year already won by a group 2 car it was not difficult to forecast the possibility of this event being won by one of these cars too. Ford, of course, used group 4 cars, three being fuel injected and one (the carburettor practice car of Waldegard) being refettled for use by the local driver 'Iaveris'. Ford suffered from unavailability of rally engines prepared by their usual company, and they started this event where reliability of the engines is paramount, anxiously. Toyota suffered the loss of a crucial service car the night before the event, and trusted that the remaining vehicles could adequately provide for their two group 2 Celicas. Datsun, their chief 'group' rivals, entered five cars either officially or on loan to local drivers, with countless vehicles in support.

Hot weather provided even tougher conditions for the drivers, of which the greatest single irritation came from dust. Waldegard was the lucky driver to start first, and this advantage helped him to gain an initial lead on penalties, although when troubles began to delay him, first Darniche was able to lead him through the stages, then Andersson with the Toyota, followed by several of the Datsuns as well. On the first day both Mikkola and Clark retired with engine troubles, Toyota lost Therier, both the Audis retired (although not before Demuth had showed remarkable speed) and only one Polonez remained. The Datsuns continued steadily, needing nothing except fuel and tyres. Ragnotti lost time with a puncture on a stage and found his time loss increased by consequent lateness at the next control. By the second day Waldegard's troubles had begun to slow him. Punctures, loss of front brakes, clutch failure, electrical trouble: all these things helped to reduce his lead systematically. Meanwhile, Darniche was going better and his poor start was being forgotten. By halfway he was up to third place with only Andersson between him and Waldegard.

The weather was yielding and at the start of the second part of the rally there was the hint of rain in the air. Rain on asphalt roads in Greece creates unbelievably slippery conditions, but whether this would help or hinder Darniche remained to be seen. However, it was the tyres rather than the weather that made the difference; Waldegard's tyres, that is. Three more punctures brought the Ford driver's lead down to virtually sixty seconds and then after having to change tyres once more for a long asphalt stage, Darniche took over the lead. But only for one stage. He then had a puncture, he changed the wheel at the end of the stage, drove down to his service crew — and promptly had another. It was a suspension failure that had caused this and although his service crew soon rescued him there was no point in continuing. Waldegard had no more trouble although Andersson now in second place did. Two stages from the end his engine failed and he had to retire. The Datsuns which had never impressed anyone by their speed (the five cars only produced two fastest times between them throughout the whole rally) now really impressed with their reliability. Skoda lost one car through rear suspension trouble but their other car finished an outstanding eighth, Ladas were ninth and tenth and the remaining Polonez made the finish in twelfth place.

The organizers' new long length of special stage made little difference to the finishing chances of the top teams since rally car reliability improves every year, but it meant that fewer privateers reached the end. As the tighter timing

The one that got away. Bjorn Waldegard suffered a lot of niggling problems with tyres and exhaust in particular, but he was spared the terminal engine failures which stopped his team-mates Mikkola and Clark

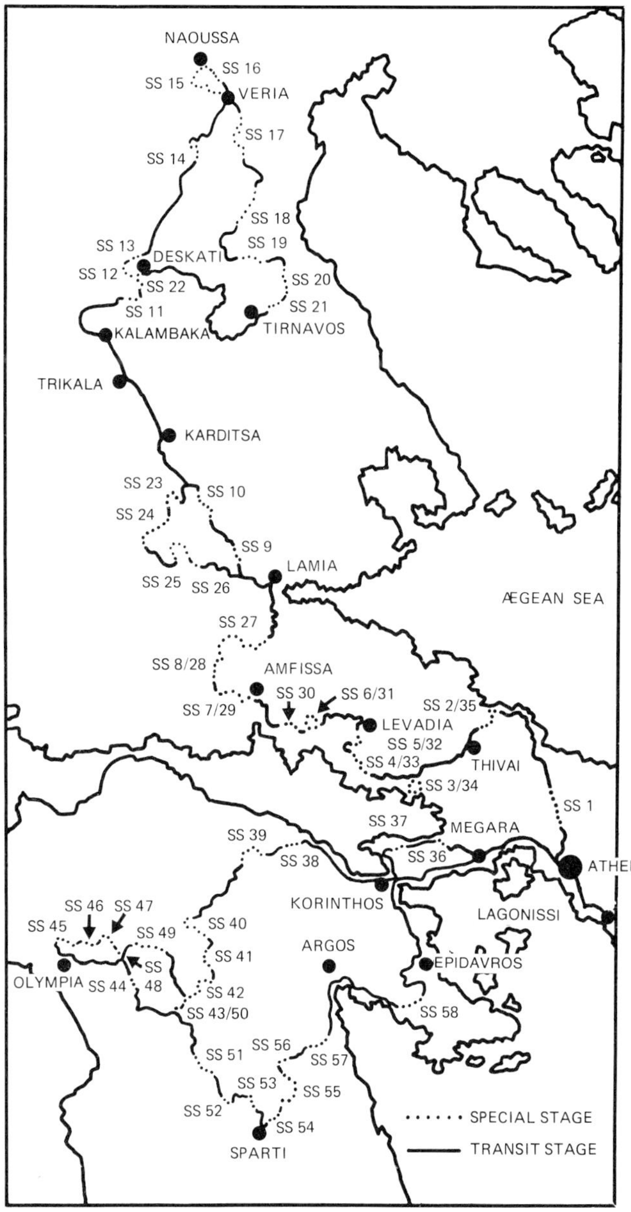

Bernard Darniche set himself a seemingly impossible task on the Acropolis. Even factory Stratos had never done well

26 Acropolis Rally

28-31 May 1979 Greece

Overall results

POSITION	DRIVER/NAVIGATOR	NATIONALITY	COMP NO.	CAR	GROUP	TOTAL STAGE TIME
1st	Bjorn Waldegard/Hans Thorszelius	S	1	Ford Escort RS	G4	13h.35m.06s
2nd	Timo Salonen/Seppo Harjanne	SF	8	Datsun 160J	G2	14h.07m.04s
3rd	Harry Kallstrom/Claes Billstam	S	3	Datsun 160J	G2	14h.11m.39s
4th	Jean Ragnotti/Jean-Marc Andrie	F	9	Renault 5 Alpine	G2	14h.19m.16s
5th	'Iaveris'/Costas Stefanis	GR	14	Ford Escort RS	G4	14h.36m.01s
6th	George Moschous/'Simetra II'	GR	21	Datsun 160J	G2	14h.54m.27s
7th	Evangelo Gallo/Demetro Petropoulos	GR	15	Datsun 160J	G2	15h.04m.08s
8th	Vaclav Blahna/Jiri Motal	CS	31	Skoda 130RS	G2	16h.09m.22s
9th	Nikolai Elizarov/Viktor Moskovskih	SU	42	Lada 1600	G2	16h.12m.20s
10th	Sergei Vukovich/Anatoli Brum	SU	49	Lada 1600	G2	16h.33m.11s
19th	Manuel Halivelakis/Theodore Korakis	GR	148	Toyota Corolla	G1	18h.23m.38s

155 starters. 20 finishers. No group 3 or Ladies finishers. 9 A-priority drivers.

World Championship positions after Round 5
Ford 68 points, Datsun 57, Fiat 41, Renault 24, Opel 22, Lancia and Saab 18, Mercedes-Benz 17, Toyota 16, Vauxhall 14, Audi 11, Porsche 8, Skoda and Volvo 6, Lada 4.

Leading positions World Championship for Drivers after Round 5
Waldegard 71 points, Mikkola 51, Alen 34, Darniche, Blomqvist and Mehta 20, Salonen 15, Kallstrom 14, Airikkala and Andersson 12.

Leading retirements

DRIVER/NAVIGATOR	NATIONALITY	COMP NO.	CAR	GROUP	CAUSE	STAGES COMPLETED
Tomasz Ciecierzynski/Jacek Rozanski	PL	30	Polonez 2000	4	overheating	0
Freddy Kottulinsky/Michael Schwagerl	S/D	28	Audi 80	4	Panhard rod mounting	1
Achim Warmbold/Horst Rausch	D	10	Porsche 911	4	shock absorbers	2
Maciej Stawowiak/Jacek Lewandowski	PL	16	Polonez 2000	4	accident	3
Stasis Brundza/Arvidas Girdauskas	SU	36	Lada 1600	2	shock absorbers	6
Harald Demuth/Arwed Fischer	D	23	Audi 80	4	driver illness	7
Hannu Mikkola/Arne Hertz	SF/S	4	Ford Escort RS	4	engine	9
Jean-Luc Therier/Michel Vial	F	11	Toyota Celica	2	differential	9
Roger Clark/Jim Porter	GB	7	Ford Escort RS	4	engine	13
'Siroco'/Costas Fertakis	GR	12	Lancia Stratos	4	rear suspension	30
Anders Kullang/Bob de Jong	S/NL	6	Opel Kadett GT/E	2	connecting rod	39
'Leonidas'/Andreas Arkentis	GR	24	Renault 5 Alpine	2	clutch	46
Svatopluk Kvaizar/Jiri Kotek	CS	41	Skoda 130RS	2	rear suspension	47
Bernard Darniche/Alain Mahe	F	2	Lancia Stratos	4	rear suspension	50
Ove Andersson/Henry Liddon	S/GB	5	Toyota Celica	2	piston	56

Rally leaders
Waldegard stages 1-48, Darniche 49 and 50, Waldegard 51-end.

Leading special stage positions

	1st	2nd	3rd	4th	5th	6th
Waldegard	30	16	2	2	—	—
Darniche	15	15	6	2	—	1
Mikkola	3	2	1	—	1	—
Kullang	2	2	2	8	7	5
Andersson	1	13	17	6	5	4
'Iaveris'	1	3	3	1	5	9
Salonen	1	1	9	10	8	7
Moschous	1	1	—	—	2	7
Ragnotti	1	—	4	4	9	5

The route

		Special stages	Total distance
Etape 1	Athens (Monday 0930) — Kalambaka (Monday 1904)	1 mixed, asphalt 11 km, gravel 31 km 9 gravel 190 km	601 km
Etape 2	Kalambaka (Tuesday 0004) — Kalambaka (Tuesday 0927) (4 stages cancelled)	1 mixed, asphalt 9 km, gravel 35 km 7 gravel 139 km (reduced from 11 gravel 201 km)	About 500 km (reduced from 592 km)
Etape 3	Kalambaka (Tuesday 1227) — Lagonissi (Wednesday 0049)	1 asphalt 8 km 12 gravel 215 km	712 km
Etape 4	Lagonissi (Wednesday 1900) — Olympia (Thursday 0330)	1 asphalt 14 km 8 gravel 118km	489 km
Etape 5	Olympia (Thursday 0630) — Epidavros (Thursday 1404)	2 asphalt 29 km 12 gravel 155 km	435 km
Etape 6	Epidavros (Thursday 1604) — Athens (Thursday 1834)	— —	142 km
		48 stages — 874 km	About 2885 km

7 stages wet, 20 in darkness.

Previous winners

1969 Pauli Toivonen Porsche 911
1970 Jean-Luc Therier Renault Alpine A110
1971 Ove Andersson Renault Alpine A110
1972 Hakan Lindberg Fiat 124 Spider
1973 Jean-Luc Therier Renault Alpine A110
1974 No rally
1975 Walter Rohrl Opel Ascona
1976 Harry Kallstrom Datsun Violet
1977 Bjorn Waldegard Ford Escort RS
1978 Walter Rohrl Fiat Abarth 131

Skodas regularly come to the Acropolis, and the best place this year was eighth for Vaclav Blahna, who regularly achieves good results in rallies in Eastern Europe

had been intended to help these drivers, the experiment failed. Progressively the 'little' man is being squeezed out of the Acropolis Rally. Mikkola's engine failure let Waldegard go well ahead in the Driver's Championship, while we cannot forget that out of the three WCR events he has entered this year, Darniche has won one and retired when leading the other two!

THIS PAGE *First time lucky? Timo Salonen has a habit of succeeding early in his careers with teams (remember Quebec 1977?), this time coming second overall and winning group 2 with Datsun, his latest contract*

Long, dusty roads are the Greek rally tradition. 'Iaveris', a local driver lent a factory car which was run by David Sutton Cars, is seen here in the evening of the first day. This dust gives the first driver on the road a great advantage, as on the Safari Rally, though later during the event cars were started at intervals of greater than one minute

FACING PAGE *Ove Andersson seems always to be out of luck in Greece. Not since he won in 1971 has he had a result there. This year he retired two stages from the finish when in second place, well ahead of the pursuing Datsuns*

This year the competitive distance was increased, a move not entirely popular but one in line with many other events. Here is the German Audi driver Harald Demuth studying one of his pacenote books. With the stages and many of the road sections pacenoted, he had 800 pages for his co-driver Arwed Fischer to read

Few people expect the little Renault 5 Alpines to succeed on the toughest rallies, even after their convincing display on the Bandama in 1978. This is Jean Ragnotti, fully recovered from his accident earlier in the year, on possibly the last important official outing for these cars

1 *Billy Coleman gained his A-priority through good regular results on European Championship rallies in 1979, but he was unlucky to retire just before the end of the Elba Rally, seen here*

1

2

3

4

2 *Hannu Mikkola also drove for Mercedes-Benz as well as Ford. On the Safari he was unlucky to lose the lead in the latter stages of the event*

3 *'Lucky' finished the year as Mitropa Cup champion, but earlier he finished second here at the Costa Smeralda Rally in Sicily. His co-driver has been Fabrizia Pons, who previously had proved an accomplished rally driver herself*

4 *The Karlstad trotting track races are always spectacular at the Swedish Rally. Here are Hannu Mikkola (left) and Anders Kullang in action. This year the races were held anticlockwise*

5 *Per Eklund's Triumph TR7V8 was a welcome sight on the gravel roads at San Remo even though he suffered an early delay and eventually had to retire*

6 *Timo Salonen joined the Datsun team at the Acropolis and immediately started getting results. On the final day after the troubles of Darniche and Andersson, the Finn finally reached second place overall, first in group 2*

5

6

32

32 *Stig Blomqvist was a surprise entry at the Janner Rally in Austria with a borrowed Lancia Beta Monte Carlo, not the turbocharged model seen later in the year in Italy*

TOYOTA

calberson
Renault elf
calberson

Motogard Rally of New Zealand

Ford escaped an almost unforgivable defeat in New Zealand by a closer margin than they would care to admit. For sure they would have won the rally outright, but when the three-night event finally finished at Auckland all their back-up cars had failed or been delayed and second lay Timo Salonen with his group 2 Datsun 160J. Ford stood to gain 18 points — and Datsun 17. Only after the finish, indeed the following day, did a chain of events occur which absolved them from this close margin, when the official Datsun team was disqualified. They had refused to allow the scrutineers to inspect their engines in New Zealand. They stated that this would have nullified the special development work aimed at eliminating valve problems because Datsun engineers would not have been able to examine the opened engines under laboratory conditions. Instructions had been taken from Japan on this matter, and exclusion was preferred. Thus Ford finished in the top four places and their grasp on the World Championship was considerably strengthened.

New Zealand stand precariously in the World Championship calender. While the question of how the future world series should be formed still raged — whether to include well-heeled but distant events like Brazil and Bandama, or whether to have cheaper and proven rallies like the 1000 Lakes and Swedish, New Zealand was included this year despite being extremely expensive to attend and poorly financed as well. Three teams attended: two (Ford and Vauxhall) through the enthusiasm of the local teams, who subsequently would buy the cars and keep them in that country, and the third (Datsun) who delivered the cars direct from Japan, which

was obviously considerably nearer than Europe. It was this division of responsibility which substantially led to their downfall. With Japan responsible for the preparation of the cars (but not present at executive level on the event), the local dealers responsible for the mechanics and service and Team Datsun Europe, under Andy Dawson who was present as a driver and a manager, for the drivers it was inevitable that some problems would occur, though nobody anticipated just how serious these would be. Even the Vauxhall team, who sent Airikkala's Chevette 2300HS in very good time, had terrible trouble with a missing crate of spares. Though he retired early in the event, Airikkala had to drive several stages using Goodyear tyres instead of the contracted Dunlops which did not arrive.

New Zealand's rallying progresses despite all the problems of import controls, unavailability of parts and the sheer distance from the centre of the rallying world. But even since the last WCR round there, in 1977, the quality of their sport had noticeably improved. Rally tyres were widely available, and there was no need to include a special class for non-homologated cars. But in many ways enthusiasm still exceeded their expertise. As in Britain there is a mania for group 4 cars. Considerable numbers of BDA Escorts were entered but nearly all of them retired, even though this time the rally was not a marathon but an event which was of ordinary length by world standards. The organizers were keen, uncontroversial, eager to do the right thing, and only in some small matters, like the undue complexity in the time control systems, could they learn much from elsewhere.

Fords were everywhere at the start. Only four cars out of the top twenty seeds were anything other than Ford. Three were in the colours of Masport, the national dealer team while another was run by Masport but in Rothmans decor. All were very smart, even the many private cars were spotless. The Vauxhall was clean even if less visually attractive, despite a previous long

FACING PAGE *Hannu Mikkola caught up again with Bjorn Waldegard's score in the World Championship for Drivers by winning, in Waldegård's absence, the Motogard Rally in New Zealand. Seen here at the end of the second division, when his head gasket was failing, he is cruising through one of the few asphalt stages in the rally*

THIS PAGE *Motogard is the trading name of Motor Specialties Limited, a New Zealand company that actively supported and promoted the rally. They got good value out of their decals as well*

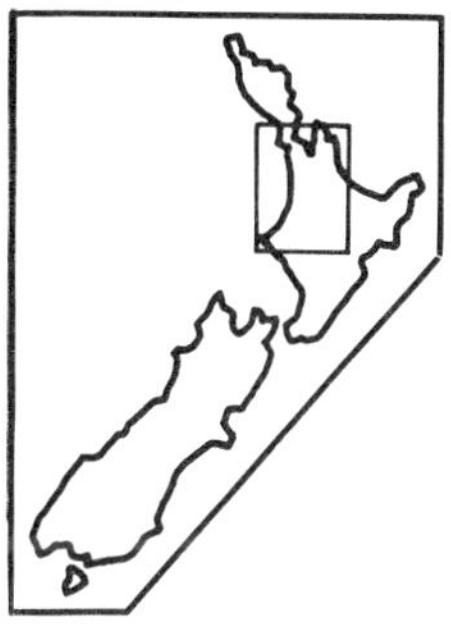

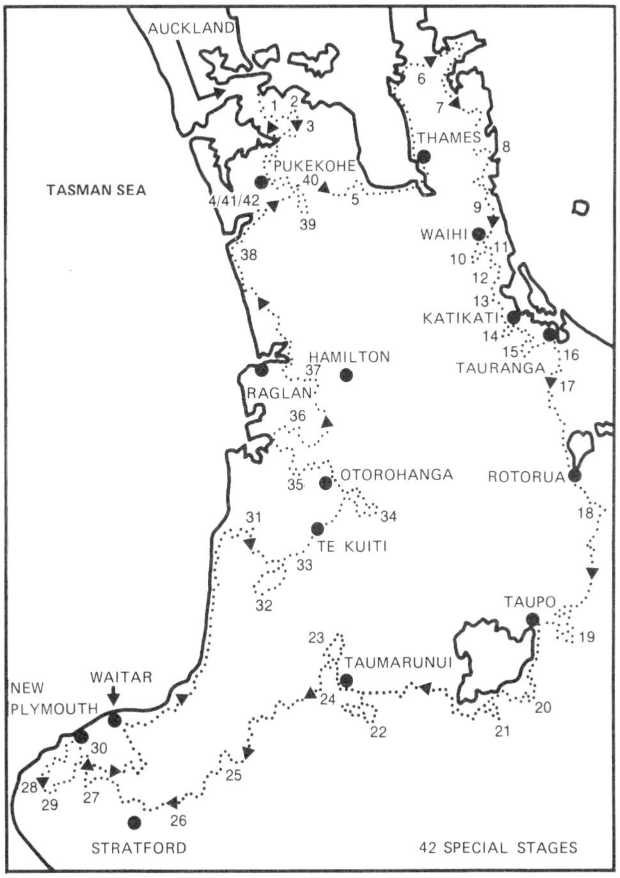

10 Motogard Rally of New Zealand

14-18 July 1979 New Zealand

Overall results

POSITION	DRIVER/NAVIGATOR	NATIONALITY	COMP NO.	CAR	GROUP	TOTAL STAGE TIME
1st	Hannu Mikkola/Arne Hertz	SF/S	1	Ford Escort RS	G4	8h.05.78m.
—	Timo Salonen/Seppo Harjanne	SF	4	Datsun 160J	G2	8h.22.31m. excluded
2nd	Blair Robson/Chris Porter	NZ	5	Ford Escort RS	G4	8h.27.05m.
3rd	Ari Vatanen/David Richards	SF/GB	3	Ford Escort RS	G4	8h.29.68m.
4th	Paul Adams/Mike Franchi	NZ	9	Ford Escort RS	G4	8h.29.90m.
—	Andy Dawson/Kevin Gormley	GB	6	Datsun 160J	G2	8h.36.75m. excluded
5th	Shane Murland/Peter Parnell	NZ	29	Vauxhall Chevette 2300HS	G4	9h.04.39m.
6th	David Parkes/Stuart Green	NZ	19	Ford Escort 1600GT	G2	9h.09.57m.
7th	Brian Green/Robert Orr	NZ	16	Ford Escort RS	G4	9h.12.61m.
8th	Roger Goss/Colin Green	NZ	27	Mazda RX3	G2	9h.26.25m.
9th	Malcolm Stewart/Doug Parkhill	NZ	30	Ford Escort Mexico	G2	9h.27.35m.
10th	Bob Robb/Malcolm Gavin	NZ	26	Datsun 710	G2	9h.37.55m.
11th	Alfred Goldsbury/Russell Thomson	NZ	28	Fiat 131 Racing	G1	9h.38.53m.

82 starters. 39 finishers. 2 excluded as above, another 14 excluded for lateness. 23 classified. 4 A-priority drivers. No group 3 or ladies starters.
Note: 1. Salonen and Dawson excluded for failing to dismantle engines after finish when requested. 2. Penalties given in hours, minutes and hundredths of a minute.

World Championship positions after Round 6
Ford 86 points, Datsun 63, Fiat 41, Renault and Vauxhall 24, Opel 22, Lancia and Saab 18, Mercedes-Benz 17, Toyota 16, Audi 11, Mazda 10, Porsche 8, Volvo and Skoda 6, Lada 4.

Leading positions in World Championship for Drivers after Round 6
Waldegard and Mikkola 71 points, Alen 34, Blomqvist and Mehta 20, Salonen and Robson 15, Kallstrom 14, Airikkala, Andersson and Vatanen 12.

Leading retirements

DRIVER/NAVIGATOR	NATIONALITY	COMP NO.	CAR	GROUP	CAUSE	STAGES COMPLETED
Hugh Armstrong/David Murie	NZ	17	Ford Escort RS	G4	head gasket	9
Jim Donald/Kevin Lancaster	NZ	7	Ford Escort RS	G4	connecting rod	16
Tony Teesdale/Gary Smith	NZ	15	Ford Escort RS	G2	halfshaft	16
Bob Couch/John Couch	NZ	14	Ford Escort RS	G4	differential	17
Pentti Airikkala/Rodger Freeth	SF/NZ	2	Vauxhall Chevette 2300HS	G4	electrics	18
Howard Collier/David Cooke	NZ	12	Ford Escort RS	G4	head gasket	18
John Woolf/Grant Whittaker	NZ	10	Mazda RX3	G2	rear axle	18
Leo Leonard/Neil Cruikshanks	NZ	13	Ford Escort RS	G4	no oil pressure	19
Mike Marshall/Jeff Beaumont	NZ/AUS	11	Ford Escort RS	G4	head gasket	20
Paddy Davidson/Paul Greaves	NZ	18	Ford Escort TC	G2	accident	29

Rally leaders
Airikkala stage 1 and 2, Mikkola 3-end.

Leading special stage positions:

	1st	2nd	3rd	4th	5th	6th		1st	2nd	3rd	4th	5th	6th		1st	2nd	3rd	4th	5th	6th
Mikkola	22	8	2	2	3	1	Airikkala	3	1	3	3	4	3	Salonen	—	4	13	8	5	2
Vatanen	8	20	2	1	—	—	Dawson	2	4	6	7	7	6	Green	—	—	3	—	—	2
Adams	7	1	7	6	4	1	Robson	1	1	5	8	11	8	Donald	—	—	2	2	1	2

The route

		SPECIAL STAGES	TOTAL DISTANCE
Etape 1	Auckland (Sunday 1400) — Thames — Tauranga (Monday 0607) (1 stage cancelled — fords too deep)	3 asphalt — 17 km 5 mixed — 39 km 6 gravel — 56 km (reduced from 7 — 66 km)	540 km (reduced from 546 km)
Etape 2	Tauranga (Monday 1600) — Taupo — Taumarunui — New Plymouth (Tuesday 1154)	2 asphalt — 21 km 4 mixed — 85 km 6 gravel — 182 km	673 km
Etape 3	New Plymouth (Tuesday 2030) Otorohanga — Auckland (Wednesday 1625) (1 stage cancelled — local objection)	2 asphalt — 22 km 8 mixed — 208 km (reduced from 9 — 212 km) 4 gravel — 61 km	780 km (reduced from 797 km)
		40 stages — 658 km	1993 km

Mostly clear weather, some rain, one stage icy. Most stages night.

Previous winners

1969 Grady Thomson Holden Monaro
1970 Paul Adams BMW 2002tii
1971 Bruce Hodgson Ford Cortina Lotus
1972 Andy Cowan BLMC Mini 1275 GT
1973 Hannu Mikkola Ford Escort RS1600
1974 cancelled
1975 Mike Marshall Ford Escort RS1800
1976 Andy Cowan Chrysler Avenger
1977 Fulvio Bacchelli Fiat Abarth 131
1978 Russell Brookes Ford Escort RS

Oversize? Wrong cylinder head? Or just a complete breakdown in communications? Even when all was said and done, nobody in New Zealand had any definite idea whether the Datsun engines held any guilty secrets or not

night's vigil with engine trouble. And the Datsuns, locally called '2 litres' rather than 'Violet' or '160J' were present. But no sooner had the rally started than it rained. The first test was around a stock-car stadium, cars being started side by side, two by two. Whatever else might happen this was most exciting, and none more so than the first heat, when Mikkola and Airikkala fought together, with the Chevette coming from behind and overtaking the Ford in a moment of unforgettable daring and skill. The rain then hung back for the rest of the afternoon while the now dirty rally cars went eastwards from Auckland towards Thames and then Tauranga. The first leg (called 'division') — and indeed all three — were mostly held at night, and earlier rain had caused havoc. One stage was cancelled because of an impassable water crossing, on another many cars were blocked and ultimately time-barred through congestion on a slippery hill. On stage three Mikkola began his attack and pulled out consistently until by morning he was 1½ minutes in front of his team-mate Vatanen and another 2½ in front of Airikkala, who was just leading Salonen with the Datsun. The Finns were in the top four places.

The second leg brought more havoc. On the first stage more water delayed drivers, and then there was a spate of mechanical crises. Airikkala had electrical trouble (the fault was quickly diagnosed later), Marshall and Collier had head gasket trouble, while Woolf, Couch, Teesdale had transmission faults. But for Ford even more serious was the gradual head gasket trouble for Mikkola and Vatanen. As the second division headed south-west towards New Plymouth, plans were hatched for

Panic Stations! For a long time it seemed impossible that Vatanen's engine would hold together long enough to reach the finish, but eventually it did, in no small measure due to the skill of the mechanics. Here Bob Marris removes a plug to study what new damage has occurred

When he tried hard, Ari Vatanen went well — witness the old familiar Vatanen driving style. He drove far more maturely than on his previous visit to New Zealand two years before

both gaskets to be changed before the day halt. An hour was allowed for service, given a clear run the jobs might just be done in time. In fact they weren't, but the lenient penalty for time control lateness meant that neither lost their places. Eight minutes now separated the leading Fords, whilst Adams and Salonen were neck-and-neck for third place, only one minute ahead of Robson. Sixth after a long earlier delay was Dawson.

The third division back to Auckland gave Mikkola the chance to spare his engine, but Vatanen was too near Salonen to take any risks. And as he tried to hold his place the engine began to fail again. He lost minutes and minutes, often stopping to refill with water in mid-stage, and ultimately he fell behind Salonen. Adams did likewise, being delayed by clutch trouble and punctures, and Robson consistently rose up the field. Vatanen eventually reached the end in fourth place, behind Mikkola, Salonen and Robson, but then the whole Datsun affair blew up. It was a silly thing to happen. The championship year was becoming exciting enough without situations like this to spoil the remaining interest in the manufacturers' series.

Delayed in the later stages of the rally by punctures and clutch trouble was local driver Paul Adams, winner nine years previously of the New Zealand Rally, who fell from third to fourth place when Vatanen's score was recounted. Because of this Adams lost his chance of becoming an FIA A-priority driver

While the Datsuns were excluded this Chevette, fitted with the old-type Lotus head, was allowed to qualify, and indeed the car gained Vauxhall ten World Championship points. Nowadays, the Vauxhall HS heads give more power, but local regulations permit non-homologated parts where homologated parts are not readily available and substitutes do not increase performance. Shane Murland came fifth overall

Andy Dawson eventually reached the finish line in sixth position. Note the dual registration plates (all cars on the New Zealand roads must be locally registered)

Rally of 1000 Lakes

Markku Alen and his Fiat confirmed even more his command of the 1000 Lakes Rally, when with Ilkka Kivimaki he won this event for a third time: indeed ever since he began to use the Fiat Abarth 131 he has only ever been beaten once on this event — and that was by a rock that stopped him in the 1977 rally! This time his victory was because of his consistency rather than his speed, by his steadiness under pressure rather than the car's mechanical superiority. For much of the second part of the rally it seemed that the Ford of Ari Vatanen would overhaul the Fiat, but eventually Vatanen just could not keep up the pressure. During the first half, after a puncture had delayed him, it was Alen's turn to maintain the pressure on Hannu Mikkola when Mikkola's Ford was leading. Mikkola had to retire when his engine failed — leaving Alen with his chance of success.

In group 4 we had Fiat, Ford, Vauxhall, Leyland, Audi and Polonez — all works entered, whilst in group 2 there were Datsun, Opel and Toyota, again all works entered, with Ford and Chrysler (Talbot?) privately entered. This rally places low emphasis on the mechanical element, and there were few technical developments. Fuel injection was fitted to the Triumphs, designed to improve the efficiency of the engines rather than simply to add power, but other teams selected proven specifications on this occasion. Fords kept to carburettors, the newly built Chevette was simply a replica of previous ones, while Datsun used minor engine changes and better transmission ratios this year. The official Toyota Celicas were probably being used for the final time on a major rally as work on the new group 4 cars was in hand and Opel had their Dutch team's Kadett GT/E on the final official outing with this type of car.

The drivers' lists produced few surprises, though the Austrian Franz Wittmann was having his first professional drive, with Audi (he had never rallied a front wheel drive car before — and eventually was the highest placed driver in the team) and Datsun contracted Erkki Pitkanen who had been their team driver the year before. Seen for the first time successfully on WCR events this year were group 2 Ford Escort RSs with sixteen valve twin-cam engines. These cars produce some 200 bhp from their 1850 cc engines, more than Toyotas and Datsuns and equal to the very best Opels, but they still have limitations with the rear axle location.

If any rally is like a Grand Prix it must be the 1000 Lakes: even the local name 'Jyvaskylan Suurajot' can be translated roughly as the 'Big Race' of Jyvaskyla. It is the nearest example to pure driving sport one can find in rallying, where the car matters the least and the man behind the wheel the most. The winner of the 1000 Lakes can justly be considered the man of the moment in rallying; very few winners do not fit into the mould of rallying's superstars. Alen and Mikkola were and are above all others in their element while Salonen, Vatanen and Airikkala are all anxious to challenge them. Behind both groups there is another rank of driver who will doubtless rise up the scale given time; people like Henri Toivonen. There were Finnish national championship contenders with little experience elsewhere but who need to prove themselves against the international stars — people like Gronholm. Then there were those who have enjoyed incredible success in years gone by and are still highly competitive, such as Lampinen (even Pauli Toivonen, the Monte Carlo winner in 1966, still competes regularly) — and all

the other foreign drivers fighting their way through. Bjorn Waldegard said publicly that it is virtually impossible for a foreigner to win. Stig Blomqvist is the only one to have succeeded since 1960!

The rally lasts only two nights and usually has the shortest competitive distance of any in the World series, and for these reasons many felt its future within the World Championship is limited. There was a distinct air of tension on this subject, particularly since future decisions had to be made immediately after the event. All the stages were on gravel roads, all could be practised (albeit within speed limits and in unmarked cars) although a high proportion of annually identical stages made the task easier. The rally was again based entirely on the town of Jyvaskyla, in central Finland. As usually the rally was not so much a rally of the Lakes as much as a rally of 1000 Jumps, where

skills can avert damaging landings and training will dictate the correct angle each jump should be taken.

Waldegard equalled the best time on the first stage but Alen pulled ahead until stage eight, when he lost about a half-minute with a puncture, which put him a quarter-minute behind Mikkola. Mikkola held his lead until the head gasket failed towards the end of the night leg, a problem which cost not only his victory but also his chances in the

Another year, perhaps? It took Markku Alen many years before he finally gained his first 1000 Lakes win, and Ari Vatanen is going through the same phase too. His chase of the leader in the second half was most exciting

Markku Alen on his way to his third 1000 Lakes victory in four years. Just as on the fourth-placed Fiat of Ulf Gronholm, the front spoiler has been damaged

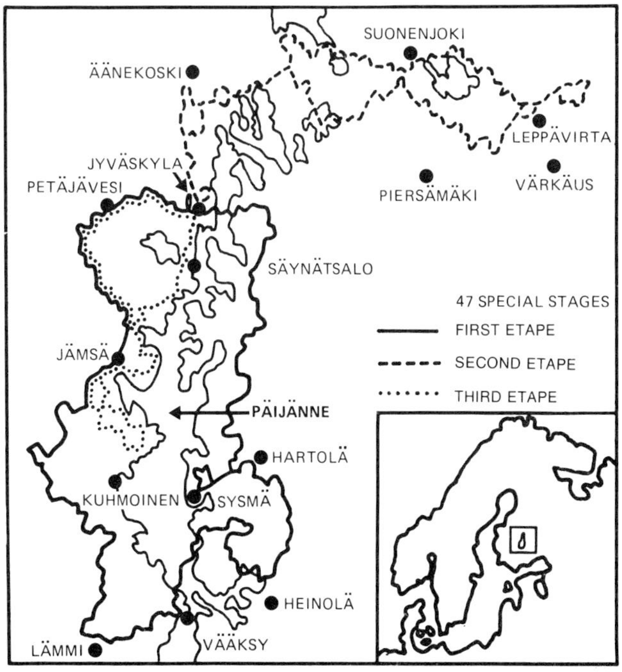

29 Jyvaskylan Suurajot Rally of 1000 Lakes

24-28 August 1979 Finland

Overall results

POSITION	DRIVER/NAVIGATOR	NATIONALITY	COMP NO.	CAR	GROUP	TOTAL STAGE TIME
1st	Markku Alen/Ilkka Kivimaki	SF	1	Fiat Abarth 131	G4	4h.01m.11s
2nd	Ari Vatanen/David Richards	SF/GB	8	Ford Escort RS	G4	4h.02m.42s
3rd	Bjorn Waldegard/Claes Billstam	S	5	Ford Escort RS	G4	4h.07m.15s
4th	Ulf Gronholm/Bob Rehnstrom	SF	18	Fiat Abarth 131	G4	4h.10m.41s
5th	Timo Salonen/Seppo Harjanne	SF	6	Datsun 160J	G2	4h.11m.50s
6th	Lasse Lampi/Pentti Kuukkala	SF	24	Ford Escort RS	G2	4h.14m.14s
7th	Tapio Rainio/Erkki Nyman	SF	20	Toyota Celica	G2	4h.14m.20s
8th	Per Eklund/Hans Sylvan	S	4	Triumph TR7V8	G4	4h.17m.48s
9th	Erkki Pitkanen/Juhani Paalama	SF	15	Datsun 160J	G2	4h.20m.01s
10th	Pekka Vilpponen/Ranuo Kangasniemi	SF	52	Ford Escort RS	G4	4h.20m.24s
13th	Peter Geitel/Rolf Mesterton	SF	26	Chrysler Avenger	G1	4h.27m.12s
31st	Kyosti Hamalainen/Matti Lammi	SF	12	Mercedes-Benz 300D	Diesel	4h.48m.28s
46th	Carita Ekroos/Tarja Soderstrom	SF	62	Opel Ascona	G2	5h.05m.18s*

128 starters, 74 finishers, *Ladies winner, no group 3 class, 12 A-priority drivers.

World Championship positions after Round 7

Ford 102 points, Datsun 77, Fiat 59, Toyota 26, Renault and Vauxhall 24, Opel 22, Lancia and Saab 18, Mercedes-Benz 17, Audi 11, Mazda 10, Porsche 8, Leyland 7, Skoda and Volvo 6, Lada 4.

Leading positions in World Championship for Drivers after Round 7

Waldegard 83 points, Mikkola 71, Alen 54, Vatanen 28, Salonen 23, Blomqvist, Darniche and Mehta 20, Robson 15, Kallstrom 12.

Leading retirements

DRIVER/NAVIGATOR	NATIONALITY	COMP NO.	CAR	GROUP	CAUSE	STAGES COMPLETED
Harald Demuth/Arwed Fischer	D	58	Audi 80	G4	accident	1
Timo Makinen/Henry Liddon	SF/GB	7	Toyota Celica	G2	oil pump	2
Pentti Airikkala/Risto Virtanen	SF	3	Vauxhall Chevette 2300HS	G4	engine	3
Leo Kinnunen/Erkki Salonen	SF	21	Porsche 911	G4	accident	4
Bjorn Johansson/Ragnar Spjuth	S	16	Opel Kadett GT/E	G2	clutch	5
Anders Kullang/Bruno Berglund	S	10	Opel Kadett GT/E	G2	piston	8
Henri Toivonen/Juha Paajanen	SF	14	Fiat Abarth 131	G4	accident	15
Hannu Mikkola/Arne Hertz	SF/S	2	Ford Escort RS	G4	head gasket	17
Pauli Toivonen/Juhana Korhonen	SF	31	Chrysler Sunbeam	G2	intercom	21
Simo Lampinen/Juhani Markkanen	SF	9	Triumph TR7V8	G4	distributor	24

Rally leaders

Alen and Waldegard stage 1; Alen 2-7; Mikkola 8-17, Alen 18-end.

Leading special stage positions:

	1ST	2ND	3RD	4TH	5TH	6TH		1ST	2ND	3RD	4TH	5TH	6TH		1ST	2ND	3RD	4TH	5TH	6TH
Alen	22	20	2	—	—	—	Waldegard	2	—	21	10	10	2	Gronholm	—	—	10	9	6	8
Vatanen	20	14	5	4	2	1	Rainio	1	—	1	7	5	8	Salonen	—	—	2	7	13	9
Mikkola	7	5	3	—	—	—	H. Toivonen	—	1	3	3	2	2	Vilpponen	—	—	1	—	3	1

The route:

		SPECIAL STAGES	TOTAL DISTANCE
1st leg	Jyvaskyla (Friday 1800) — Vaaksy — Jyvaskyla (Saturday 0822)	20 — 208 km	642 km
2nd leg	Jyvaskyla (Saturday 1422) — Leppavirta — Jyvaskyla (Sunday 0225)	18 — 118 km	522 km
3rd leg	Jyvaskyla (Sunday 0320) — Jyvaskyla (Sunday 0905)	8 — 99 km	285 km
		425 km	1450 km

(Note: Special stage number 20 cancelled before event)

All stages gravel, half stages in darkness, nearly all dry.

Previous winners

1969 Hannu Mikkola Ford Escort TC
1970 Hannu Mikkola Ford Escort TC
1971 Stig Blomqvist Saab 96 V4
1972 Simo Lampinen Saab 96 V4
1973 Timo Makinen Ford Escort RS 1600
1974 Hannu Mikkola Ford Escort RS 1600
1975 Hannu Mikkola Toyota Corolla
1976 Markku Alen Fiat Abarth 131
1977 Kyosti Hamalainen Ford Escort RS 1800
1978 Markku Alen Fiat Abarth 131

Fuel vaporisation caused by high under-bonnet temperatures on the complex fuel injection system caused Per Eklund long delays, but still he reached 8th position with the Triumph TR7V8

race for the Drivers' Championship, which Waldegard took up in his place, having started the event dead-level. So Alen was back in the lead again, eager to use his opportunities to the full but mindful that the Fords behind him must be superior in performance. Psychologically he had the lead over Waldegard, but the challenge would be coming from Vatanen. Airikkala's Chevette had retired, Henri Toivonen had been lying fifth in the local importer's team Fiat Abarth 131 but had left the road when his intercom system did not work, and Gronholm was struggling to keep ahead of the group 2 cars. The TR7V8s were suffering fuel starvation problems and the other group 4 cars were nowhere in the race. In group 2 the Opel had blown up, a dramatic end to an abortive season but the Datsuns were proving much more competitive than in 1978. Makinen retired with oil pump problems in his Toyota and Rainio could not hold Salonen's Datsun when misfiring trouble afflicted him. Only slightly slower was Lasse Lampi's group 2 Ford.

In the second part of the rally Vatanen strove hard to close the gap on Alen, which he consistently succeeded in doing but then he first had a puncture and secondly went off the road. Eventually he made a lucky second place. Waldegard gained a 12-point World Championship for Drivers' lead and Ford pulled ahead to a 25-point lead in the manufacturers series, ahead of Datsun.

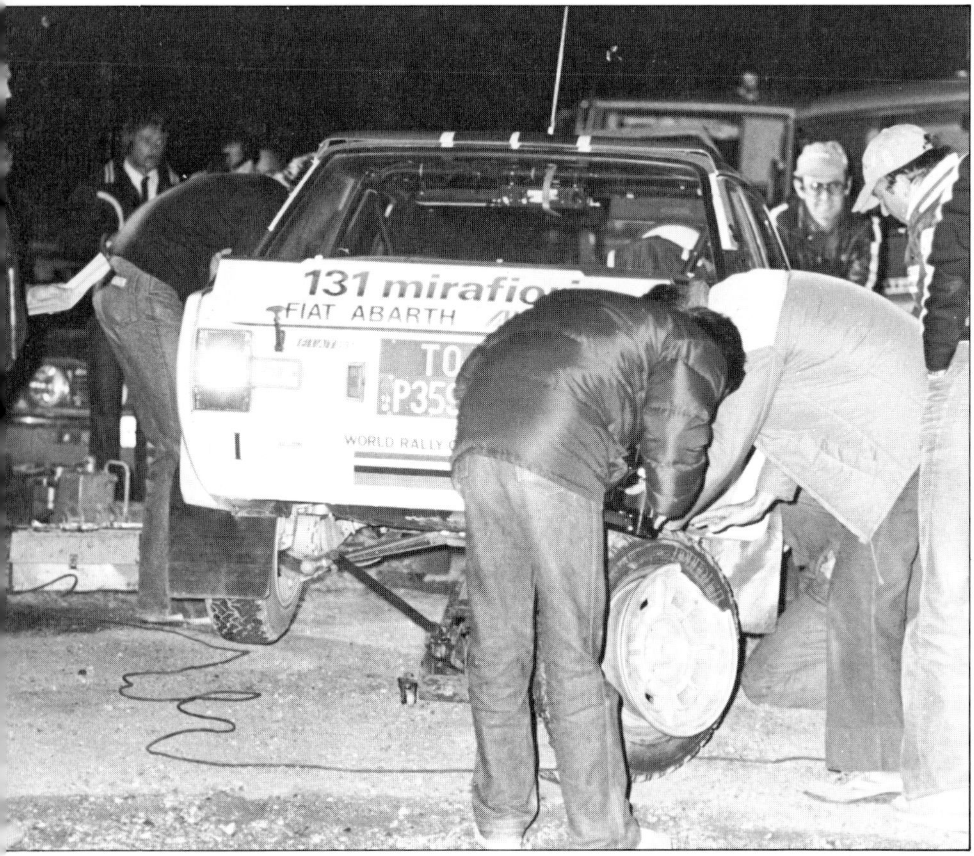

Timo Salonen proved once again that his 1000 Lakes performances are reliable and an asset to any team. This year he was fifth and best group 2 driver, with his Datsun 160J which showed considerably better performance than a year ago

Back in a competitive car in Europe again after a long spell, Timo Makinen showed all his old determination —for the first stage and a half! Here he is attacking the famous series of jumps at Humalamaki just before engine trouble intervened

Markku Alen's mechanics change the wheel which cost him the lead on the eighth stage. Note the broken rim

The 1000 Lakes was once again one of the few World rallies which catered for diesel cars; this year they have to be homologated before they can compete. Here is Kyosti Hamalainen with his Mercedes-Benz, who won the category and came in the top half of the field at the finish. He won the rally outright in 1977 driving a Ford Escort RS1800

The best non-Scandinavian driver this year came from France: Jean-Paul Luc who finished 20th overall, an excellent performance with such a big car

Despair. Never once has any of the Dutch team's Opel Kadett GT/Es reached the finish of a World championship rally in 1979 — here is Anders Kullang (far left) recognising the inevitable defeat while the engine still smoulders, several minutes after arriving at this service point

Criterium Molson du Quebec

It comes as a shock to find an event which does not match up to expectation in World Championship rallying. The only saving grace for the Criterium Molson du Quebec was that most rally followers half-expected that things would not be up to scratch. The record books will recall that Waldegard beat Salonen (Ford, then Datsun), while back-up team drivers Vatanen beat Dawson (Ford, then Datsun again). Apart from these two teams' activities it is hard to muster any great memories of this North American rally. Through his win, Waldegard has virtually squeezed out any remaining hope that Mikkola had harboured for the Drivers' series, while accepting the balance of probabilities Ford must expect to be the world champion make for the first time.

Datsun continued to be the fly in Ford's ointment; all the time they remain the only company which can conceivably deny Ford their ultimate success. The group 2 category gives Datsun the chance of slightly greater points whenever they score a good position, but except at the Safari they have never shown anything like winning form. For Quebec, more powerful engines were said to have been produced by Japan — team engineer Kudo quoting 183 bhp, but even if this was conservative, their cars are still rated a good 50-60 bhp less than the Fords, and that advantage can never be matched by sheer reliability on a sprint event like Quebec. Or so you might think. Actually, Salonen's Datsun very nearly won this time. . . .

Ford started off in the manner one has come to expect. A classic steamroller situation existed, not what type of car but which driver would be allowed to win. Vatanen jokingly said before the first stage that the man who was quickest on the first stage would receive team

manager Peter Ashcroft's blessing. Waldegard could just have been listening to this, for when the first stage times were announced, the two Fords were equal! Furthermore, one second behind was Rod Millen, quicker than the two official Datsuns with a similar Datsun he runs for the local importer. He had quietly watched the leading cars through the opening corners, worked out the best line and stormed through, six seconds quicker than the next similar car. However, he did not hold this advantage — this was his first ever practice rally — but it attracted considerable attention at the time. Meanwhile Waldegard took the lead momentarily, but Vatanen started to pull forward and by the end of the first leg was seventeen seconds ahead of his team-mate, the next best being Salonen nearly 1½ minutes behind. Taisto Heinonen was the best outsider, driving what was supposed to be a replica Toyota Team Europe group 2 Celica but which neither sounded nor went like one, but after driving nearly all an eight-kilometer stage on a flat tyre he fell behind the Datsuns. Leading group 1 was a surprise, the new Mitsubishi Mirage front wheel drive 1600 cc car of Hendrik Blok, the American. This was the international debut for the model, and Blok had already survived an alarming looking accident in which he had demolished a road sign and almost overturned. Yet only ten seconds behind came John Nixon's group 1 twin cam Celica.

So far the organization had proved irritating rather than inept and to be fair, the weather on the second day would have disrupted even a military display. Torrential rain fell from the skies, leading immediately to two stage cancellations. Later that day it led to the ignominy of the Ford works cars when both stopped in deep water on the first of the traditional long forest stages. Seven minutes for Waldegard, thirteen for Vatanen: the lead was now Salonen's. Road penalties had delayed the other two Datsuns, and Heinonen had driven one too many laps of the stage at the Trois Rivieres racetrack, which meant that at the end of the second leg Waldegard was back in second place notwithstanding his delay. Vatanen was sixth. The third leg was easily the longest part of the route and both Fords expected to be able to pull well up, assuming the spate of cancelled stages was stemmed. Luckily for them the third day was clearer and only local objectors at Trois Rivieres stood in the way of a full programme, even if this was excessively long drawn-out.

In clear conditions the Datsun team waited for defeat, hoping fervently that Fords would suffer further misfortune while they kept clear of trouble. This did not work out entirely, as Millen carelessly lost nineteen road minute penalties and then retired in mid-stage with propeller shaft collapse, but when the rally reached the long forests again,

Bjorn Waldegard charges through the water lying on the track at Trois Rivieres. Three stages later he did the same — and his Escort RS drowned out for seven minutes, and very nearly cost him the rally

Timo Salonen at the asphalt stage in Shawinigan village, in the third leg on the rally when Waldegard was chasing him for the lead. The large man behind is Andre Lariviere, the President of the organising committee

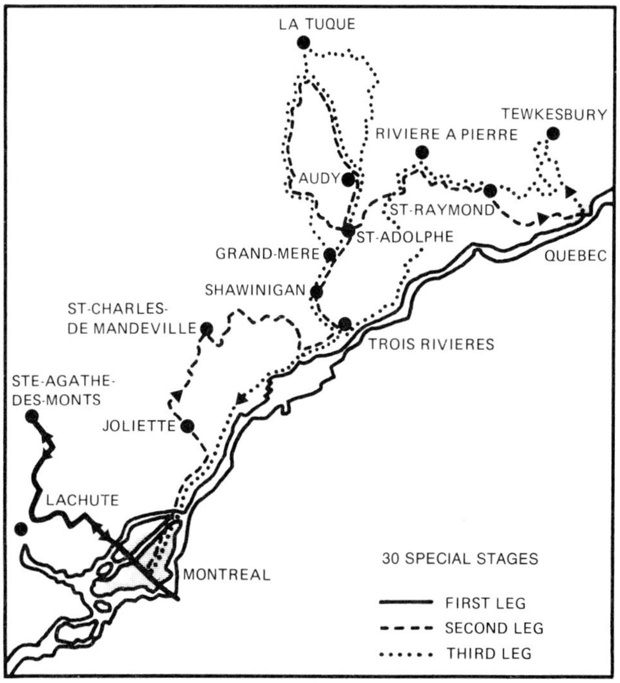

6 Criterium Molson du Quebec

13-16 September 1979 Canada

Overall results

POSITION	DRIVER/NAVIGATOR	NATIONALITY	COMP NO.	CAR	GROUP	TOTAL STAGE TIME
1st	Bjorn Waldegard/Hans Thorszelius	S	2	Ford Escort RS	G4	3h.35m.32s
2nd	Timo Salonen/Seppo Harjanne	SF	3	Datsun 160J	G2	3h.36m.10s
3rd	Ari Vatanen/David Richards	SF/GB	1	Ford Escort RS	G4	3h.41m.50s
4th	Andy Dawson/Kevin Gormley	GB	20	Datsun 160J	G2	3h.50m.55s
5th	Taisto Heinonen/Erkki Nyman	SF	4	Toyota Celica	G2	3h.56m.21s
6th	Hendrik Blok/Doug Shepherd	USA	5	Mitsubishi Mirage	G1	4h.41m.56s
7th	Jack Swayze/Izim Okeren	CDN	39	Datsun 160J	G1	4h.50m.27s
8th	Claude Laurent/Jacques Marche	F	30	Peugeot 104ZS2	G2	4h.52m.35s
9th	Nicole Ouimet/Yves Fontaine	CDN	11	Datsun 510	G2	4h.54m.05s
10th	Paul Bourgeoys/Robert Blouin	CDN	35	Mitsubishi Colt	G1	5h.06m.01s

39 starters. 13 finishers. No ladies, diesel or group 3 starters. 3 A-priority drivers.
Note: There were errors in some times for the final stage which were never officially corrected. The times given here are correct. No changes in positions are involved.

World Championship positions after Round 8
Ford 120 points, Datsun 94, Fiat 59, Toyota 38, Renault and Vauxhall 24, Opel 22, Lancia and Saab 18, Mercedes-Benz 17, Mitsubishi 13, Audi 11, Mazda 10, Porsche and Peugeot 8, Leyland 7, Volvo and Skoda 6, Lada 4.

Leading positions in World Championship for Drivers after Round 8
Waldegard 103 points, Mikkola 71, Alen 54, Vatanen 40, Salonen 38, Darniche, Blomqvist, Mehta and Dawson 20, Robson 15.

Leading retirements

DRIVER/NAVIGATOR	NATIONALITY	COMP NO.	CAR	GROUP	CAUSE	STAGES COMPLETED
Jean-Paul Perusse/Marie-Pierre Laforest	CDN	6	Renault 5 GTL	G2	accident	3
Jean-Paul Luc/Bruno Charbonnier	F	9	Citroen 2400CX	G2	accident	4
John Nixon/Lynn Nixon	CDN	33	Toyota Celica	G1	differential	12
Rod Millen/John Bellefleur	NZ/CDN	24	Datsun 160J	G2	propeller shaft	26
Jon Woodner/Jerry Hinkle	USA	7	Triumph TR7V8	G4	engine	after last stage

Rally leaders
Vatanen and Waldegard stage 1, Waldegard 2, (3 cancelled), Vatanen 4-14, Salonen 15-27, Waldegard 28, (29 cancelled), Salonen 30, Waldegard 31 and 32.

Leading special stage positions:

	1st	2nd	3rd	4th	5th	6th		1st	2nd	3rd	4th	5th	6th		1st	2nd	3rd	4th	5th	6th
Vatanen	15	6	—	—	—	1	Millen	—	1	6	6	4	2	Laurent	—	—	—	—	1	—
Waldegard	9	12	1	—	—	—	Dawson	—	—	3	9	10	1	Swayze	—	—	—	—	1	—
Salonen	1	3	13	4	1	—	Heinonen	—	—	1	3	6	10	Woodner	—	—	—	—	—	7

The route

		SPECIAL STAGES	TOTAL DISTANCE
Etape 1	Montreal (Thursday 1200) — St. Agathe des Monts — Montreal (Thursday 2400) (1 stage cancelled due to crowd control)	2 asphalt — 17 km 5 gravel — 32 km (reduced from 6 — 42 km)	307 km
Etape 2	Montreal (Friday 0700) — Trois Rivieres — Quebec (Friday 2100) (2 stages cancelled due to heavy rain and 1 stage cancelled due to crowd control)	3 asphalt — 31 kms) (reduced from 4 — 35 km) 4 gravel — 54 km (reduced from 6 — 97 km)	649 km
Etape 3	Quebec (Saturday 0830) — Montreal (Sunday 0600) (1 stage cancelled due to local objection and 2 stages cancelled before rally)	3 asphalt — 37 km (reduced from 4 — 45 km) 8 gravel — 246 km	969 km
		25 — 417 km	1925 km

Dry first and third etapes, wet second etape. Half the special stages held in darkness.

Previous winners

1973 Walter Boyce Toyota Corolla
1974 Jean-Paul Perusse Fiat Abarth 124
1975 John Buffum Porsche 911
1976 Taisto Heinonen Renault 17 Gordini
1977 Timo Salonen Fiat Abarth 131
1978 Walter Rohrl Fiat Abarth 131

Taisto Heinonen, Canadian champion for the third year running, with his disappointing group 2 Toyota Celica. Not only did the engine not give the expected power, but he lost time with a puncture and by making one too many laps at Trois Rivieres

Claude Laurent was the only private European driver to finish, with this Peugeot 104ZS2 — but he earned the company World Championship points

Fords began living on borrowed luck. Waldegard smashed his gearbox on a rock, but at this point in the route there was enough service time for this to be replaced. One stage later he overtook Salonen for the lead — and then lost it on the following stage after a puncture! Finally on the last stage of all, a repeat of an earlier one, Waldegard smashed his gearbox *again* — and the Ford mechanics had no spare. Waldegard had to drive the 300 kilometres back to the finish, topping up regularly.

The Quebec Rally succeeded through two factors only: the rally itself was above average in excitement with the lead changing seven times, something which is quite unusual, and the sponsors (Molson) themselves supported the event in a way that many other organizers would envy. But what were they backing? It is always sad to see people not understanding what they should do, simply through a failure to keep in touch and to observe the lessons being learned by others and thereby profiting from the experience. The Quebec Rally raises once again the questions which the Rally Commission have been facing: whether the future world of rallying must suffer from lessons being learned publicly the hard way — or whether only events of proven merit, irrespective of location, should be counted. The compromise solution dreamed up by the Rally Commission after the 1000 Lakes did not fully tell us which path will have to be followed.

Nicole Ouimet was the only lady driver in the event; furthermore she finished an amazing ninth place overall. Not only this, but without a time penalty incurred on a section where heavy traffic delayed competitors she would have come seventh

Rod Millen, the New Zealander, earned his place with the Datsun team by some remarkably forceful driving. Unfortunately his co-driving incurred nineteen minutes of road penalties, and when Millen decided after that he could safely drive flat-out, his 160J collapsed beneath him

Hendrik Blok quietly took sixth place and best group 1 in this Mitsubishi Mirage, the first time this model had been used on an International rally

Jean-Paul Perusse's Quebec cocktail: Renault on the Rocks!

Rallye San Remo

The Italians have got reasons for everything. A private Lancia success which (in the eyes of enthusiasts) disgraced the official Fiat group entries was ultimately described as an excellent boost for the Fiat group — the new Lancia Delta road car was announced immediately afterwards. The only thing not yet fully explained is how an Italian car shod with Michelin tyres came to win. . . . You cannot easily beat the Italians on their home ground, as witness the failures of a remarkable number of foreign teams who entered the rally. Many of the visiting drivers assumed that the newly devised formula which used a lot of gravel roads would favour them. Sadly they found that the Italian cars were not only built for asphalt, as had been supposed. The only entirely foreign entry to finish was Tony Pond and Ian Grindrod, who came fourth with their group 4 Sunbeam. While the cars were all still running, the sight of the Sunbeams, the TR7V8s, a Datsun and a Chevette 2300HS made the event very attractive.

While the event might have been visually attractive to outsiders, the change in format was far from attractive to privateers. The use of gravel roads (for the first time since 1975) came with mixed feelings. These roads were extremely abrasive; even long-accepted standards of tyre wear on the British forest tracks were nothing compared with the systematic stripping of the tyre treads caused by the rock-based roads in Italy. This brought endless problems of tyre management and expense. But the change in format in which the rally now straddled the width of northern Italy by crossing from San Remo over to San Marino was much less arguable. It caused long, tiring road sections, great difficulties in training and considerably increased expense (once again).

Even the visits to attractive places like Sienna and the Republic of San Marino itself hardly compensated. It was said that the old, all-asphalt format was too soft for the tough World Championship series, but whereas last year San Remo boasted a thirty-six per cent finishing rate, this year there was thirty-nine! And of course the number of starters as a whole was considerably reduced this year.

Ford did not enter and Datsun sent just one car. The World Championship was losing steam rapidly. What was more, neither Mikkola nor Waldegard competed, and furthermore still there was uncertainty about the actual rules of the World Championship itself. Nobody was quite sure how many rounds counted. The FIA Year Book stated nine out of the twelve yet the BPICA (the constructors' association) had been told by the Rallies Commission that the number was to be seven. Of this seven, some thought that only five European events could be counted, others said that this year — unlike 1980 — any seven could count. On the basis of the BPICA's understanding Ford felt pretty confident, and when the only Datsun on the entry list retired, the rule books were sought again. If (what an if!) Datsun won the last three rounds and Ford did not score at all — even on the RAC — Datsun and Ford would end up with equal points, and what would happen then? Suffice it to say, this situation was not clearly explained.

The rally was more interesting than this conjecture suggests. An almost unknown driver took the lead on the first stage; Fabrizio Tabaton, a graduate of Cesare Fiorio's Autobianchi rally championship training ground. 'Tony' was not happy with his car, but on the second stage he got into his stride, and took the lead when Tabaton left the road in dramatic style. He never lost the lead. The Fiats of Alen and Rohrl went well on the gravel stages, which began on the second day, but already 'Tony' had built up a buffer. He was even quickest overall on the first gravel stage as well. The Alitalia Fiats were having trouble with their transmissions, Alen in particular being delayed through servicing work. As soon as the gravel stages arrived, Salonen with the Datsun suddenly became highly competitive, but his engine failed him. A valve spring broke, this was replaced, but on the way to the next stage the valve itself gave up. Jean-Pierre Nicolas with Talbot France's Sunbeam was having handling troubles and then the distributor broke, and ultimately he retired.

When Salonen had gone, Opel had group 2 well in hand, but on the second leg Verini retired with transmission trouble, as did Lampinen's group 4 TR7V8 in which a rear suspension bolt broke. His team-mate Eklund went out on the third leg with engine trouble — the oil had vanished — but his rally had been troubled ever since a brake adjuster jammed on the first day, and the Swede was lucky to avoid a serious accident. The only Fiat to be spared serious trouble was that of Bettega, the

Abarth 131 driver who had been contesting the Italian international championship for the factory this year. Like Tabaton, he is another ex-Autobianchi driver. The Fiat factory had also entered another car — a Ritmo for Fusaro, which was still continuing despite a lot of delays. Group 2 was now in the hands of Dario Cerrato, the Conrero driver, who had only graduated from a Kadett GT/E on to the Ascona on this event. Ultimately he was the only group 2 driver to finish in the top ten. In group 1, Angelo Presotto was well ahead of his rivals with his Escort RS.

'Tony' was facing increasing pressure as the long six-day rally progressed. This time last year another private Stratos driver had gone into the final leg in the lead, with Alen in a similar car catching him fast. Then that driver (Vudafieri, who this year had gone off the road early on) had lost his cool and crashed. 'Tony's' job was easier, a six-minute lead over Rohrl was not expected to be lost. He used up over a half-minute on the very first test on the final leg with the wrong tyres (Rohrl

The victory of 'Tony' Fassina with the private Jolly Club Stratos was very popular. Even the Fiat Group themselves stated that it created favourable publicity, as the new Lancia Delta production car was being announced at the same time

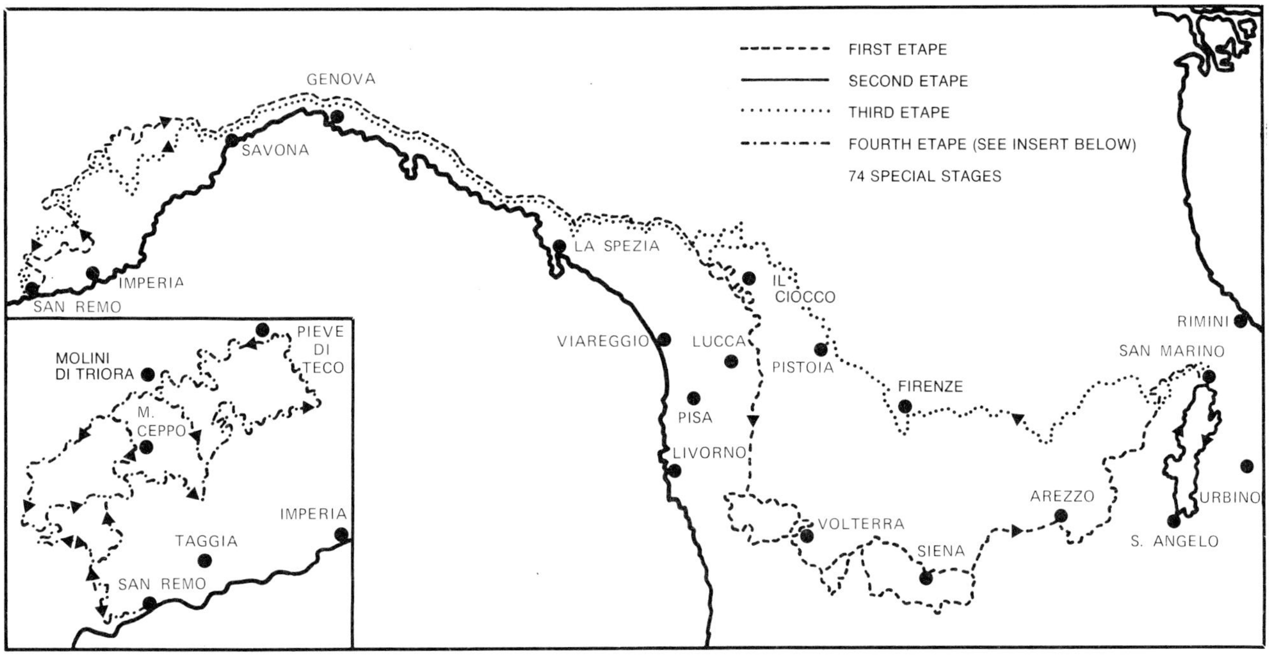

21 Rallye San Remo

1-7 October 1979 Italy

Overall results

POSITION	DRIVER/NAVIGATOR	NATIONALITY	COMP NO.	CAR	GROUP	TOTAL STAGE TIME
1st	'Tony'/Mauro Mannini	I	2	Lancia Stratos	G4	12h.37m.17s
2nd	Walter Rohrl/Christian Geistdorfer	D	6	Fiat Abarth 131	G4	12h.41m.31s
3rd	Attilio Bettega/Maurizio Perissinot	I	12	Fiat Abarth 131	G4	12h.55m.59s
4th	Tony Pond/Ian Grindrod	GB	11	Talbot Sunbeam	G4	13h.05m.22s
5th	Dario Cerrato/Lucio Guizzardi	I	18	Opel Ascona	G2	13h.11m.15s
6th	Markku Alen/Ilkka Kivimaki	SF	1	Fiat Abarth 131	G4	13h.18m.00s
7th	Angelo Presotto/Max Sghedoni	I	20	Ford Escort RS2000	G1	13h.26m.14s
8th	Antonio Tognana/Luciano Tedeschini	I	21	Opel Kadett GT/E	G1	13h.46m.38s
9th	'Nico'/Giogio Barban	I	23	Lancia Stratos	G4	14h.06m.56s
10th	Paolo Pasutti/Rinaldo Danelutti	I	26	Porsche 911	G3	14h.14m.25s

67 starters, 26 finishers. No lady crews started, 8 A-priority drivers

World Championship positions after Round 9
Ford 120 points (best seven results count, not nine as originally specified), Datsun 94, Fiat 75, Toyota 38, Lancia and Opel 36, Renault and Vauxhall 24, Saab 18, Mercedes-Benz 17, Mitsubishi 13, Talbot 12, Audi 11, Mazda 10, Porsche and Peugeot 8, Leyland 7, Skoda and Volvo 6, Lada 4.

Leading Positions in World Championship for Drivers after Round 9
Waldegard 103 points, Mikkola 71, Alen 60, Vatanen 40, Salonen 38, Darniche, Blomqvist, Mehta, Dawson and 'Tony' 20.

Rally Leaders
Tabaton stage 1, 'Tony' 2-end.

Leading Retirements

DRIVER/NAVIGATOR	NATION-ALITY	COMP NO.	CAR	GROUP	CAUSE	STAGES COMPLETED
Adartico Vudafieri/Mario Mannucci	I	15	Fiat Abarth 131	G4	accident	1
Fabrizio Tabaton/Marco Genovesi	I	16	Lancia Stratos	G4	accident	2
Jean-Pierre Nicolas/Jean Todt	F	4	Talbot Sunbeam	G4	withdrawn	25
Timo Salonen/Seppo Harjanne	SF	9	Datsun 160J	G2	engine valve	29
Simo Lampinen/Fred Gallagher	SF/GB	5	Triumph TR7V8	G4	rear suspension	43
Maurizio Verini/'Rudy'	I	7	Opel Ascona	G2	differential	43
Per Eklund/Hans Sylvan	S	10	Triumph TR7V8	G4	engine main bearings	51
Jean-Louis Dumont/Robert Rorife	B	14	Vauxhall Chevette 2300HS	G4	rear axle	63

Leading special stage positions:

	1st	2nd	3rd	4th	5th	6th		1st	2nd	3rd	4th	5th	6th		1st	2nd	3rd	4th	5th	6th
Rohrl	25	17	15	4	1	1	Bettega	3	9	12	14	14	9	Tabaton	1	—	—	—	1	—
'Tony'	24	21	6	5	5	3	Pond	2	—	14	14	8	11	Salonen	—	6	1	3	—	—
Alen	16	11	12	9	6	3	Eklund	1	—	3	5	7	7	Nicolas	—	2	1	2	2	3

The route

		SPECIAL STAGES	TOTAL DISTANCE
Etape 1	San Remo (Monday 0800) — Il Ciocco — Sienna — San Marino (Tuesday 2107) (1 stage cancelled through timing error, 1 stage cancelled through no authorization)	16 asphalt — 178 km 21 gravel — 254 km (reduced from 23 gravel — 276 km)	1554 km
Etape 2	San Marino (Wednesday 1100) — San Marino (Wednesday 1947)	10 gravel — 22 km	199 km
Etape 3	San Marino (Wednesday 2300) — San Remo (Thursday 1943) (2 stages cancelled through no authorization, 4 stages cancelled through damage to roads)	2 gravel — 43 km (reduced from 8 gravel — 147 km) 8 asphalt — 82 km	About 800 km
Etape 4	San Remo (Friday 2100) — San Remo (Saturday 0710)	9 asphalt — 203 km	416 km
		66 stages — 962 km	About 2950 km

Some stages damp, mostly dry and dusty (gravel). Half stages at night. Stages cancelled: 22, 36, 52, 53, 54, 55, 56 and 57.

Previous winners

1969 Harry Kallstrom Lancia Fulvia
1970 Jean-Luc Therier Renault Alpine A110
1971 Ove Andersson Renault Alpine A110
1972 Amilcare Ballestrieri Lancia Fulvia
1973 Jean-Luc Therier Renault Alpine A110
1974 Sandro Munari Lancia Stratos
1975 Bjorn Waldegard Lancia Stratos
1976 Bjorn Waldegard Lancia Stratos
1977 Jean-Claude Andruet Fiat Abarth 131
1978 Markku Alen Lancia Stratos

reached the end of that test with a badly handling car; all four of his tyres were found to be deflating), but he kept his cool and won. Of all the performances, however, the most promising must have been that of Pond — the first time for him or his team at this event, limited training, a car that had to be prepared outside the factory because of strikes — and fourth place too. As the best non-Italian car to finish, San Remo must have been a rewarding experience indeed. It would be nice if things were not quite the same another year, however.

Tony Pond's fourth place was an achievement in reliability for this British group 4 car as much as for the whole Talbot team who had to prepare the car privately in the middle of a strike at the factory. This was the most important result in Pond's career

The new format produced some stages in spectacular areas (this was close to San Marino) but did not produce any particular difference in the results, which would have been very similar had the rally been all held on the traditional asphalt stages nearer San Remo

Markku Alen watches as his Fiat Abarth 131 receives transmission repairs. Of the three official 131s, two had serious transmission troubles

Vanni Fusaro came to the official Fiat team after success in the Autobianchi series and then victory in the 1978 Mitropa championship. Twelfth place with this Ritmo did not sound much, but it was the first time one of these cars had survived a big rally, and Fusaro overcame troubles during the event

End of a Shooting Star. Tabaton's Stratos had been leading the rally when this accident occurred on the second stage

Dario Cerrato has been increasingly successful with Conrero Opel Kadett GT/Es, and his first event with a group 2 Ascona at San Remo resulted in a group win and fifth place overall

Timo Salonen's Team Datsun Europe 160J was hopeless on asphalt stages but went incredibly well on gravel stages before valve trouble, an old Datsun weakness, caused retirement

RALLYE SANREMO
7° TROFEO FIAMM
16
MAGNETI MARELLI
NOVOLAN
CODELLO

Mobil
conrero
OPEL
ascona
18
NOVOLAN
MICHELIN

Datsun
Castrol

Tour de Corse

The Corsicans may believe that Corsica is for them, but French rally drivers certainly reckon that the Tour de Corse is their own event. It is officially the French round in the World Championship, and of the 112 starters only five drivers came from abroad! All the finishers were French and the winner was the uncrowned champion of them all. Bernard Darniche with his Chardonnet Lancia Stratos outpaced and (more important) outdistanced all his rivals. Only once, after the first special stage, did Darniche fail to lead the rally — and that was because of Bernard Beguin, the current French national champion. On the second stage Beguin began to suffer a terminal transmission problem and Darniche was never again headed. It was a long, long event, demanding as much reconnaissance as possible (even many leading drivers could only cover the high-speed sections twice in available time), and the variety of the high-speed sections was itself unique. Sometimes the sections were simply timed to the minute, then there were orthodox special stages, and the exclusive 'chronometric' sections. These were non-stop sections covering distances up to one hundred kilometres at a time, timed like special stages but with an alternative (and complicated) penalty system. On these sections, unlike the scratch timing on the special stages themselves, minimum and maximum times were specified. On one section nobody managed to record even the maximum permitted time!

The organizers always wonder why so few foreign teams go to Corsica each year, and this year the matter was more acute than ever. It is held very close to the RAC Rally which is popular with most teams, the French are traditionally specialists in asphalt rallies and, of course, the matter of the training is very

daunting. Only local drivers are willing to tackle the sections without pace-notes, which for a foreign driver are essential just to keep within the overall time limits. And this year the amount of new route was so great that even an experienced Corsican rally expert like Jean-Pierre Nicolas stated that he had to make new notes for sixty per cent of the speed sections. Even allowing for certain duplication of these sections, Jean Ragnotti's co-driver calculated that more than 1000 kilometres had to be reconnoitred. At a rally like Bandama, this is not so serious, since there reconnaissance can be made at high-speed, but on the narrow, twisty three-dimensioned Corsican roads it can take hours to cover in daylight a road that on the rally will be covered in minutes. Maybe these are some of the reasons why Corsica does not attract so many foreigners. But having said that, the challenge of the route has always been demanding in its own way as any rally in the world, which makes the decision to increase the length of the event even more mysterious.

The next strange thing about the Tour de Corse 1979 was that there were no official cars at all! The nearest to this was the Renault 5 Alpine entered by the local dealers, an ex-works car driven by the factory driver Ragnotti, whilst Chardonnet-Lancia, Fiat-France, Talbot and Opel all entered cars from the national teams. Datsun's chances of the World Championship for Makes had been so slim after San Remo, they did not enter either officially from Japan or from Team Datsun Europe and since no Datsuns were on the entry list (private or otherwise) Ford gained the Championship without even entering the rally! The ones most likely to beat those semi-official cars which entered were,

Bernard Beguin started the rally with the determination to win. He won the first section but transmission trouble intervened on the second

Bernard Darniche sweeps along to his fifth Tour de Corse victory, seen here on the penultimate section at Levie on the Sunday morning

of course, the Porsches, many of which were 3-litre models prepared to group 4 and one of which (that of Jacques Almeras) was said to develop more than 300 bhp.

The sheer endurance demanded from the crews and cars was without parallel. On the high-speed sections (over ninety per cent of the route is closed to other traffic, whether this is special stage, 'chronometric' section, tight road section or any liaison section except those on Routes Nationales) the driver is forever changing direction, changing gear, listening to the next instruction from his co-driver, concentrating on driving as smoothly as he can. At this Darniche is a master, but even he had trouble. Mahe, his constant co-driver, misread one instruction. In an instant the Lancia was off the road and the wing was damaged. Then on the penultimate section he came round one corner to find rocks in the road — just as happened to Waldegard at Monte Carlo. His steering was damaged and he stopped listening to Mahe, driving every subsequent corner by sight. Ragnotti and Mouton also had punctures here. Mouton, on her way to her fifth Ladies' prize on this event, had a very troubled rally. Punctures and a broken injector pipe had seriously delayed her in the early stages, and all the rest of the event had been spent fighting back. Before those rocks she had risen to fourth

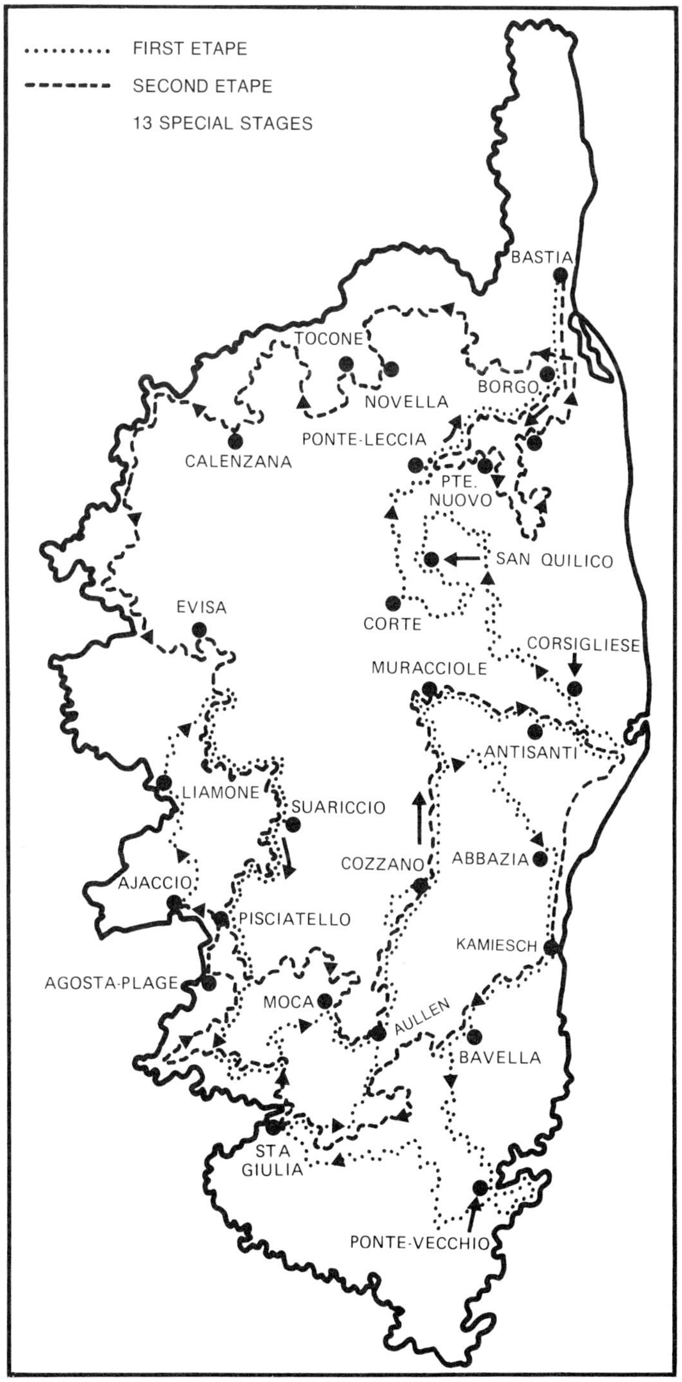

23 Tour de Corse

2-4 November 1979 France

Overall results

POSITION	DRIVER/NAVIGATOR	NATIONALITY	COMP NO.	CAR	GROUP	TOTAL STAGE TIME
1st	Bernard Darniche/Alain Mahe	F	1	Lancia Stratos	G4	14h.36m.46s
2nd	Jean Ragnotti/Jean-Marc Andrie	F	6	Renault 5 Alpine	G2	15h.12m.52s
3rd	Pierre-Louis Moreau/Patrice Baron	F	16	Porsche 911	G4	15h.23m.06s
4th	Alain Coppier/Josepha Laloz	F	29	Porsche 911	G3	15h.30m.26s
5th	Michele Mouton/Francoise Conconi	F	3	Fiat Abarth 131	G4	15h.53m.38s*
6th	Bernard Picone/Robert Cianelli	F	85	Opel Kadett GT/E	G1	16h.09m.29s
7th	Paul Rouby/Alain Garcon	F	43	Renault 5 Alpine	G2	16h.28m.15s
8th	Jean-Pierre Mari/Patrick de la Foata	F	114	Toyota Starlet	G1	17h.41m.56s
9th	Jean Bondrille/Vincent Fattaccio	F	47	Opel Kadett GT/E	G2	17h.44m.44s
10th	Jean-Charles Martinetti/Philippe Gabrielli	F	54	Peugeot 104ZS2	G2	18h.04m.51s

112 starters. 14 finishers. *Ladies winner. No diesel starters. 5 A-priority drivers.
Note: a sixth A-priority driver Francis Vincent withdrew because of engine trouble before the start.

World Championship positions after Round 10
Ford 120 points, Datsun 94, Fiat 87, Lancia 54, Opel 49, Toyota 48, Renault 41, Porsche 32, Vauxhall 24, Saab 18, Mercedes-Benz 17, Peugeot 15, Mitsubishi 13, Talbot 12, Audi 11, Mazda 10, Leyland 7, Skoda and Volvo 6, Lada 4. FORD NOW CHAMPION.

Leading positions in World Championship for Drivers after Round 10
Waldegard 103 points, Mikkola 71, Alen 60, Vatanen and Darniche 40, Salonen 38, Ragnotti 25, Blomqvist, Mehta, Dawson and 'Tony' 20.

Leading retirements

DRIVER/NAVIGATOR	NATION-ALITY	COMP NO.	CAR	GROUP	CAUSE	STAGES COMPLETED
Jean-Claude Andruet/'Biche'	F	5	Fiat Abarth 131	G4	front suspension	2
Alain Beauchef/Daniel Brichot	L	8	Ford Escort RS	G1	no fuel	2
Jacques Almeras/Jean-Claude Perramond	F	9	Porsche 911	G4	rear suspension	2
Bernard Beguin/Jean-Jacques Lenne	F	10	Porsche 911	G4	transmission	2
Francis Serpaggi/Denise Emmanuelli	F	12	Lancia Stratos	G4	fuel starvation	2
Yves Loubet/Rene Alemany	F	40	Opel Kadett GT/E	G2	accident	2
Jean-Louis Clarr/Jean-Francois Fauchille	F	7	Opel Kadett GT/E	G1	accident	11
Jean-Pierre Manzagol/Jean-Francois Filippi	F	39	Renault 5 Alpine	G2	accident	12
Jean-Pierre Nicolas/Jean Todt	F	4	Talbot Sunbeam	G4	accident	13
Christian Gardavot/Jean-Luc Claret	F	25	Porsche 911	G3	oil cooler	14

Rally leaders
Beguin stage 1, Darniche stage 2-end.

Leading special stage positions:

	1ST	2ND	3RD	4TH	5TH	6TH		1ST	2ND	3RD	4TH	5TH	6TH		1ST	2ND	3RD	4TH	5TH	6TH
Darniche	9	7	4	2	—	—	Nicolas	3	4	—	4	1	—	Mouton	—	4	7	6	2	—
Ragnotti	4	2	5	3	2	—	Coppier	2	—	—	1	7	2	Manzagol	—	1	—	3	4	2
Moreau	4	1	2	2	2	—	Beguin	1	1	—	—	—	—	Picone	—	1	—	1	1	4

The route

		SPECIAL STAGES	TOTAL DISTANCE
Etape 1	Ajaccio (Friday 1400) — Kamiesch — Muracciole — Bastia (Saturday 0900)	4 chronometric sections (339 km) 7 special stages (205 km)	967 km
Etape 2	Bastia (Saturday 1800) — Aullene — Quenza — Ajaccio (Sunday 1330)	5 chronometric sections (405 km) 6 special stages (199 km)	1066 km
		9 chronometric sections (744 km)	2033 km
		13 special stages (404 km)	

All asphalt route, mostly dry but some rain on first etape. Most stages at night.

Previous winners

1969 Gerard Larrousse Porsche 911
1970 Bernard Darniche Renault Alpine A110
1971 rally not held
1972 Jean-Claude Andruet Renault Alpine A110
1973 Jean-Pierre Nicolas Renault Alpine A110
1974 Jean-Claude Andruet Lancia Stratos
1975 Bernard Darniche Lancia Stratos
1976 Sandro Munari Lancia Stratos
1977 Bernard Darniche Fiat Abarth 131
1978 Bernard Darniche Fiat Abarth 131

place. Her team-mate Andruet also had punctures and had given up hope when suspension trouble had cost him twenty minutes' delay — after the second of the twenty-two stages.

The most telling effect from the length of the event was on the gearboxes of the cars. One could hear just how carefully Darniche was nursing his car along, but the Renault 5 Alpine drivers Ragnotti and Manzagol both had great trouble changing gear, and the Porsches which finished third and fourth were both stuck in third gear during the later stages. Almeras's powerful Porsche had gone off the road on the first section and retired with a broken wishbone after the second, and the only group 4 Porsche to reach the finish at all was that of the Corsican Pierre-Louis Moreau. He was third overall, having the previous year finished as best in group 3. This year this award went to Alain Coppier, an experienced French private driver who only this year has turned to driving more powerful cars. Jean-Pierre Nicolas was plagued with electrical trouble with the Talbot Sunbeam but eventually retired after hitting one of the country's famous wild pigs —

Jean Ragnotti storms up the Col de Bavella in the second etape with his reliable Renault 5 Alpine entered by Doria, the local dealers which was so heavy that the front suspension was seriously damaged. In group 1 the Opel France driver Jean-Louis Clarr, never a man to finish the Tour de Corse without some accident, had a long battle in the first half with the Corsican Bernard Picone who drove a similar Kadett GT/E, and on the second leg it was Clarr who retired again after a crash. An interesting car to finish second in group 1 was a Toyota Starlet. Corsica in 1979 may not have been so important in world terms as in earlier years but the drivers who entered it will remember it forever. It must have been the toughest asphalt rally of all time.

First important result on World championship rallies for the Toyota Starlet, which finished eighth overall and second in group 1

Pierre-Louis Moreau from Calvi was the best placed local driver, coming third with his group 4 Porsche and gaining A-priority for the coming season

Jean-Pierre Nicolas drove a French built Talbot Sunbeam group 4 car, which suffered electrical trouble before hitting a pig in the second part of the event

One of the biggest surprises of the event was the speed of this Opel Kadett GT/E driven by the Corsican Bernard Picone, who matched the times of the official French Opel driver Jean-Louis Clarr

The start was delayed while an argument raged over pro-nationalist Corsican stickers being placed on the rally cars. Here Darniche waits patiently whilst this was resolved, as the effigy of Napoleon on the steps in the background silently looks on

SUNBEAM
Shell
Shell
Shell
TALBOT
4
ESSO
FERODO

chardonnet
TOUR DE CORSE
LIBERTA
PER I PATRIOTTI
A RISCOSSA

Lombard RAC Rally

At least the rally had virtually all the stars you could wish to see. The route was one of the most compact and toughest in memory — but all the time something was missing from this year's RAC Rally. It seemed as if it had all happened before. Hannu Mikkola won for the second time, the Escort won for the *eighth* time; technically there was virtually nothing new to see. Once again Mikkola took over the lead as soon as the 'real' forest stages started — again it was at the expense of Markku Alen's Stratos. For some while the order lay; Mikkola, Vatanen, Brookes and Pond. Substitute Waldegard for Vatanen and you had last year's finishing order, with Pond being the best non-Ford driver. Things did not quite work out like that. Pond (with a Talbot Sunbeam instead of a TR7V8) crashed and Vatanen lost two places due to a time control mistake, but all the time the RAC, rather like the Tour de Corse before it, had that air of *dèja vue*.

For all that, however, the RAC attracted the crowds and the teams. Much of the layout of the route was designed to reduce public discontent caused by the spectator traffic, but the added compactness of this year's event was much appreciated by crews if not by the spectators. It was a great surprise to see so many teams on the entry list, bearing in mind that hardly any of them had any chance of beating the Fords. Some teams, like Audi, openly admitted that their presence was solely in the cause of experience. Others, like Talbot and Vauxhall have been contesting the British championship season while the Fiat and Lancia teams came as a result of demand by the local dealers. Every year the presentation of the Lombard RAC Rally improves.

Technical interest this year was very slight. Fords had a new clutch, Saab had more powerful engines, Toyota had their 16-valve car on its first important event since this engine was banned at the end of 1977 (in other words, the team were back two years in development). Datsun had two new cars which, particularly the one driven by Salonen, at last confirmed that they had the edge on their great rival Toyota — although meanwhile Toyota had been elevated to group 4. Fords had pursued a policy of reliability and proven specification — their clutches were aimed more at trouble-free gearbox removal rather than better performance — and this was clearly the way to go. Ford had one new car, for Waldegard, but this was troublesome and a great disappointment for World Championship leader. The three types of car most likely to beat Ford were; Talbot — a single entry for Pond, at a power disadvantage although of proven reliability, Vauxhall — Airikkala had one eye on the British championship; this year he started as firm favourite with a better car but with a team that still could not match the immense experience of Ford — and Lancia. Ever since Waldegard drove his tail-less Stratos through the forests of Britain, the British enthusiasts have seen no reason why a Stratos should not win this event. This year the car used was prepared away from the factory and had not been used for over a year. Although it suffered disconcerting engine and brake troubles, once again it led the rally and even if it did not win, the spectators were happy. A splendid sight were the five smart Triumph TR7V8s, even if between them they could only gain one fastest stage time all rally. John Buffum's had fuel injection while the others, carburettors. How those cars were reminiscent of the Datsun 240Zs of the early sixties!

Last year the first stage produced a strange result. Danielsson had the honour of leading the rally; this year that honour fell to Jean-Luc Therier, the French Toyota driver. It was the only happiness for Toyota this time; a miscellany of problems afflicted the team from that moment onwards. Then Markku Alen got to grips with his Stratos, its superior traction important for the slippery spectator stages. The Italian dream of winning the RAC Rally with a Stratos began to fade as soon as the rally reached the Yorkshire forests. As Hannu Mikkola began to apply the pressure, the brakes of the Stratos began to give trouble and the engine kept misfiring. Just after the Escort overtook the Stratos, the Stratos went off the road for nine minutes and all hope for Alen disappeared. But just as Waldegard had previously enraptured the crowds when in a hopeless position, Alen continued to fight. Mikkola's team mate Waldegard was in miseries. A small excursion on the first stage put him out of the top runners. Then on the first night he had a puncture and found when he stopped to change the wheel that the jack would not work. In the Kielder forests the Stratos was far from happy, Alen saying that the corrogations in the road made the car almost undriveable, while his fellow Fiat group driver Walter Rohrl was unable to make his car work well at all. The Ford takeover was proceeding as expected. The only cars other than Ford and the Stratos in the top ten were Pond's Talbot, and Salonen's Datsun.

The morning of the start of the second half dawned foggy and icy, some unpleasant driving obviously lay in store. Gone already were the two Saabs; Blomqvist and Stromberg both having been delayed before ultimately retiring, while only one of the three Toyotas was still going. Two of the five Triumph TR7V8s were missing as well. Gradually some cracks in the giant Ford armour were appearing. Roger Clark retired when he had valve trouble and Ari Vatanen was penalised ten minutes at Machynlleth. All the while the amazing Salonen was going better and better, the only group 2 driver in the top ten. Pond retired, which made Salonen the

Bjorn Waldegard had a miserable rally: here he is changing the rear axle as a precaution

Hannu Mikkola on the last day at Great Orme asphalt special stage, near Llandudno. By now his lead was secure

28 Lombard RAC Rally

18-21 November 1979 Great Britain

Overall results

POSITION	DRIVER/NAVIGATOR	NATIONALITY	COMP NO.	CAR	GROUP	TOTAL STAGE TIME
1st	Hannu Mikkola/Arne Hertz	SF/S	1	Ford Escort RS	G4	8h.03m.38s
2nd	Russell Brookes/Paul White	GB	10	Ford Escort RS	G4	8h.14m.07s
3rd	Timo Salonen/Stuart Pegg	SF/ZA	12	Datsun 160J	G2	8h.16m.22s
4th	Ari Vatanen/David Richards	SF/GB	6	Ford Escort RS	G4	8h.19m.53s
5th	Markku Alen/Ilkka Kivimaki	SF	2	Lancia Stratos	G4	8h.20m.23s
6th	John Taylor/Phil Short	GB	18	Ford Escort RS	G4	8h.24m.01s
7th	Pentti Airikkala/Risto Virtanen	SF	7	Vauxhall Chevette 2300HS	G4	8h.25m.57s
8th	Walter Rohrl/Christian Geistdorfer	D	3	Fiat Abarth 131	G4	8h.26m.37s
9th	Bjorn Waldegard/Hans Thorszelius	S	4	Ford Escort RS	G4	8h.29m.12s
10th	Greg Carr/Fred Gocentas	AUS	23	Ford Escort RS	G4	8h.30m.31s
19th	Alan Carter/David West	NZ/GB	27	Ford Escort RS	G1	9h.04m.01s
34th	Marja-Liisa Korpi/Eija Heinio	SF	88	Ford Escort RS	G1	10h.00m.52s*
74th	Joe McHale/Christy Farrell	IRL	147	VW Golf LD	Diesel	12h.17m.13s

175 starters. 74 finishers. No group 3 starters. *Ladies winner. 13 A-priority drivers.

World Championship positions after Round 11
Ford 132 points (best 7), Datsun 104 (best 7), Fiat 92, Lancia 65, Opel 49, Toyota 48, Renault 41, Porsche 32, Vauxhall 31, Saab 18, Mercedes-Benz 17, Peugeot 15, Mitsubishi 13, Talbot 12, Audi 11, Mazda 10, Leyland 7, Skoda and Volvo 6, Lada 4.

Leading positions in World Championship for Drivers after Round 11
Waldegard 103 points (best 7), Mikkola 91, Alen 68, Vatanen and Salonen 50, Darniche 40, Ragnotti 25, Rohrl 21, Blomqvist, Mehta, Dawson and 'Tony' all 20 etc.

Leading retirements

DRIVER/NAVIGATOR	NATIONALITY	COMP NO.	CAR	GROUP	CAUSE	STAGES COMPLETED
Holger Bohne/Peter Diekmann	D	25	Ford Escort RS	G4	wet electrics	4
Lief Asterhag/Mike Broad	S/GB	19	Toyota Celica	G4	clutch	8
Ola Stromberg/Bo Reinicke	S	22	Saab 99 Turbo	G2	water pump	11
Bror Danielsson/Ulf Sundberg	S	14	Ford Escort RS	G4	no fuel	14
Stig Blomqvist/Bjorn Cederberg	S	5	Saab 99 Turbo	G2	accident	16
John Buffum/John Brown	USA/GB	26	Triumph TR7V8	G4	accident	16
Terry Kaby/Brian Rainbow	GB	34	Triumph TR7V8	G4	oil pressure	16
Jean-Luc Therier/Michel Vial	F	21	Toyota Celica	G4	injection pump	16
Henri Toivonen/Phil Boland	SF/GB	20	Ford Escort RS	G4	clutch	30
Bjorn Johansson/Ragnar Spjuth	S	24	Opel Kadett GT/E	G2	engine	41
Tony Pond/Ian Grindrod	GB	17	Talbot Sunbeam	G4	accident	41
Roger Clark/Neil Wilson	GB	8	Ford Escort RS	G4	engine	45

Rally Leaders
Therier stage 1, Alen 2-10, Mikkola 11-end.

Leading special stage positions:

	1st	2nd	3rd	4th	5th	6th		1st	2nd	3rd	4th	5th	6th		1st	2nd	3rd	4th	5th	6th
Mikkola	24	7	5	5	3	5	Pond	4	2	5	3	4	5	Waldegard	2	6	7	8	5	2
Alen	13	12	7	3	4	2	Salonen	3	3	6	8	5	2	Rohrl	2	1	2	1	2	5
Vatanen	8	13	6	9	4	1	Brookes	2	7	7	6	7	5	Wilson	1	4	7	5	3	4

Note: Malcolm Wilson/Terry Harryman (Ford Escort RS G4 GB) 15th overall.

The route

		SPECIAL STAGES	TOTAL DISTANCE
Etape 1	Chester (0900 Sunday) — Pickering — Carlisle — Chester (2000 Monday) —	3 asphalt —11.5 miles 3 mixed —9 miles 28 gravel —221 miles	1020 miles
Etape 2	Chester (0930 Tuesday) — Llandrindod Wells — Machynlleth — Chester (1630 Wednesday)	1 asphalt —3 miles 1 mixed —2 miles 23 gravel —168.5 miles	772 miles
		59 stages —415 miles	1792 miles

Mostly dry weather with wet surfaces, some ice, a little snow, some rain, some fog. Most stages at night.

Previous winners

1969 Harry Kallstrom Lancia Fulvia
1970 Harry Kallstrom Lancia Fulvia
1971 Stig Blomqvist Saab 96V4
1972 Roger Clark Ford Escort RS1600
1973 Timo Makinen Ford Escort RS1600
1974 Timo Makinen Ford Escort RS1600
1975 Timo Makinen Ford Escort RS1800
1976 Roger Clark Ford Escort RS1800
1977 Bjorn Waldegard Ford Escort RS1800
1978 Hannu Mikkola Ford Escort RS

best non-Ford and both Rohrl and Airikkala gradually rose up the field. Malcolm Wilson who had been up with the leading Fords in the early stages went off the road in Wales, and the remaining Triumphs tried unsuccessfully to improve their positions. Eventually the tenth best driver was Greg Carr from Australia.

Organizationally it is difficult to see how future RAC Rallies can be improved: the format is so well operated. It is just a pity that so few teams and drivers have been able to succeed on this event. Just before this year's event, Mikkola stated he expected to compete on the 1980 event in a private Ford, a telling comment on how ineffective are the other teams on this particular rally.

Russell Brookes obliges the next generation. In 1978 he was third overall, this time he was second

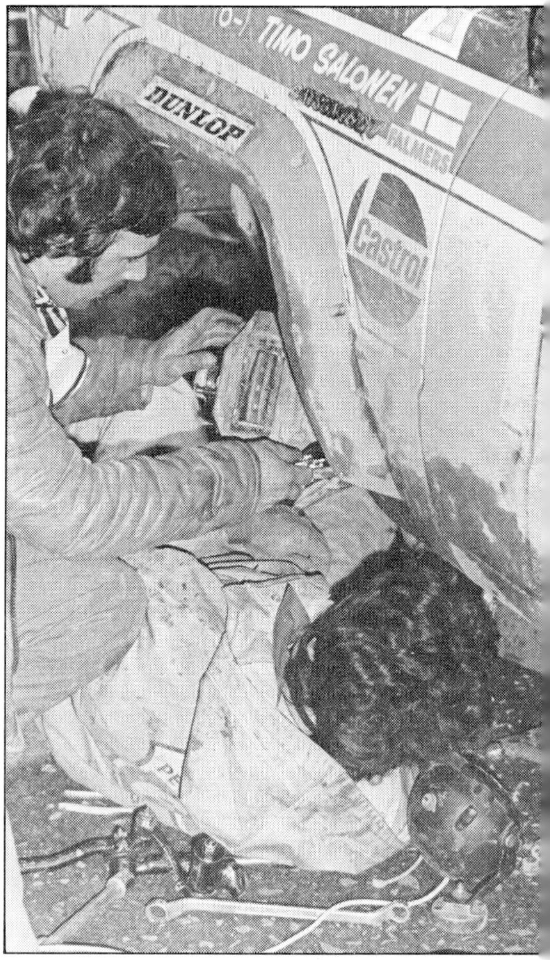

Tony Pond once again led the challenge of the non-Ford cars, this time with his Sunbeam group 4 car. Untypically his rally ended off the road with the car on its roof, but the message about the potential of this car and the skill of its driver was clear

Timo Salonen's third place was a great surprise, helped a little by the difficult conditions in the second half of the event. His most serious problem was the old Datsun steering trouble. Here at Devil's Bridge urgent repairs are put in hand

A most unhappy driver on the RAC Rally was Pentti Airikkala, here having his rear axle changed after bending it on the first evening. Despite his troubles he clinched the British Open Championship as a result of the rally

Per Eklund leaves the picturesque start in Chester in front of a small section of the RAC Rally's legendary crowds

Not the most impressive Stratos performance ever, but once again Markku Alen put a Lancia into the lead of the RAC Rally until brake troubles slowed him and then put him off the road

Ari Vatanen finished second best driver on stage times with his Rothmans Ford Escort RS, his car virtually unmarked – a far cry from his early days as a rally driver

Bandama Rally

The last big rally of the nineteen-seventies gave a fascinating, almost frightening, insight into the nineteen-eighties. Mercedes entered officially without any of the charade of 'private involvement' that they had used before — and won the longest and fastest of the World Championship rallies completely and comprehensively. Four cars entered and took the four top places. It was an ideal event for them, their 450SLC 5.0 was suited to this event in a way that nobody expects them to be so on the tighter European rallies, but the most impressive thing was not that they won, nor by what margin, nor by how much money they spent in doing it — but by the whole range of ideas they employed in doing it. It made other manufacturers seem to be playing with rallies. It almost made a joke of everything that others had been taken so seriously in the past. Not everything went perfectly: there were touching little human fallibilities — like the two times mechanics failed to fix bonnet catches and bonnets flew up. There were also mechanics faults (electrical failure for Mikkola, a bonnet failure for Waldegard of its own accord, a broken fan for Vic Preston, brake trouble for Waldegard and so on) but compared with the complete devastation of the other teams these were trifling. It came almost as an incidental that Mikkola was first, that Waldegard finished second and took the World Rally Drivers Championship: so incidental that this situation could have been one of countless instructions fed into the Mercedes computer along with the records of all the mechanical stresses and details of the route.

Mercedes came with four cars, Peugeot with four as well, while the only other team to compete seriously was Toyota with two. Toyota had the distinction of creating the most interesting technical news: they had two group 4 Liftback models — variants of the RA45 model homologated earlier in the year. They had used the normal notchback model with the more recently evolved 4-valve engine on the RAC Rally, but here they used the older 2-valve engines — apparently on specific instructions from Japan. The Peugeots had their sump mountings modified after the Safari — the cause of their agonising troubles there, while Mercedes had done outwardly little more than change their final axle ratio — lower. Despite Bandama being the fastest championship rally in the world, Mercedes felt that acceleration to cruis-

Mercedes' delight was Peugeot's despair. This is Timo Makinen driving as hard as he knows how, but constant problems on the car slowed him and eventually caused retirement on the last day

ing speeds in the region of 140-180 kph was the most important thing.

Teams entering a rally like the Bandama expect a certain wastage of their entries: there are just too many unforseeable things to be able to cater for everything in advance. Vast stretches of the route had been re-graded shortly before the rally this year. The type of pace-notes required for this event will guide a driver to take the smoothest line through bends and avoid the bad holes — and these were largely useless on the sections of the route concerned. Trees fall down in unpredicted places (the huge tropical trees are one of the most impressive features of the landscape) and sometimes it is easier to cut a hole through a fallen tree than move it. Wal-

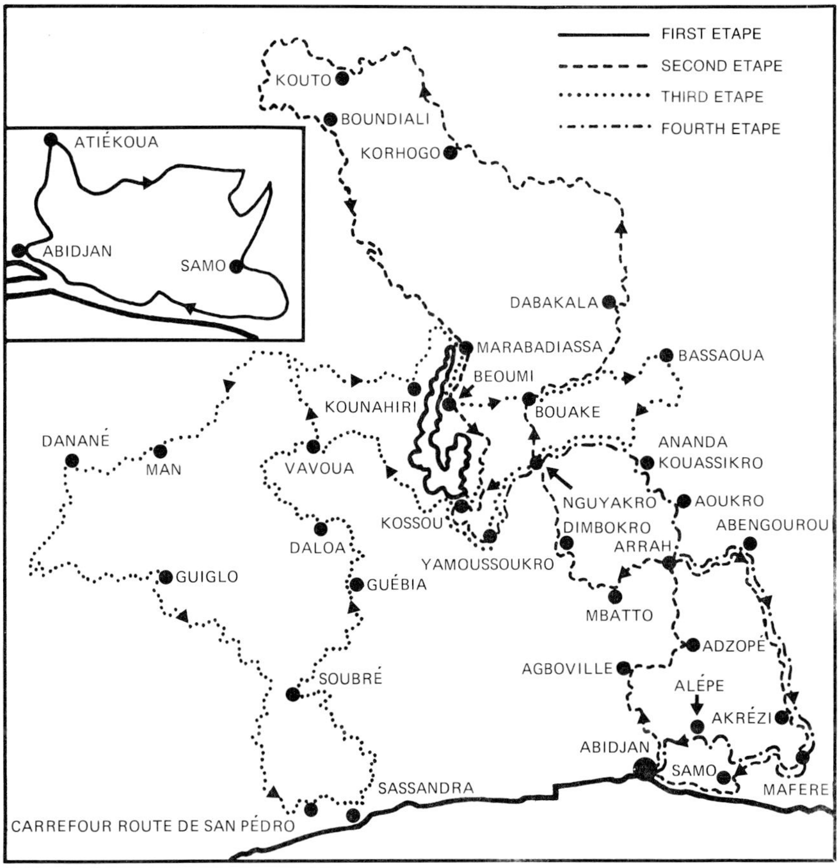

Hannu Mikkola and Arne Hertz en route to victory, but Waldegard was always within reach and his second place brought the ultimate championship. The Mercedes 450SLC 5.0s were both magnificent and historic: the first World Championship victory by an 8-cylinder car and the first World Championship win with a car using an automatic gearbox

11 Bandama Rally

9-14 December 1979 Ivory Coast, West Africa

Overall results

POSITION	DRIVER/NAVIGATOR	NATIONALITY	COMP NO.	CAR	GROUP	TOTAL PENALTY
1st	Hannu Mikkola/Arne Hertz	SF/S	6	Mercedes-Benz 450SLC 5.0	G4	3h.23m.
2nd	Bjorn Waldegard/Hans Thorszelius	S	4	Mercedes-Benz 450SLC 5.0	G4	3h.58m.
3rd	Andrew Cowan/Klaus Kaiser	GB/D	10	Mercedes-Benz 450SLC 5.0	G4	4h.10m.
4th	Vic Preston Jnr/Mike Doughty	EAK	3	Mercedes-Benz 450SLC 5.0	G4	4h.17m.
5th	Ove Andersson/Henry Liddon	S/GB	5	Toyota Celica Liftback	G4	6h.08m.
6th	Alain Ambrosino/Robert Schneck	F	9	Peugeot 504 V6 Coupé	G4	8h.58m.
7th	Michel Mitri/Jean-Pierre Fornado	F	18	Datsun Violet	G2	12h.25m.
8th	Jean-Pierre Faure/Alain Manfredini	F	55	Datsun Violet	G1	13h.48m.

57 starters. 8 finishers. No Diesel or ladies finishers. No group 3 starters. 6 A-priority drivers.

Final World Championship positions
Ford (150) 122 points, Datsun (122) 108, Fiat 92, Lancia 65, Toyota 58, Opel 49, Renault 41, Mercedes-Benz 35, Porsche 32, Vauxhall 31, Peugeot 23, Saab 18, Mitsubishi 13, Talbot 12, Audi 11, Mazda 10, Leyland 7, Volvo and Skoda 6, Lada 4.

Leading final World Championship for Drivers
Waldegard (120) 112 points, Mikkola 111, Alen 68, Salonen 50, Vatanen 50 (note: Salonen more second places than Alen), Darniche 40, Ragnotti 25, Cowan 22, Rohrl 21, Blomqvist, Mehta and 'Tony' 20. WALDEGARD NOW CHAMPION.

Leading retirements

DRIVER/NAVIGATOR	NATION-ALITY	COMP NO.	CAR	GROUP	CAUSE	CONTROLS VISITED
Jean-Pierre Nicolas/Jean de Alexandris	F	1	Peugeot 504 V6 Coupé	G4	differential	2
Andy Dawson/Naguib Saad	GB/CI	19	Datsun 160J	G2	rear wheel bearing	4
Adolphe Choteau/Yves Taravel	F	16	Peugeot 504 V6 Coupé	G4	engine	11
Jean-Luc Therier/Michel Vial	F	8	Toyota Celica Liftback	G4	accident	14
Jean-Claude Lefebvre/Christian Delferrier	F/B	12	Peugeot 504 V6 Coupé	G4	engine	24
Bruno Saby/Daniel le Saux	F	21	Renault 5 Alpine	G2	rear suspension	24
Carlos Torres/Miguel Oliveira	P	15	Ford Escort RS 2000	G1	alternator	31
Timo Makinen/Jean Todt	SF/F	2	Peugeot 504 V6 Coupé	G4	electrics	44
Jean-Francois Vincens/Felix Giallolacci	F	14	Mitsubishi Lancer	G2	too late at finish	50
Samir Assef/Gilbert Fourcade	RL/F	11	Peugeot 504 V6 Coupé	G4	too late at finish	50

Rally leaders
Controls 1 and 2 — many cars without penalty, 3-9 Cowan, 10 Cowan and Mikkola, 11 and 12 Cowan, 13-18 Mikkola, 19-23 Waldegard, 24-end Mikkola.

This Range Rover (four-wheel drive) completed over half of the route, despite the very high averages required. Maybe this will be forerunner of similar transmissions in rallying

The route

		CONTROLS	TOTAL DISTANCE
Etape 1	Abidjan (Sunday 1000) — Alepe — Abidjan (Sunday 1400)	Start — 7	238 km
Etape 2	Abidjan (Monday 1000) — Bouake — Yamoussoukro (Tuesday 1400)	8 — 27	2232 km (reduced from 2278 km)
Etape 3	Yamoussoukro (Wednesday 1200) — Daloa — Yamoussoukro (Thursday 1520)	28 — 39	2420 km
Etape 4	Yamoussoukro (Friday 0200) — Alepe — Abidjan (Friday 1030)	40 — 50	732 km
			5622 km (reduced from 5668 km)

800 km approximately asphalt, the rest gravel. Total scheduled time 55h.30m. (Winners time 58h.53m.). Total of 50 sections of which only 16 not attainable by the leading crews within the time allowance. No special stages. Rally held in dry conditions with some wet roads and very humid climate.

Previous winners

1971 Robert Neyret Peugeot 504
1972 no finishers
1973 Edgar Herrmann Datsun 180B
1974 Timo Makinen Peugeot 504
1975 Bernard Consten Peugeot 504
1976 Timo Makinen Peugeot 504 V6 Coupé
1977 Andrew Cowan Mitsubishi Lancer
1978 Jean-Pierre Nicolas Peugeot 504 V6 Coupé

degard collided with one such. Another fallen tree was discovered by Mikkola, at that time the first Mercedes driver on the road, alongside a bus parked on the side of the road. He warned the other team drivers by radio — and Andersson the first non-Mercedes driver to arrive went straight into it. And perhaps the biggest unnatural hazard were the other vehicles themselves. There are no special stages on the Bandama, no closed roads: drivers fight against time and against all and every other vehicle on the road.

The biggest natural hazard this year was dust. There was a short classifying loop on the first day, in which the British driver Andy Cowan was quickest (Mikkola being delayed here with his electrical trouble), so he was allowed to restart the second loop in clear conditions. As soon as the night arrived, instructions came from the Mercedes aeroplane above that he was to stop and allow the two Scandinavian drivers to come past. The aeroplanes were used as a satellite to bounce radio waves rather than the older system of being the relay station. He was then instructed to follow the others through in case of trou-

ble. Behind him as a long-stop was Preston, who had to drive in the hanging dust of all his teammates — but in turn creating even more dust for the drivers of other cars behind.

Peugeot lost their first car almost immediately: Nicolas, last year's winner, had a crownwheel and pinion failure, caused apparently through poor alignment in manufacture. On the second loop they lost Lefebvre with engine trouble and Makinen had a long delay with differential then other troubles. After this he and the local driver Ambrosini then carried spare differentials in case of further trouble. Ambrosini incurred a one-hour penalty on the third loop by arriving at a control an half-hour early (there were few controls where that was physically possible!) but ultimately, after Makinen retired on the final loop, it did not matter. The large majority of the 57 starters retired early — including the second Toyota driver Therier, who left the road in dust whilst hurrying to a service crew with overheating trouble. By midway only 15 were left. Eleven started the short final loop, and two of these were excluded for exceeding the two-hour maximum lateness allowance. This was a particularly cruel end; the leading drivers themselves were losing nearly 1½ hours here.

Some drivers love and others hate the Bandama: many compare it with the Safari, the other open-road rally in the World Championship in 1979. They say the Bandama has better organization but less varied roads. But soon, even in Africa, people will be worried whether open-road championship rallying is acceptable any more. This year there were no serious incidents with other vehicles on the roads, but that in the opinion of many drivers was more by luck than judgement. With the degree of involvement now being shown by companies like Mercedes-Benz, rallying stands to progress so much more than ever before, but all the time it must always be accountable and justifiable. One only has to recall why Mercedes pulled out of motor sport in the nineteen-fifties to understand the responsibilities that accompany this corresponding opportunity.

Nearing the end of a long tough rally, Mike Doughty (hands on hips) has hallucinations as his Mercedes is transported on the Alepe ferry. On his left, Vic Preston Jnr looks worried!

No problems with crowd control

Mercedes self-service! The reliability of the Mercedes caused havoc at service points later during the rally. Here is Bjorn Waldegard welding the bonnet catches at Bouake on the third etape

The hazards of open road rallying. On this occasion Michel Mitri was travelling in the same direction as the truck. Often the trucks are considerably bigger

An inside view of the Toyota Celica Liftback, showing the oil reservoir on the right and the safety fuel tank in the middle. A transparent partition separates the rear portion from the drivers' cockpit

One of the best results was Andersson's fifth place with this Toyota Celica Liftback. Note the damaged driver's door, caused by a fallen tree. Hannu Mikkola, the first car on the road, had seen the tree earlier and radioed a warning to his fellow Mercedes teammates

HUILE

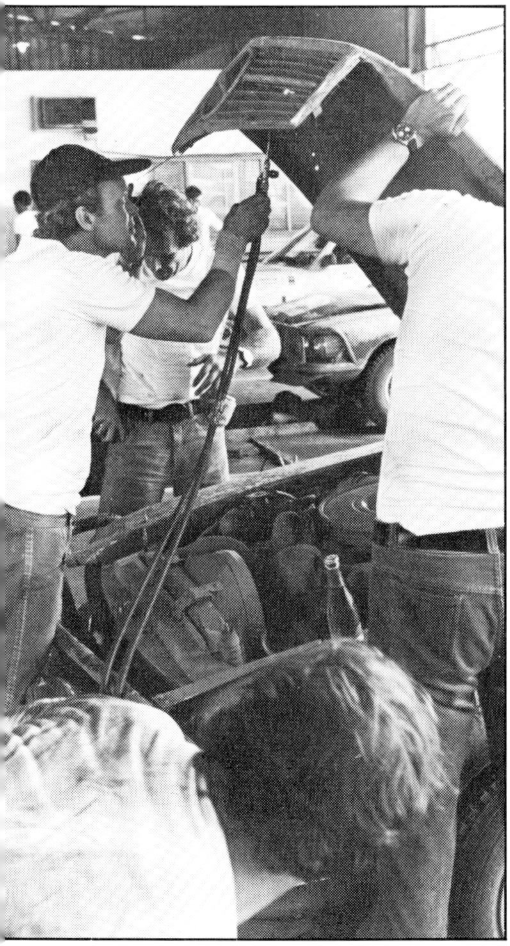

TOYOTA

New cars

The most daunting prospect facing manufacturers of rally cars in 1979 has been the uncertainty regarding the new regulations that will apply in 1982. Until the rules are announced and clarified, many manufacturers have stated that they will defer long-term competition model plans. The biggest involvement started in 1979 has been the Opel Ascona 400, but the decision to proceed with this was made some time ago and the programme has been running late.

Audi produced a new version of their stylish two-door 80 rally cars, and announced that because the rally car had overtaken full production it was necessary to compete with the car in group 4 guise. It is known that Audi have long-term ambitions in rally competition and have been developing their team with a view to the future, so the team cannot be content with their present 160 bhp, 930 kg car, which would not be competitive in group 2 let alone group 4. It is presumed that the basis of the group 4 car is to enable this model to be a starting point for further development, since it is easier to

Audi 80

Saab 99 Turbo 2 door

Saab 99 Turbo 2 door

Saab 99 Turbo 3 door

homologate special parts for group 4 than group 2. Whether this process of 'evolution' will enable parts to be used that will make the car materially more effective in competition remains to be seen. The most interesting story to emerge from Audi concerns their hopes to use a four-wheel drive car in competition in the future. During 1979, FIA decided that four-wheel-drive will be permitted in international rallies from the start of 1980, a move which has considerably interested American manufacturers who would like to compete on such endurance-style events as the Safari.

Saab introduced a two-door version of the 99 Turbo and were concerned with a succession of homologation changes during the year. In January 1978 the three-door Saab Turbo was homologated in group 4 (652) and then in October into group 1 (5722), under which it competed on the RAC with group 2 modifications. In February 1979 the two-door Saab Turbo was homologated into group 4 (658) — as Blomqvist's car ran in the Swedish — and the 900 Turbo was homologated on the same day in group 2 (1694). The next month the two-door Turbo was accepted into group 2 (1695) as the company preferred the kudos of group 2 successes rather than the greater opportunity of evolution.

A definite 'evolution' project has been started by Vauxhall, who announced a small-run high-performance version of the Chevette 2300HS, developed by Dealer Team Vauxhall and called the 2300HSR. In styling terms the design was highly acclaimed, but the theories behind the subtle changes were far more pertinent. The 'power bulge' on the bonnet enables future induction improvements, the reshaped front spoiler permits extra airflow to the radiator, the twin-plate clutch provides for future power increases and changes to the rear anti-roll bar link mountings enable long-sought changes to the rear suspension design.

First seen as a prototype in 1978, Chrysler (later Talbot) homologated their Sunbeam 16-valve car (marketed as the 'Lotus') into group 4, with only the restriction on rear axle location design to limit the car's capabilities. Peugeot brought out a revised model of the 104ZS called the 104ZS2, which gained WCR points in private hands in Quebec and Corsica while the Mazda RX7 which surprised in circuit racing was used by a private Japanese team on the Monte Carlo Rally and won its class. Denied the chance of gaining success, being only permitted to run on the Welsh Rally on condition that the driver forfeited awards, was an unusual TR7V8. Called a 'Strange Rover', it was in fact the four-wheel-drive chassis from a Range Rover with a Triumph body. Despite its appearance the car finished the route in style. Not all the modifications had officially been accepted by the FIA!

There has been considerable confusion during the year about the intentions of the Japanese companies Toyota and Datsun to re-enter group 4, using 16-valve engines which were banned when the '100-off' rule was abandoned. Team Datsun Europe expected to be able to use 16-valve engines during 1979, but this never happened. Toyota on the other hand had their car approved and these first appeared at the Castrol non-championship rally in Britain, in preparation for the RAC. Renault in Argentina started to produce a 12 fitted with a 1397 cc Renault 5 Alpine engine, called a '12 Alpine'. This was used without success in the Codasur Rally, although they challenged the victorious Peugeots.

Saab 99 Turbo 3 door

Vauxhall Chevette 2300HSR

Chrysler/Talbot Sunbeam Lotus

Chrysler/Talbot Sunbeam Lotus

Peugeot 104ZS2

'Strange' Rover

'Strange' Rover

Renault 12 Alpine

Corsa

In group 2 the SEAT 124 Especial was homologated with a 2-litre engine, and at the time of going to press the situation ended there. At the end of the year the international scene loses some old friends, that is when certain homologations finally expire. This happens automatically at the end of the fifth year after cessation of production. Farewell therefore to: Renault-Alpine A110 (1565 cc), Porsche Carrera 2.7 and Fiat Abarth 124 — all cars which will be fondly remembered by drivers and enthusiasts alike — and all incredibly successful as well.

The following pages illustrate those cars which are new to international rallying. Their quantity suggests that many manufacturers and entrants consider that there is still room for the competitive but untypical car. No specific captions are given to the grouped photographs.

Group 4 homologations in 1979

Homologation no:	656	Jan.	Polonez 125pn (1481 cc)
	657		Polonez 2000 (1995 cc)
	658	Feb.	Saab 99 Sedan Turbo (2-door)
	659		Audi 80
	660		Porsche 924 Turbo
	661	March	Mercedes-Benz 450SLC 5.0
	662		Chrysler/Talbot Sunbeam
	663	May	Toyota Celica 2000GT RA45
	664	July	Renault 12 Alpine
	665		Morgan Plus 8 (racing only)
	666	Nov.	Opel Ascona 400

Alfa Romeo Alfasud TI

Autodelta have used a group 2 1.5 Alfasud TI in Italian international championship rallies, started at the Targa Florio in Sicily. The 1489 cc engine developed a healthy 155 bhp with 15.5 mkg torque, dry sump, twin Weber carburettors and a weight of around 850 kg. Unfortunately the car has suffered serious transmission and shock absorber problems on gravel roads and in six entries it only finished once, at Ciocco, when it was second in its group. A limited slip was fitted for the non-championship Giro d'Italia but this time the engine failed. The regular driver was Federico Ormezzano. Interestingly, Autodelta were also campaigning their group 2 Alfetta GTV with Pregliasco at the same time, which is 50 bhp more powerful but weighs around 130 kg more.

Belle Epoque

Alfa Romeo 2300 TI

A surprise at the Brazil Rally was the entry of four official Alfa Romeo 2300 TIs, from the *Fiat* company of Brazil. In that country these cars are built by Fiat, the same team also running Fiat 147s as well! Drivers included Wilson Fittipaldi, brother of Emerson and former racing driver in his own right, and Mario Figueiredo, who was well known in the early seventies as an accomplished Datsun driver in Portugal. The cars were prepared in a short period of time, and there was considerable trouble with the location of the rear axle. This is by long bottom and short diagonal-links which attach to the differential and which frequently failed.

The cars were heavy by European standards, at about 1200 kg, but the engine was the old twin overhead cam unit based on the Italian 1900/2000 of the fifties and sixties which gives about 170 bhp and which is very reliable.

Fiat 147 Alcohol

One of the most important aspects of the Brazil Rally was the inclusion of a class for cars powered with engines that use alcohol rather than petrol. Brazil has great interest in promoting alcohol as an alternative fuel and already this is widely used as an additive. FIA rules forbid the use of alternative fuels in rallying, so the cars did not qualify for overall awards, but such was the speed of the little Fiat 147s (similar to the 127s in Europe) that the car of Anna Cambiaghi would have finished fourth. 1300 cc engines were fitted, giving about 100 bhp in twin carburettor form with a compression ratio raised from around 7:1 to 12:1. Cold starting was tricky and fuel consumption was about thirty-five per cent greater than on equivalent cars.

North

Ford Fiesta 1600 and BDA

In preparation for the eighties when virtually all mass-produced small cars in Europe are expected to be of front-wheel-drive layout, Ford of Britain, in conjunction with Germany, have undertaken a continuation of the development of the Fiesta model mentioned in *World Rallying 1* (page 126). Bigger engines were chosen as the basic 1300 cc unit would not be competitive, notably the 1600 cc unit, which is used in countries where severe emission restrictions are in force. For the Monte Carlo Rally one car was prepared in England and another in Germany; both finished this long event and Ari Vatanen came tenth overall. Since then a programme of development on both asphalt and forest roads has been undertaken using Roger Clark as the driver. Although this has been Ford's first front-wheel-drive competition car, no transmission design faults have been revealed, although fitting of the early driveshafts was faulty and led to delays on the Monte Carlo. If anything, the engine (an old push-rod design) has proved more troublesome.

As a parallel development programme, Haynes of Maidstone have built a Fiesta with a 1700 cc 220 bhp BDA engine, to test the strength of the transmission further, and to improve traction. On the Monte Carlo Rally, the racing tyres and the studs helped minimize this problem, which was soon evident when this powerful version of the Fiesta was used on secret forest tracks. In the first half of the season the car was used only once, on the national York Rally with John Taylor driving. This model is not homologated so cannot be used on bigger events. A BDA-engined car built privately by Burton Engineering has been very successful in international Rallycross, however, after being shown at the Performance Car Show at the beginning of the year.

The most interesting discovery during testing has been the highly critical settings for the front suspension geometry. It has been a long and difficult year for Ford with this model, not helped by the pressures of running the group 4 cars, but many feel that Vatanen's results on the Monte Carlo Rally may have given an insight into this model's suitability for top rallying.

North

Lancia Beta Monte Carlo Turbo

The most exciting cars to be found on the special stages for the first time in 1979 must be the group 5 Lancia Beta Monte Carlos, seen at the Giro d'Italia. Clearly the immediate purpose of these entries was to secure the publicity from winning the event, but behind this, Lancia personnel were thinking all the while of the feasibility of using a car like it in properly homologated form on international rallies in 1982 if the regulations permit. Few modifications from the specification used in long-distance racing were made for the Giro; the most noticeable being the shortened tail and wing. The excitement generated by watching these cars on the stages was immense, and was understandable considering they put out 370 bhp from their KKK turbocharged 1425 cc engines. In rally form the cars weighed about 800 kg. During the initial nighttime special stages at the start of the Giro, when all the leading runners were still in action, the special stages times for these cars were disappointing, though this could have been due to factors other than the design.

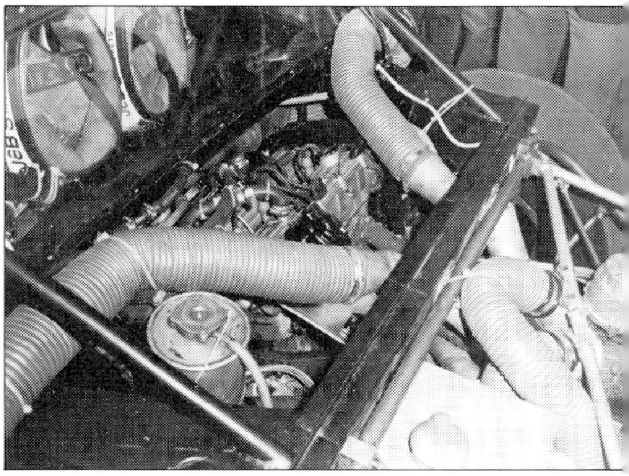

Mercedes-Benz 450SLC 5.0

Mercedes appeared on the Safari with a re-engined version of the 450SLC that they had used on the South American Event in 1978. This engine is said to have better torque and is built with alloy instead of cast iron. Power is given as 300 bhp instead of 225, and the three-speed automatic gearbox permitted speeds of 95, 160 and 220 kph in the gears. Pending full production of this model, the car was entered in group 4. Of the three 450SLC 5.0s that were entered on the Safari, two of them held the lead at one time or another, but the elusive win did not come until Bandama.

Mitsubishi Mirage (Colt GLX)

A surprise on the Quebec World Championship Rally was the group 1 victory of Hendrik Blok, the Californian tuning specialist and rally driver, at the wheel of a new Mitsubishi Mirage front wheel drive. Previously this model had only been used on national events in Japan, where it had achieved local success. Not only did it win the group but finished sixth overall. The engine was standard giving 88 bhp (1600 cc), but the suspension had been tuned to cope with the gravel roads.

Opel Ascona 400

Homologated during the latter part of the year but not actually used in competition during the season was the Ascona 400 group 4 car. It had been hoped to effect homologation in mid-season but production schedules for Opel prevented this. The essential difference for the group 4 car is the engine, which has 16 valves, twin overhead camshafts and is of 2.4 litres. A big engine for a four-cylinder, the work in converting this unit for sale as a completed or knocked-down competition unit to teams in many countries was entrusted by Opel to Cosworth, although individual tuners in various countries are already seeking to obtain the best conversions possible. The other major change from the Ascona group 2 car is the aerodynamic bodywork. Fifteen-inch wheels are used. Testing has been carried out mainly in Cyprus, where these pictures were taken, but naturally the attention of the Eurohandler Team has been divided between the development of this model and Jochi Kleint's chase for the European title. Ascona group 1 development is also under way, using a model called the i2000 with specialist competition parts marketed on completed vehicles that have been fitted out by Irmscher.

Nieborg

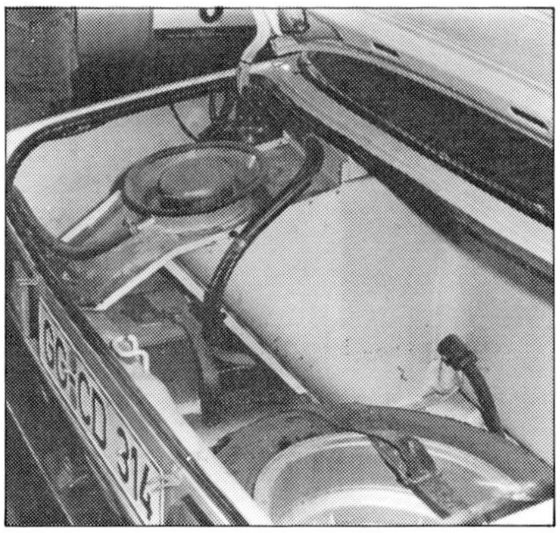

Nieborg

Opel Manta

The British DOT company undertook a programme of development of the Opel Manta model for rallies, and originally it was intended that this car would make its first official competition appearance in 1978. Almost as soon as work began, it became apparent that the next rally car would be the Ascona, not the Manta. Not all the project was valueless, however, since the floor pan and the suspension were identical to the Ascona, but inevitably the impetus to proceed was lost, particularly when their other cars were being so successful. The engine used on the only rally this car entered (the Gwynedd) was a 2-litre 16-valve model originally prepared by Dr Shrick, with fuel injection. A 5-speed ZF gearbox was fitted, while the transmission was via a shortened Commodore rear axle, using 5-link attachments. It was necessary to fit 14-inch rather than the 15-inch wheels originally specified, as the latter could not be supplied by Goodyear, with whom DOT Britain has a tyre contract. On the event itself, which was very snowy, the driver (Culcheth) started well, led by halfway but finished only fifth. Eventually, the car was sent to Germany as a test vehicle and has not been rallied again since.

North

North

Porsche 924 Turbo

Jurgen Barth had originally hoped to compete on the Monte Carlo Rally with a pair of 924 Turbos, sponsored by Datacom. Two pre-production cars were obtained, but due to a steel strike, the production of this model was delayed so that homologation was not available in time for the event. In order not to waste the opportunity of driving at Monte Carlo, the cars were then converted back to normal 924s, and Barth himself finished an excellent twentieth place. After the event was over, homologation for the Turbo model was obtained and work began with the Safari in mind. The engine used gave a mild 170 bhp compared with the 125 of the ordinary 924, and the car was still very heavy. Reinforced suspension was fitted and Bilstein shock absorbers replaced the Sachs units. On the event the car hit an unmarked bump and this moved the location of a bump stop. This in turn caused too great travel on the suspensions and created unexpected shock absorber trouble. An oil tube also broke, but the car finally failed within sight of the end when the shaft between the transaxle and the gearbox broke. The other car, driven by Alex Janda suffered serious problems when dust penetrated the injectors, causing misfiring, which appeared to have been due to electrical failure.

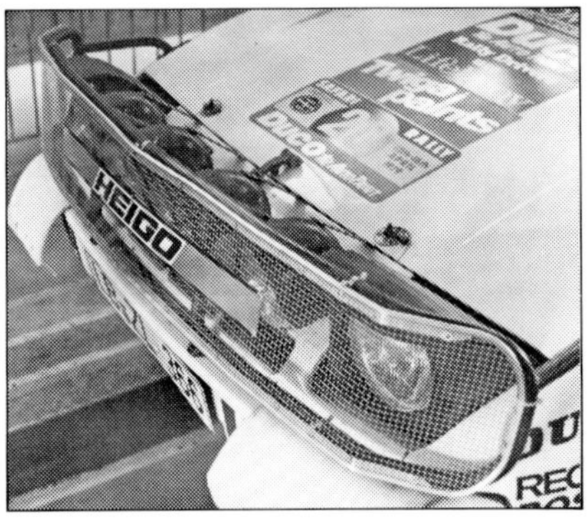

Renault 5 Turbo

A year after the car was shown at the Paris Salon and then at the annual sporting press conference, Renault produced the 5 Turbo at the Giro d'Italia. The whole car had been changed from normal 5 Alpines; the engine was centrally mounted behind the seats and the transmission led to rear wheel drive. The same size engine was used (1397 cc) and the Garrett turbocharger was set at 1.4 boost, which produced about 250 bhp — almost double that of the regular Alpine team cars. Aerodynamic work had produced a lip at the rear of the roof, while wide wings front and rear were joined by a horizontal 'running board'. Where engines are placed on normal Alpines, a spare wheel is fitted to the Turbo, but the location of the fuel tank remains behind the seats. Initial speed over the special stages on the Giro was most promising (Frequelin gained one fastest time overall), but engine trouble ensued and caused the car's ultimate retirement. At that time it was not known when or even if the car would be used again, one of the problems being that few rallies cater for prototypes in which the basic model is not homologated. The starting number on the Giro was 598, although it was entered in the special prototype class.

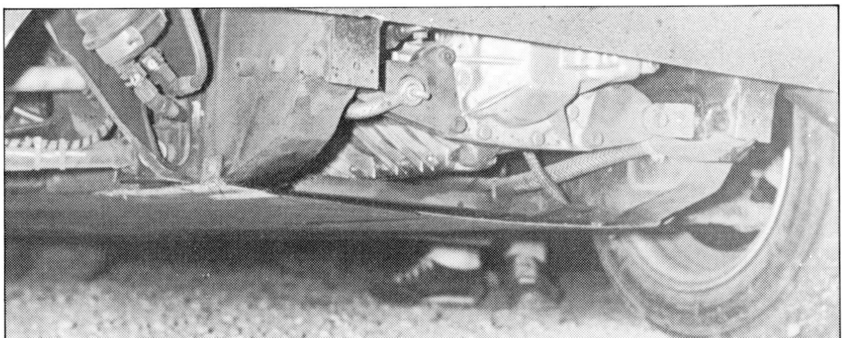

Taylor

Toyota Celica RA45

Toyota returned to group 4 rallying on the RAC Rally with their 16-valve Celica, which was banned at the end of 1977 when the '100-off' rule was discontinued. In May the Celica 2000GT type RA45 was homologated into group 4 with an 8-valve engine. This was effectively an identical model to that already being used in group 2, and as such there was no purpose in using this in competition. Only when the 16-valve engine was accepted as an evolution of the group 4 RA45 model — in November 1979 — was it possible to return it to group 4 rallying. Toyota were following the example of Leyland who had previously evolved their 8-valve four-cylinder TR7 into a 16-valve four-cylinder model for competition purposes, before the eight cylinder car was introduced. The advantage of this method of homologation is that evolution is accepted with only fifty models being built. The car was used at the Castrol Rally in Wales, but brake troubles caused delays, and on the RAC many different troubles hit the cars and only Rainio's car reached the finish. Externally the cars are the same as the old group 2 cars, and in the RAC, Rainio's car was, in fact, a converted group 2 car.

World Championship for Rallies 1979

In 1979 the World Championship for Rallies was officially divided, for the first time, between manufacturers and drivers but based on the same events. The drivers' series followed the trial FIA Cup for Drivers which was held successfully in 1978. The main problem with the FIA Cup was the complication of the scoring system, and for 1979 the drivers' series used a much simpler system, as follows: 20 for 1st, 15 for 2nd, 12 for 3rd, 10 for 4th, 8 for 5th, 6 for 6th, 4 for 7th through to 1 for 10th overall. There were no added points for groups. The scoring system for the manufacturers' series was unchanged from last year, except in so far as the number of points to count. The total number of rounds to count was reduced from nine to seven, with a maximum of five in Europe to count. These changes applied to both series.

During the year a change in the system for the two championships was ordered for the 1980 season. There was to be a reduced number of events in the manufacturers' series and the same number of events in the drivers'. Furthermore the two WCR events which were no longer to be eligible in the manufacturers' series (Swedish and 1000 Lakes) were also to be included in the European Championship with Coefficient 4.

The only important change in the running of World Rallies in 1979 was that any car which competed in the Diesel category had to be homologated in its own right within groups 1 through to 4.

In 1980, seven best scores will count, irrespective of where they were gained, in both drivers' and manufacturers' series. The details of the qualifying events are given at the calendar on the final page of this book.

	Monte Carlo	Sweden	Portugal	Safari	Acropolis	New Zealand	1000 Lakes	Quebec	San Remo	Tour de Corse	RAC	Bandama	Total	Official Total
1 Ford	16	16	18		18	18	(16)	18	(12)		18		150	122
2 Datsun		(8)	14	18	17	(5)	14	17			16	12	122	108
3 Fiat	14	12		15			18		16	12	5		92	92
4 Lancia	18								18	18	11		65	65
5 Toyota			16				10	12		10		10	58	58
6 Opel		13	9						14	13			49	49
7 Renault	11				13					17			41	41
8 Mercedes-Benz				17								18	35	35
9 Porsche	8								9	15			32	32
10 Vauxhall		14				10					7		31	31
11 Peugeot								8		7		8	23	23
12 Saab		18											18	18
13 Mitsubishi								13					13	13
14 Talbot (Chrysler)									12				12	12
15 Audi			11										11	11
16 Mazda						10							10	10
17 Leyland							7						7	7
18 Volvo		6											6	6
19 Skoda					6								6	6
20 Lada					4								4	4

World Championship for Drivers 1979

	Monte Carlo MC	Sweden S	Portugal P	Safari EAK	Acropolis GR	New Zealand NZ	1000 Lakes SF	Quebec CDN	San Remo I	Tour de Corse F	RAC GB	Bandama CI	Total	Position
Bjorn Waldegard (S)	15	15	15	(6)	20		12	20			(2)	15	(120) 112	1
Hannu Mikkola (SF)	8	8	20	15		20					20	20	111	2
Markku Alen (SF)	12	10		12			20		6		8		68	3
Timo Salonen (SF)					15		8	15			12		50	4
Ari Vatanen (SF)	1					12	15	12			10		50	5
Bernard Darniche (F)	20									20			40	6
Jean Ragnotti (F)					10					15			25	7
Andrew Cowan (GB)				10								12	22	8
Walter Rohrl (D)				3					15		3		21	9
Stig Blomqvist (S)		20											20	10
Shekhar Mehta (EAK)				20									20	
'Tony' Fassina (I)									20				20	
Ove Andersson (S)			12									8	20	13
Andy Dawson (GB)			10					10					20	14
Pentti Airikkala (SF)		15											15	15
Blair Robson (NZ)						15							15	
Russell Brookes (GB)											15		15	
Harry Kallstrom (S)				2	12								14	18
Attilio Bettega (I)									12				12	19
Pierre-Louis Moreau (F)										12			12	
Michele Mouton (F)	4									8			12	21
Jean-Claude Andruet (F)	10												10	22
Paul Adams (NZ)						10							10	
Ulf Gronholm (SF)							10						10	
Tony Pond (GB)									10				10	
Alain Coppier (F)										10			10	
Vic Preston Jnr. (EAK)												10	10	
Carlos Torres (P)			8										8	28
Rauno Aaltonen (SF)				8									8	
'Iaveris' (GR)					8								8	
Shane Murland (NZ)						8							8	
Taisto Heinonen (SF)								8					8	
Dario Cerrato (I)									8				8	

Jean-Pierre Nicolas F, Bjorn Johansson S, Harald Demuth D, George Moschous GR, David Parkes NZ, Lasse Lampi SF, Hendrik Blok USA, Bernard Picone F, John Taylor GB and Alain Ambrosino F — all 6 points.

Ola Stromberg S, Freddy Kottulinsky D, Mike Kirkland EAK, Evangelo Gallo GR, Brian Green NZ, Tapio Rainio SF, Jack Swayze CDN, Angelo Presotto I, Paul Rouby F and Michel Mitri F — all 4 points.

Guy Frequelin F, Lars Carlsson S, Joaquim Santos P, Vaclav Blahna CS, Roger Goss NZ, Per Eklund S, Claude Laurent F, Antonio Tognana I, Jean-Pierre Mari F and Jean-Pierre Faure F — all 3 points.

Jacques Almeras F, John Haugland N, Jorge Ortigao P, Mikolai Elizarov SU, Malcolm Stewart NZ, Erkki Pitkanen SF, Nicole Ouimet CDN, 'Nico' I and Jean Bondrille F — all 2 points.

Sven-Inge Neby S, Marques Baptista P, Sandro Munari I, Sergei Vukovich SU, Bob Robb NZ, Pekka Vilponnen SF, Paul Bourgeoys CDN, Paolo Pasutti I, Jean-Charles Martinetti F and Greg Carr AUS — all 1 point.

Subject to official confirmation.

Co-drivers

Gunnar Palm, himself probably the winner of more important rallies as co-driver than anyone else, helped instigate the Halda Trophy for the most successful co-driver each year, as judged by a panel of Swedish experts. The decision must be made before the RAC Rally each year, and the award for 1979 was given to Arne Hertz, the regular co-driver of Hannu Mikkola. Serious consideration was given to Hans Thorszelius, but it will be remembered that Bjorn Waldegard did not compete exclusively with Thorszelius in 1979. The co-drivers who have been awarded this trophy in the past are: 1973 Henry Liddon, 1974 Mario Mannucci, 1975 and 1977 Hans Thorszelius, 1976 Alain Mahe and 1978 Ilkka Kivimaki.

Co-drivers who have accompanied the winning drivers in each of the World Championship rounds are featured next.

- Bjorn Cederberg (Swedish)
- Mike Doughty (Safari)
- Arne Hertz (Portugal, New Zealand, RAC, Bandama)
- Ilkka Kivimaki (1000 Lakes)
- Alain Mahe (Monte Carlo, Tour de Corse)
- Mauro Mannini (San Remo)
- Hans Thorszelius (Acropolis, Quebec)

Bjorn Cederberg

Hans Thorszelius

Mauro Mannini

Mike Doughty

Ilkka Kivimaki

Alain Mahe

Arne Hertz

Obituary

Jerzy Landsberg
Almost a year after he survived a terrible accident in which his co-driver Marek Muszynski had died, **Jerzy Landsberg** suffered another accident on the Crocus Rally, near Krakow, in his native Poland. He was leading the rally as he tackled the Rabkowa-Znamierowice stage, near Nowy Sacz, when his car left the road on a fast bend. Other drivers reported that there is a deceptive place where at first sight it seems that one must take a different route, and it was here that the accident occurred. His co-driver **Janusz Szajng** died immediately and Landsberg passed away a week later.

Landsberg had been Polish National Champion no fewer than four times despite driving private cars, often sponsored by Stomil, the tyre company for which he worked, and then Marlboro. He started his career on motorcycles, rally co-driving and then driving progressing through nationally built cars to Renaults and Opels. This year he had been driving Opel Kadett GT/E cars including one supplied specially by Eurohandler. Apart from his obvious success at home and often in Western Europe, Landsberg will be remembered for the way he achieved his rally successes without the help of official teams in his own country. In 1978 he earned the Polish honour of 'Master of Sport'. He died at the age of 38.

Jerzy Landsberg below *Janusz Szajng with moustache*

Stop Press

The list of A-priority drivers set out in our chapter on World-Class Drivers earlier in the book was finalized after New Zealand Rally. The following have earned their A-priority status since then: Attilio Bettega I (3rd San Remo), Pierre-Louis Moreau F (3rd Tour de Corse), Andrew Cowan GB (3rd Bandama), Jochi Kleint D (1st ECR), Billy Coleman IRL (3rd ECR), Mauro Pregliasco I (4th ECR) and Bernard Beguin F (5th ECR). Kleint's priority continues until the end of 1982, the others' until the end of 1980. Furthermore the priorities for several of the drivers already mentioned earlier have been extended: 'Tony' Fassina's victory at San Remo gives him priority until the end of 1982, Jean Ragnotti's second place in Corsica and Russell Brookes' second on the RAC until the end of 1980. Also Antonio Zanini's second place on the ECR revives his status until the end of 1980. The records of the new drivers will be set out in *World Rallying 3* next year.

Errata
World Rallying 1
pp 46. Danielsson *10th* RAC Rally, 1976.
pp 52. Mouton 7th Monte Carlo, 1978. *(Lancia Stratos).*
pp 55. 'Tony' 4th San Remo, 1976. *(Lancia Stratos).*
pp 83. Car no. 33 crewed by *Andrzej Jaroszewicz/Ryszard Zsyskowski.*
pp 83. Munari retired *after* leading.
pp 99. *Aldo* Pasetti.
pp 99. *1971 Ove Andersson Renault Alpine A110.*
pp 109. *1976 Sandro Munari Lancia Stratos.*

European Championship for Rallies

Rally	Janner	Arctic	Boucles de Spa	Galway	Costa Brava	Sachs Winter	Hanki	Targa Florio	YU	Costa Smeralda	Saarland	Zlatni Piassatzi	Circuit of Ireland	Firestone	Arbo	Elba	Lucien Bianchi	Alpin	Welsh	Four Regions	Lorraine	South Swedish	Scottish
Country	A	SF	B	IRL	E	D	SF	I	YU	I	D	BG	GB	E	A	I	B	F	GB	I	F	S	GB
Round No.	1	2	3	4	5	6	7	8	9	10	11	12	13	14	15	16	17	18	19	20	21	22	23
Coefficient	1	4	2	2	3	3	2	2	1	1	1	4	3	2	1	4	2	3	2	3	2	2	4
Jochi Kleint (D)	(4)		40		(30)	(36)					(10)					40							40
Antonio Zanini (E)					60							80								45			
Billy Coleman (IRL)				40	36								45										
Mauro Pregliasco (I)					45			20		12						48							
Bernard Beguin (F)																					40		
Attilio Bettega (I)										20						60				60			
Pentti Airikkala (SF)													60										80
Guy Colsoul (B)			16									40					40						
Michele Mouton (F)																					24		
Attila Ferjancz (H)												16			6								
Holger Bohne (D)			24			45					15												
Walter Rohrl (D)						60																	
'Tony' (I)																80							
Josef Haider (A)	24					24					6				12								
Jean-Louis Clarr (F)																		30			20		
'Didi' (B)			20		24							48											
Ulf Gronholm (SF)		60					30																
Jean-Claude Andruet (F)																					30		
Yves Loubet (F)																		36					
Angelo Presotto (I)								16			1					32				24			
Malcolm Wilson (GB)																			24				60
Achim Warmbold (D)						9																	
Leo Kinnunen (SF)		80																					
Stig Blomqvist (S)													18						6			40	16
Jorge de Bagration (E)																							
Bernard Darniche (F)																							
Per Eklund (S)							8																48
Harald Demuth (D)						30									15								
Adartico Vudafieri (I)								40															
Dario Cerrato (I)								24												36			
Russell Brookes (GB)																			30				4
Vaclav Blahna (CS)			8						20			24											
Hermes Delbar (B)			6														20						
Jose-Luis Sallent (E)					18									30									
Brian Nelson (GB)				20																			
Hannu Mikkola (SF)																			40				24
Reinhard Hainbach (D)			12			18					8												
Franz Wittmann (A)	40														20								
Aldo Pasetti (I)								30												30			
'Siroco' (GR)												60											
Francis Vincent (F)																		60					
Ari Vatanen (SF)																							
	1	2	3	4	5	6	7	8	9	10	11	12	13	14	15	16	17	18	19	20	21	22	23

Scoring Basic Points: 20 for 1st, 15 for 2nd, 12 for 3rd, 10 for 4th, 8 for 5th, 6 for 6th, 4 for 7th, 3 for 8th, 2 for 9th and 1 for 10th.
These points are then multiplied by the coefficient concerned.
Best eight scores only to count.

	Hessen	Antibes	Donegal	Orense	Ciocco	Ypres	Skoda	Polish	Hunsruck	Danube	Taurus	Madeira	Halkidikis	Sachs Baltic	Manx	Tour de France	Vin	Cyprus	Warsaw	OASC	Chataigne	Espagne	Algarve	Total Points	Position
	D	F	IRL	E	I	B	CS	PL	D	R	H	P	GR	D	GBM	F	CH	CY	PL	A	F	E	P		
	24	25	26	27	28	29	30	31	32	33	34	35	36	37	38	39	40	41	42	43	44	45	46		
	3	2	1	1	1	3	1	4	2	1	1	1	3	1	2	4	1	3	2	2	1	3	2		
Kleint	45					(6)		60	(20)				60					45				45		**(481) 375**	**1**
Zanini								80														36		**301**	**2**
Coleman								48	16															**185**	**3**
Pregliasco													45											**170**	**4**
Beguin		40				60															20			**160**	**5**
Bettega																								**140**	**6**
Airikkala																								**140**	**6**
Colsoul						18						4										3		**121**	**8**
Mouton		30														48					15			**117**	**9**
Ferjancz							10	40			20									12				**104**	**10**
Bohne									8					8										**100**	**11**
Rohrl									40															**100**	**11**
'Tony'												20												**100**	**11**
Haider									6											24				**96**	**14**
Clarr																40					4			**94**	**15**
'Didi'																								**92**	**16**
Gronholm																								**90**	**17**
Andruet																60								**90**	**17**
Loubet		20														32								**88**	**19**
Presotto					12																			**85**	**20**
Wilson																								**84**	**21**
Warmbold	60													12										**81**	**22**
Kinnunen																								**80**	**23**
Blomqvist																								**80**	**23**
De Bagration				20																		60		**80**	**23**
Darniche																80								**80**	**23**
Eklund														20										**76**	**27**
Demuth																				30				**75**	**28**
Vudafieri					20							15												**75**	**28**
Cerrato					15																			**75**	**28**
Brookes															40									**74**	**31**
Blahna										20														**72**	**32**
Delbar						45																		**71**	**33**
Sallent				10																		12		**70**	**34**
Nelson			20			24																		**64**	**35**
Mikkola																								**62**	**36**
Hainbach									24															**60**	**37**
Wittmann																								**60**	**37**
Pasetti																								**60**	**37**
'Siroco'																								**60**	**37**
Vincent																								**60**	**37**
Vatanen																		60						**60**	**37**
	24	25	26	27	28	29	30	31	32	33	34	35	36	37	38	39	40	41	42	43	44	45	46		**etc.**

Individual awards: Co-drivers **Gunter Wanger**
Ladies **Michele Mouton**

ECR1 JANNER (A) 12-14 January 1979 *Coeff 1*

1	Wittmann/Nestinger	Porsche 911	16101
2	Stohl/Engseth	Lada 1600	16267
3	Haider/Pattermann	Opel Kadett GT/E	16607
4	Grunsteidl/Neverla	VW Golf GTi	17006
5	Smolej/Ostmann	Opel Kadett GT/E	17081
6	Stigler/Stigler	VW Golf GTi	17119
7	Lietz/Stocker	Ford Escort RS	17201
8	Decker/Kolar	VW Golf GTi	17299
9	Kleint/Wanger	Opel Kadett GT/E	17375
10	Weinmesser/Holzer	Opel Kadett GT/E	17513

56 starters, 28 finishers

ECR2 ARCTIC (SF) 2-3 February 1979 *Coeff 4*

1	L. Kinnunen/Kuukkala	Porsche 911	14622
2	Gronholm/Rehnstrom	Fiat Abarth 131	14737
3	Grondahl/Lammi	Saab 96 V4	14739
4	K. Aho/Kaipainen	Opel Kadett GT/E	14827
5	Geitel/Mesterton	Chrysler Avenger	14846
6	J. Kinnunen/Verkala	Ford Escort RS	15036
7	Jouhki/Piironen	Ford Escort RS	15042
8	Valtaharju/Anttila	Ford Escort RS	15074
9	Pitkanen/Harjanne	Chrysler Avenger	15152
10	Sundstrom/Sorjonen	Chrysler Avenger	15175

51 starters, 35 finishers

ECR3 BOUCLES DES SPA (B) 2-4 February 1979 *Coeff 2*

1	Kleint/Wanger	Opel Ascona	4h.35m.25
2	Smolej/Ostmann	Opel Kadett GT/E	4h.36m.53
3	Bohne/Diekmann	VW Golf GTi	4h.41m.32
4	'Didi'/Pauly	Fiat Abarth 131	4h.42m.00
5	Colsoul/Lopes	Opel Kadett GT/E	4h.42m.36
6	Hainbach/Fabisch	Ford Escort RS	4h.45m.50
7	Blahna/Raichl	Skoda 130RS	4h.46m.14
8	Delbar/Lux	Porsche 911	4h.46m.27
9	Kvaizar/Kotek	Skoda 130RS	4h.49m.21
10	Plas/Nijs	Fiat Ritmo	4h.56m.23

147 starters, 48 finishers

ECR4 GALWAY (IRL) 9-11 February 1979 *Coeff 2*

1	Coleman/O'Donoghue	Ford Escort RS	5h.59m.53
2	O'Connell/O'Connell	Ford Escort RS	6h.04m.30
3	Smith/Turkington	Porsche 911	6h.12m.27
4	Nelson/Cole	Ford Escort RS	6h.16m.25
5	Carter/Neville	Ford Escort RS	6h.18m.04
6	Cathers/McCanny	Chrysler Avenger	6h.20m.33
7	Windsor/Goff	Ford Escort RS	6h.21m.26
8	Everett/Bowie	Ford Escort RS	6h.24m.27
9	Bonner/Bonner	Chrysler Sunbeam	6h.26m.47
10	McCartney/Law	Chrysler Sunbeam	6h.28m.19

114 starters, 31 finishers

ECR5 COSTA BRAVA (E) 16-18 February 1979 *Coeff 3*

1	Zanini/Petisco	Fiat Abarth 131	4h.47m.05
2	Pregliasco/Reisoli	Alfa Romeo Alfetta GTV	4h.59m.21
3	Coleman/Porter	Ford Escort RS	5h.03m.55
4	Kleint/Wanger	Opel Kadett GT/E	5h.07m.49
5	'Didi'/Pauly	Fiat Abarth 131	5h.08m.58
6	Sallent/Puvill	Opel Kadett GT/E	5h.16m.47
7	Dorche/Bourgoin	Opel Kadett GT/E	5h.16m.53
8	Franquesa/Brucart	SEAT 124/1800	5h.21m.52
9	Casanovas/Villalba	Ford Escort RS	5h.26m.07
10	Canela/Blancafort	VW Golf GTi	5h.27m.03

111 starters, 49 finishers

ECR6 SACHS WINTER (D) 23-25 February 1979 *Coeff 3*

1	Rohrl/Geistdorfer	Fiat Abarth 131	9695
2	Bohne/Diekmann	VW Golf GTi	10013
3	Kleint/Wanger	Opel Ascona	10271
4	Demuth/Fischer	Audi 80	10297
5	Haider/Pattermann	Opel Kadett GT/E	10379
6	Hainbach/Fabisch	Ford Escort RS	10437
7	Fritzinger/Kehl	Toyota Celica	10551
8	Warmbold/Liddon	Toyota Celica	10632
9	Kristiansen/Jensen	Opel Ascona	11130
10	Stock/Schmuck	VW Golf GTi	11187

121 starters, 75 finishers

ECR1

ECR3

ECR5 Archives

ECR2 Top-Foto

ECR4

ECR6

ECR7 HANKI (SF) 2-4 March 1979 *Coeff 2*

1	Alen/Kivimaki	Fiat Abarth 131	13918
2	Gronholm/Rohnstrom	Fiat Abarth 131	14047
3	Lampi/Kuukkala	Ford Escort RS	14101
4	Valtaharju/Antilla	Ford Escort RS	14195
5	K. Hamalainen/Palmuare	Ford Escort RS	14291
6	Geitel/Mesterton	Chrysler Avenger	14598
7	Eklund/Sylvan	Porsche 911	14636
8	Hirvenen/Repe	Ford Escort RS	14654
9	J. Hamalainen/Muraja	Ford Escort RS	14654
10	Sillanpaa/Kylanpaa	Ford Escort RS	14797

73 starters, 44 finishers

ECR8 TARGA FLORIO (I) 16-18 March 1979 *Coeff 2*

1	Vudafieri/Mannucci	Fiat Abarth 131	2h.37m.02
2	Pasetti/Spollon	Fiat Abarth 131	2h.40m.15
3	Cerrato/Guizzardi	Opel Kadett GT/E	2h.41m.34
4	Pregliasco/Reisoli	Alfa Romeo Alfetta GTV	2h.42m.08
5	Presotto/Sghedoni	Ford Escort RS	2h.43m.42
6	Cambiaghi/Vittadello	Lancia Stratos	2h.45m.30
7	Pantaleoni/Maida	Porsche 911	2h.46m.16
8	'Apache'/Cammarata	Porsche 911	2h.48m.32
9	'Lucky'/Pons	Fiat Ritmo	2h.49m.24
10	Picciurro/Briguglia	Alfa Romeo Alfetta GTV	2h.49m.52

170 starters, 119 finishers

ECR9 YU (YU) 30-31 March 1979 *Coeff 1*

1	Blahna/Motal	Skoda 130RS	14323
2	Russling/Kosceutnig	Porsche 911	14364
3	Havel/Soukup	Skoda 130RS	14510
4	Tchubrikov/Kirov	Renault 5 Alpine	14542
5	Kuzmic/Ravnikar	BMW 2002	14883
6	Pusnik/Janja	Ford Escort RS	14912
7	Filippi/Maffei	Opel Kadett GT/E	15144
8	Kolev/Stojanov	Renault 5 Alpine	15203
9	Petkov/Gurlev	Lada 1600	15395
10	Schweizer/Siegert	Opel Kadett GT/E	15461

100 starters, 44 finishers

ECR10 COSTA SMERALDA (I) 4-7 April 1979 *Coeff 1*

1	Bettega/Perissinot	Fiat Abarth 131	3h.46m.04
2	'Lucky'/Pons	Fiat Abarth 131	3h.47m.05
3	Pregliasco/Reisoli	Alfa Romeo Alfetta GTV	3h.51m.57
4	Zordan/Della Benetta	Porsche 911	3h.53m.13
5	Verini/'Rudy'	Opel Ascona	3h.58m.19
6	Tognana/Creston	Opel Kadett GT/E	4h.00m.11
7	Cambiaghi/Vittadello	Lancia Stratos	4h.03m.04
8	Zandona/Stradiotto	Opel Kadett GT/E	4h.05m.49
9	Noberasco/da Monte	Opel Kadett GT/E	4h.06m.02
10	Presotto/Sghedoni	Ford Escort RS	4h.08m.56

109 starters, 52 finishers

ECR11 SAARLAND (D) 6-8 April 1979 *Coeff 1*

1	Hero/Horsch	Porsche 911	10393
2	Bohne/Diekmann	VW Golf GTi	10487
3	Smolej/Hopfe	Audi 80	10490
4	Kleint/Wanger	Opel Ascona	10520
5	Hainbach/Fabisch	Ford Escort RS	10603
6	Haider/Pattermann	Opel Kadett GT/E	10724
7	Ebenhoh/Oschner	Porsche 911	10950
8	Soltwedel/Muller	Ford Escort	10958
9	Werner/Meurer	Ford Escort	11015
10	Vogl/Hupf	Opel Kadett GT/E	11078

122 starters, 72 finishers

ECR12 ZLATNI PIASSATZI (BG) 7-9 April 1979 *Coeff 4*

1	Zanini/Petisco	Fiat Abarth 131	15243
2	'Siroco'/Fertakis	Lancia Stratos	15726
3	'Didi'/Pauly	Fiat Abarth 131	15766
4	Colsoul/Lopes	Opel Kadett GT/E	15780
5	Landsberg/Szajng	Opel Kadett GT/E	16436
6	Blahna/Motal	Skoda 130RS	16522
7	Ferjancz/Tandari	Renault 5 Alpine	16535
8	Kvaizar/Kotek	Skoda 130RS	16606
9	Sedivy/Janecek	Skoda 130RS	16849
10	Wozowicz/Wozowicz	Lada-Vaz 21011	17044

86 starters, 34 finishers

ECR7

ECR9 Jevtovic

ECR11 Scharnagl

ECR8 Belle Epoque

ECR10

ECR12

ECR13 CIRCUIT OF IRELAND (GB) 13-17 April 1979 Coeff 3

1	Airikkala/Virtanen	Vauxhall Chevette 2300HS	8h.29m.29
2	Coleman/O'Donoghue	Ford Escort RS	8h.40m.15
3	Fisher/Frazer	Ford Escort RS	8h.42m.51
4	Buckley/Caplice	Ford Escort RS	8h.49m.06
5	McCartney/Scott	Chrysler Sunbeam	8h.57m.31
6	Blomqvist/Cederberg	Saab 99 Turbo	8h.58m.23
7	Culcheth/Wilson	Opel Kadett GT/E	9h.04m.48
8	Lyons/Davison	Ford Escort RS	9h.14m.41
9	Logan/Ervine	Ford Escort RS	9h.21m.57
10	Cathers/Young	Chrysler Avenger	9h.31m.08

126 starters, 54 finishers

ECR14 FIRESTONE (E) 20-22 April 1979 *Coeff 2*

1	Alonso/Varela	Simca 1200TI	4h.26m.05
2	Sallent/Pubill	Opel Kadett GT/E	4h.26m.56
3	Franquesa/Blancafort	SEAT 124/1800	4h.27m.51
4	Torres/de Almeida	Ford Escort RS	4h.28m.15
5	'Correcaminos'/Rueda	SEAT 124/1800	4h.30m.35
6	Ortiz/Cabal	Simca 1200TI	4h.31m.01
7	Juncosa/Correal	Simca 1200TI	4h.36m.29
8	Martinez/Crespo	SEAT 124/1800	4h.45m.04
9	Gomes-Perez/Andicoechea	SEAT 124/1800	4h.46m.46
10	Munoz/Boto	Citroën GS	4h.49m.02

51 starters, 18 finishers

ECR15 ARBO (A) 20-22 April 1979 *Coeff 1*

1	Wittmann/Nestinger	Porsche 911	10939
2	Demuth/Fischer	Audi 80	10955
3	Haider/Pattermann	Opel Kadett GT/E	11385
4	Kottulinsky/Schwagerl	Audi 80	11451
5	Sulc/Weixelbaum	Porsche 911	11708
6	Ferjancz/Tandari	Renault 5 Alpine	12094
7	Osterer/Pabst	Porsche 911	12176
8	Lietz/Stocker	Ford Escort RS	12202
9	Essig/Oberortner	Opel Kadett GT/E	12260
10	Bittner/Polak	Opel Kadett GT/E	12268

62 starters, 42 finishers

ECR16 ELBA (I) 26-28 April 1979 *Coeff 4*

1	'Tony'/Mannini	Lancia Stratos	6h.37m.16
2	Bettega/Perissinot	Fiat Abarth 131	6h.43m.53
3	Pregliasco/Reisoli	Alfa Romeo Alfetta GTV	6h.47m.01
4	Kleint/Wanger	Opel Ascona	6h.48m.39
5	Presotto/Sghedoni	Ford Escort RS	6h.53m.58
6	Betti/Betti	Lancia Stratos	7h.04m.33
7	Dean/Dean	Ford Escort RS	7h.08m.02
8	Pasutti/Bisol	Porsche 911	7h.12m.02
9	Zandoni/Stradiotto	Opel Kadett GT/E	7h.17m.14
10	Torchio/Nizzotti	Porsche 911	7h.18m.23

190 starters, 62 finishers

ECR17 LUCIEN BIANCHI (B) 27-29 April 1979 *Coeff 2*

1	Colsoul/Lopes	Opel Kadett GT/E	5h.46m.24
2	Dumont/Rorife	Vauxhall Chevette 2300HS	5h.49m.00
3	Jacquemin/Destat	Chrysler Sunbeam	6h.01m.19
4	Delbar/Lux	Porsche 911	6h.07m.11
5	Koob/Goedert	Porsche 911	6h.16m.11
6	Horgnies/Alexisa	Ford Escort RS	6h.26m.56
7	Beauchef/Lambert	Ford Escort RS	6h.27m.10
8	Godart/Godart	Ford Escort RS	6h.34m.26
9	Neri/Materne	Lancia Stratos	6h.38m.53
10	'Chavan'/Symens	BMW 323i	6h.40m.37

90 starters, 40 finishers

ECR18 ALPIN (F) 4-6 May 1979 *Coeff 3*

1	Vincent/Huret	Porsche 911	5h.25m.27
2	Baroni/Baud	Porsche 911	5h.25m.41
3	Loubet/Mandrea	Opel Kadett GT/E	5h.38m.13
4	Clarr/Fauchille	Opel Kadett GT/E	5h.38m.42
5	Gardavot/Ferrato	Porsche 911	5h.46m.09
6	Lunel/Kerespert	Opel Kadett GT/E	5h.50m.46
7	Rouby/Martin	Renault 5 Alpine	5h.53m.43
8	Grindou/Wrons	Porsche 911	5h.54m.03
9	Collard/Chaudron	Opel Kadett GT/E	5h.59m.34
10	Lescure/Belland	Opel Kadett GT/E	6h.01m.09

96 starters, 35 finishers

ECR13 Saunders

ECR15 Archives

ECR17

ECR14

ECR16

ECR18

ECR19 WELSH (GB) 10-12 May 1979 *Coeff 2*

1	Mikkola/Hertz	Ford Escort RS	3h.25m.53
2	Brookes/White	Ford Escort RS	3h.30m.27
3	Wilson/Harryman	Ford Escort RS	3h.31m.01
4	Taylor/Short	Ford Escort RS	3h.32m.31
5	Pond/Peters	Chrysler Sunbeam	3h.32m.39
6	Toivonen/Harris	Ford Escort RS	3h.34m.08
7	McRae/Nicholson	Vauxhall Chevette 2300HS	3h.34m.44
8	Blomqvist/Cederberg	Saab 99 Turbo	3h.35m.43
9	Donald/Tucker	Ford Escort RS	3h.38m.13
10	Kaby/Rainbow	Triumph TR7V8	3h.39m.24

118 starters, 81 finishers

ECR20 FOUR REGIONS (I) 18-20 May 1979 *Coeff 3*

1	Bettega/Perissinot	Fiat Abarth 131	4h.40m.42
2	Zanini/Petisco	Fiat Abarth 131	4h.43m.40
3	Cerrato/Guizzardo	Opel Kadett GT/E	4h.45m.26
4	Pasetti/Pirollo	Fiat Abarth 131	4h.46m.58
5	Presotto/Sghedoni	Ford Escort RS	4h.52m.35
6	Pasutti/Bisol	Porsche 911	4h.53m.30
7	Gerbino/Bertone	Opel Kadett GT/E	4h.56m.16
8	Pantaleoni/Maida	Porsche 911	4h.56m.20
9	Torchio/Nizzotto	Porsche 911	4h.59m.41
10	Crucitti/Ravera	Porsche 911	5h.00m.50

183 starters, 63 finishers

ECR21 LORRAINE (F) 18-20 May 1979 *Coeff 2*

1	Beguin/Lenne	Porsche 911	3h.28m.51
2	Andruet/Lienard	Fiat Abarth 131	3h.30m.25
3	Mouton/Concoin	Fiat Abarth 131	3h.37m.14
4	Clarr/Fauchille	Opel Kadett GT/E	3h.41m.13
5	Meny/Lienere	Renault Alpine A310 V6	3h.41m.47
6	Roussely/Diss	Porsche 911	4h.02m.04
7	Haxaire/Bertolotti	Simca Rallye 3	4h.02m.09
8	Granjean/Ruer	Opel Kadett GT/E	4h.03m.19
9	Vaucard/Arnould	Simca Rallye 3	4h.04m.14
10	Belliard/Dequin	Renault 5 Alpine	4h.04m.51

74 starters, 36 finishers

ECR22 SOUTH SWEDISH (S) 25-27 May 1979 *Coeff 2*

1	Blomqvist/Cederberg	Saab 99 Turbo	3h.39m.08
2	Danielsson/Edqvist	Opel Kadett GT/E	3h.41m.38
3	Johansson/Spjuth	Opel Kadett Rallye E	3h.45m.14
4	Neby/Backman	Volvo 142	3h.48m.40
5	Nilsson/Olsson	Opel Kadett Rallye E	3h.49m.06
6	Arthusson/Fransson	Volvo 142	3h.50m.01
7	Sunner/Johansson	Opel Kadett Rallye E	3h.51m.29
8	Gustavsson/Hansson	Opel Kadett Rallye E	3h.53m.46
9	Holmberg/Georgny	Opel Kadett Rallye E	3h.54m.21
10	Johansson/Carlsson	Opel Kadett Rallye E	3h.54m.56

209 starters, 75 finishers

ECR23 SCOTTISH (GB) 9-12 June 1979 *Coeff 4*

1	Airikkala/Virtanen	Vauxhall Chevette 2300HS	4h.44m.30
2	Wilson/Harryman	Ford Escort RS	4h.50m.02
3	Eklund/Sylvan	Triumph TR7V8	4h.52m.12
4	Kleint/Wanger	Opel Kadett GT/E	4h.58m.28
5	Cowan/Syer	Ford Escort RS	5h.02m.43
6	Mikkola/Hertz	Ford Escort RS	5h.04m.16
7	Blomqvist/Cederberg	Saab 99 Turbo	5h.04m.20
8	Sanders/Ridden	Ford Escort RS	5h.04m.42
9	Brise/Rainbow	Opel Kadett GT/E	5h.09m.43
10	Brookes/White	Ford Escort RS	5h.11m.15

108 starters, 65 finishers

ECR24 HESSEN (D) 15-16 June 1979 *Coeff 3*

1	Warmbold/Liddon	Toyota Celica	6h.12m.30
2	Kleint/Wanger	Opel Ascona	6h.16m.30
3	Dawson/Fischer	Datsun 160J	6h.22m.25
4	Kristiansen/Jensen	Opel Ascona	6h.24m.19
5	Kohl/Pruefert	Porsche 911	6h.28m.28
6	Kromm/Inhester	Ford Escort	6h.34m.12
7	Guteit/Wellborn	Ford Escort RS	6h.36m.28
8	Bittner/Polak	Opel Kadett GT/E	6h.47m.14
9	Angelmaier/Angelmaier	VW Golf GTi	6h.57m.31
10	Simon/Rohringer	VW Golf GTi	6h.58m.02

103 starters, 35 finishers

ECR19

ECR21

ECR23

ECR20

ECR22

Archives

ECR24

ECR25 ANTIBES (F) 15-17 June 1979 *Coeff 2*

1	Beguin/Lenne	Porsche 911	7h.24m.19
2	Mouton/Conconi	Fiat Abarth 131	7h.41m.45
3	Cudini/Bourgoin	VW Golf GTi	7h.45m.55
4	Loubet/Alemany	Opel Kadett GT/E	7h.47m.19
5	De Meyer/Bolla	Opel Kadett GT/E	7h.52m.25
6	Gardavot/Ferrato	Porsche 911	7h.58m.43
7	Rouby/Martin	Renault 5 Alpine	8h.04m.44
8	Colard/Chaudron	Opel Kadett GT/E	8h.09m.00
9	Chatriot/'Tilber'	VW Golf GTi	8h.10m.12
10	Sintzel/Vincent	VW Golf GTi	8h.17m.27

113 starters, 35 finishers

ECR26 DONEGAL (IRL) 15-17 June 1979 *Coeff 1*

1	Nelson/Cole	Ford Escort RS	4h.55m.02
2	Fisher/Frazer	Ford Escort RS	4h.59m.22
3	J. Lyons/Semple	Ford Escort RS	5h.04m.46
4	Kidney/Moffett	Ford Escort RS	5h.05m.03
5	Coyne/Farrell	Chrysler Sunbeam	5h.07m.20
6	Bonner/Bonner	Chrysler Sunbeam	5h.09m.12
7	R. Lyons/McCanny	Chrysler Sunbeam	5h.10m.19
8	Campbell/Campbell	Ford Escort RS	5h.13m.49
9	Gallacher/McHarg	Ford Escort RS	5h.15m.04
10	McDaid/Duffy	Ford Escort RS	5h.18m.40

125 starters, 62 finishers

ECR27 ORENSE (E) 22-24 June 1979 *Coeff 1*

1	Bagration/Llopis	Lancia Stratos	2h.10m.55
2	Munoz/Valverde	Porsche 911	2h.18m.20
3	Ortiz/Cabal	Simca 1200TI	2h.19m.17
4	Sallent/Casanovas	Opel Kadett GT/E	2h.21m.07
5	Sousa/Boto	SEAT 124/1800	2h.22m.01
6	Gonzalvez/Oliveira	Porsche 911	2h.23m.14
7	Diaz/Sala	SEAT 124/1800	2h.24m.05
8	Juncosa/Correal	Simca 1200TI	2h.25m.27
9	Franquesa/Pinedo	SEAT 124/2000	2h.27m.22
10	Paradela/Garcia	SEAT 124/1800	2h.28m.39

59 starters, 20 finishers

ECR28 CIOCCO (I) 22-24 June 1979 *Coeff 1*

1	Vudafieri/Perissinot	Fiat Abarth 131	4h.07m.02
2	Cerrato/Guizzardi	Opel Kadett GT/E	4h.09m.30
3	Presotto/Sghedoni	Ford Escort RS	4h.11m.08
4	Tognana/Cresto	Opel Kadett GT/E	4h.13m.53
5	Pantaleoni/Maida	Porsche 911	4h.15m.13
6	Ormezzano/Scabini	Alfa Romeo Alfasud	4h.18m.37
7	Torchio/Nizzotti	Porsche 911	4h.20m.40
8	'Nico'/Barban	Lancia Stratos	4h.25m.23
9	Roti/Quercoli	Ford Escort RS	4h.26m.57
10	Rabino/Neri	Opel Kadett GT/E	4h.27m.01

160 starters, 55 finishers

ECR29 YPRES (B) 30 June-1 July 1979 *Coeff 3*

1	Beguin/Lenne	Porsche 911	5h.45m.52
2	Delbar/Lux	Porsche 911	5h.50m.02
3	'Gustavson'/van Oosten	Porsche 911	5h.57m.19
4	Snyers/Colebunders	Ford Escort RS	6h.01m.33
5	Nelson/Cole	Ford Escort RS	6h.06m.02
6	Colsoul/Lopes	Opel Kadett GT/E	6h.07m.28
7	'Eldis'/'Rossi'	Ford Escort RS	6h.08m.46
8	Jacquemin/Destat	Chrysler Sunbeam	6h.12m.47
9	Kleint/Wanger	Opel Ascona	6h.14m.33
10	Snoeck/Bontridder	Opel Kadett GT/E	6h.18m.51

168 starters, 55 finishers

ECR30 SKODA (CS) 30 June-1 July 1979 *Coeff 1*

1	Haugland/Bohlin	Skoda 130RS	19406
2	Pavlik/Molt	Renault 5 Alpine	19659
3	Havel/Soukup	Skoda 130RS	19720
4	Ferjancz/Tandari	Renault 5 Alpine	19912
5	Kristiansen/Thomsen	Opel Ascona	21085
6	Spiro/Else	Opel Kadett GT/E	21191
7	Lundstrom/Andersson	Toyota Corolla	21448
8	Svensson/Andersson	Opel Ascona	21887
9	Braathen/Braathen	Opel Kadett GT/E	22020
10	Berg/Jakobson	Opel Kadett GT/E	22037

86 starters, 39 finishers

ECR25 Morelli-Bertier

ECR27 Pujol

ECR29

ECR26 Taylor

ECR28 Belle Epoque

ECR30 Archives

ECR31 POLISH (PL) 5-7 July 1979 *Coeff 4*

1	Zanini/Petisco	Fiat Abarth 131	18877.1
2	Kleint/Wanger	Opel Ascona	19036.8
3	Coleman/Holmes	Ford Escort RS	19446.6
4	Ferjancz/Tandari	Renault 5 Alpine	20209.9
5	Wozowicz/Wozowicz	Lada 21011	21757.0
6	Ciecierzynski/Brzozowski	Polonez 2000	21426.2
7	Lank/Teichman	Lada 21011	22078.5
8	Sivik/Cermak	Skoda 130RS	22410.3
9	Elizarov/Moskowskich	Lada 21011	22467.8
10	Janowski/Malachowski	Zastava 1100p	22600.9

66 starters, 21 finishers

ECR32 HUNSRUCK (D) 20-21 July 1979 *Coeff 2*

1	Rohrl/Geistdorfer	Fiat Abarth 131	6h.23m.41
2	Carlsson/Ufer	Ford Escort RS	6h.34m.51
3	Hainbach/Fabisch	Ford Escort RS	6h.35m.57
4	Kleint/Wanger	Opel Ascona	6h.37m.19
5	Coleman/Neville	Ford Escort RS	6h.39m.43
6	Fritzinger/Kraistchy	Toyota Celica	6h.41m.48
7	Bohne/Diekmann	VW Golf GTi	6h.43m.41
8	Haider/Pattermann	Opel Kadett GT/E	6h.46m.59
9	Thiry/Thiry	Ford Escort RS	6h.49m.56
10	Nikola/Liski	Ford Escort RS	6h.53m.39

297 starters, 133 finishers

ECR33 DANUBE (R) 27-29 July 1979 *Coeff 1*

1	Blahna/Soukup	Skoda 130RS	4h.33m.54
2	Kolev/Stoyanov	Renault 5 Alpine	4h.47m.35
3	Petkov/Goudev	Lada 21011	4h.47m.43
4	Petrov/Tonev	Lada 21011	4h.51m.46
5	Trajbold/Trajboldova	Skoda 130RS	4h.55m.11
6	Yunpuu/Timusk	Lada 21011	4h.55m.20
7	Rajde/Valdek	Lada 21011	5h.00m.58
8	Oulteanu/Scobai	Dacia 1300	5h.19m.53
9	Rhodes/Pease	Ford Escort RS	5h.20m.48
10	Kovacs/Dekany	Lada 21011	5h.21m.23

74 starters, 30 finishers

ECR34 TAURUS (H) 10-12 August 1979 *Coeff 1*

1	Ferjancz/Tandari	Renault 5 Alpine	13201
2	Fischer/Gottlieb	Datsun Sunny	13401
3	Simor/Panics	Lada 1600	13910
4	Hidegh/Bojtai	Lada 1600	14079
5	Gal/Margo	Renault 17 Gordini	14334
6	Felian/Erdelyi	Lada 21011	14846
7	Osterer/Papst	Porsche 911	14882
8	Kovacs/Kiss	Lada 1300	14900
9	Dudacs/Doma	Lada 1200	15062
10	Hartwich/Wils	Wartburg 353	15080

81 starters, 37 finishers

ECR35 MADEIRA (P) 17-19 August 1979 *Coeff 1*

1	'Tony'/Mannini	Lancia Stratos	3h.40m.56
2	Vudafieri/Russo	Fiat Abarth 131	3h.43m.28
3	Falcon/Ortega	Isuzu Gemini	4h.20m.44
4	Rodriguez/Castro	Opel Kadett GT/E	4h.23m.00
5	Goncalvez/Oliveira	Ford Escort RS	4h.23m.58
6	Helle/Sorensen	Opel Ascona	4h.27m.34
7	Colsoul/Lopes	Opel Kadett GT/E	4h.31m.22
8	'Aledi'/Rodrigues	Chrysler Sunbeam	4h.39m.41
9	Fourmachat/Crign	Opel Kadett GT/E	4h.54m.42
10	Roda/Canario	Datsun 1200	4h.54m.55

59 starters, 16 finishers

ECR36 HALKIDIKIS (GR) 4-6 September 1979 *Coeff 3*

1	Kleint/Wanger	Opel Ascona	4h.09m.05
2	Pregliasco/Reisoli	Alfa Romeo Alfetta GTV	4h.14m.01
3	'Iaveris'/Stefanis	Ford Escort RS	4h.20m.36
4	Moschous/'Simetra II'	Datsun 160J	4h.23m.22
5	Gallo/Arketis	Datsun 160J	4h.32m.26
6	Avcioglu/Avcioglu	Fiat Abarth 131	4h.46m.32
7	'Carlo'/Kriadis	Renault 5TS	4h.51m.54
8	Karamanoglu/Alonzo	Ford Escort RS	4h.53m.34
9	Galentis/Potmandis	Lada 1300	5h.02m.49
10	Gemenis/'El Nak'	Datsun 160J SSS	5h.05m.15

49 starters, 15 finishers

ECR31 Fekete

ECR33 Fekete

ECR35

ECR32

ECR34 Fekete

ECR36

ECR37 SACHS BALTIC (D) 7-9 September 1979 *Coeff 1*

1	Eklund/Sylvan	VW Golf GTi	9028
2	Rainio/Krogell	Toyota Celica	9064
3	Warmbold/Liddon	Toyota Celica	9086
4	Kristiansen/Pedersen	Opel Ascona	9102
5	Bohne/Diekmann	VW Golf GTi	9357
6	Schewe/Merchel	Ford Escort RS	9402
7	Gunther/Ricken	Datsun 160J	9455
8	Glad/Zachariassen	Opel Kadett GT/E	9532
9	Werner/Meurer	Ford Escort RS	9546
10	Svanholt/Svanholt	Porsche 911	9623

155 starters, 93 finishers

ECR38 MANX (GBM) 14-15 September 1979 *Coeff 2*

1	Brookes/White	Ford Escort RS	13120
2	McRae/Nicholson	Vauxhall Chevette 2300HS	13134
3	Elsmore/Gallagher	Triumph TR7V8	13668
4	Kaby/McMahon	Triumph TR7V8	13925
5	McCartney/Scott	Talbot Sunbeam	14113
6	Ryan/Gray	Talbot Sunbeam	14138
7	Cathcart/Harkness	Ford Escort RS	14471
8	Bonner/Bonner	Talbot Sunbeam	14710
9	Carter/West	Ford Escort RS	14837
10	Thompson/Thomas	Ford Escort RS	14866

138 starters, 75 finishers

ECR39 TOUR DE FRANCE (F) 16-20 September 1979 *Coeff 4*

1	Darniche/Mahe	Lancia Stratos	9h.24m.50.0
2	Andruet/Lienard	Fiat Abarth 131	9h.37m.41.9
3	Mouton/Conconi	Fiat Abarth 131	9h.49m.03.0
4	Clarr/Fauchille	Opel Kadett GT/E	10h.08m.18.4
5	Loubet/Alemany	Opel Kadett GT/E	10h.11m.38.2
6	Hazard/Morel	Porsche 911	10h.18m.38.8
7	Ravenel/Buchet	Opel Kadett GT/E	10h.27m.10.1
8	Noyer/Causse	Porsche 911	10h.34m.31.7
9	Dienon/Brichot	Opel Kadett GT/E	10h.35m.57.9
10	Lemeunier/Chalvet	Opel Kadett GT/E	10h.43m.18.0

65 starters, 21 finishers

ECR40 VIN (CH) 28-30 September 1979 *Coeff 1*

1	Chapuis/Bernasconi	Fiat Abarth 131	4h.57m.11
2	Fornage/Besse	Porsche 911	5h.00m.54
3	C. Carron/Laderach	Opel Kadett GT/E	5h.03m.17
4	Reuche/Junod	Opel Kadett GT/E	5h.04m.05
5	Corboz/Duvoisin	Opel Kadett GT/E	5h.05m.35
6	Savioz/Coppet	Opel Kadett GT/E	5h.14m.03
7	Bosch/Bosch	Opel Kadett GT/E	5h.16m.27
8	Moser/Golay	Porsche 911	5h.18m.51
9	Perret/Guinchard	Opel Kadett GT/E	5h.20m.55
10	Guggisberg/Fragniere	Ford Escort RS	5h.26m.51

68 starters, 29 finishers

ECR41 CYPRUS (CY) 28-30 September 1979 *Coeff 3*

1	Vatanen/Richards	Ford Escort RS	6h.47m.43
2	Kleint/Wanger	Opel Ascona	7h.28m.11
3	Kyprianou/Vassiliades	Talbot Sunbeam	7h.49m.39
4	'Leonidas'/Arkentis	Renault 5 Alpine	8h.01m.03
5	Mavropoules/Charalambous	Talbot Avenger	8h.09m.35
6	Okhu/Diener	Lada 1600	8h.10m.31
7	Kirmitsi/Adams	Peugeot 504 Coupé	8h.43m.07
8	Mehta/Mehta	Peugeot 104ZS	9h.29m.12
9	Theocharides/Demetriades	Subaru 1400	9h.53m.07
10	Panayiotopoulos/Corres	Talbot Avenger	9h.57m.31

55 starters, 14 finishers

ECR42 WARSAW (PL) 5-7 October 1979 *Coeff 2*

1	Stawowiak/Rozanski	Polonez 2000	9600.9
2	Krupa/Mystkowski	Renault 5 Alpine	9721.6
3	Essig/Oberortner	Opel Kadett GT/E	10359.1
4	Koper/Pawlowski	Renault 5 Alpine	10361.9
5	Britth/Andersson	Ford Escort RS	10706.7
6	Dernalowicz/Lisicki	Polski Fiat 125p	10813.8
7	Radecki/Burzynski	Polski Fiat 125p	10877.1
8	Weinrich/Pihl	Opel Kadett GT/E	10877.8
9	Kobylinski/Siniarski	Polski Fiat 125p	11047.7
10	Granica/Werner	Polski Fiat 125p	11285.6

53 starters, 23 finishers

ECR37 Scharnagl

ECR39 Morelli-Bertier

ECR41

ECR38 Saunders

ECR40 Marchand

ECR42 Fekete

ECR43 OASC RALLY (A) 13-14 October 1979 *Coeff 2*

1	'Lucky'/Pons	Fiat Abarth 131	7512
2	Demuth/Fischer	Audi 80	7621
3	Haider/Pattermann	Opel Kadett GT/E	7637
4	Essig/Oberortner	Opel Kadett GT/E	8020
5	Bittner/Polak	Opel Kadett GT/E	8026
6	Ferjancz/Tandari	Renault 5 Alpine	8094
7	Havel/Kvaizar	Skoda 130RS	8274
8	Sedivy/Janecek	Skoda 130RS	8306
9	Klosch/Liendl	Ford Escort RS	8555
10	Stigler/Lukarsch	VW Golf GTi	8573

56 starters, 27 finishers

ECR44 CHATAIGNE (F) 13-14 October 1979 *Coeff 1*

1	Beguin/Lenne	Porsche 911	3h.05m.30
2	Mouton/Conconi	Fiat Abarth 131	3h.08m.39
3	Hazard/Gibaud	Porsche 911	3h.09m.31
4	Teilhol/Teilhol	Porsche 911	3h.09m.57
5	Cudini/Tilber	VW Golf GTi	3h.10m.35
6	Meny/Lienere	Renault Alpine A310 V6	3h.15m.25
7	Clarr/Fauchille	Opel Kadett GT/E	3h.15m.30
8	Lagrosse/Chevarin	Porsche 911	3h.18m.34
9	Panciatici/Tabet	VW Golf GTi	3h.20m.12
10	Malbran/Benatier	Talbot Sunbeam	3h.22m.04

89 starters, 50 finishers

ECR45 RACE (E) 19-21 October 1979 *Coeff 3*

1	Bagration/Llopis	Lancia Stratos	3h.57m.11
2	Kleint/Wanger	Opel Ascona	4h.03m.58
3	Zanini/Sabater	Fiat Abarth 131	4h.05m.18
4	Augustin/Varela	Simca 1200TI	4h.18m.38
5	Krupa/Mystkowski	Renault 5 Alpine	4h.19m.32
6	Munoz/Fernandez	Porsche 911	4h.20m.41
7	Sallent/Puvill	Opel Kadett GT/E	4h.21m.31
8	Torres/Almeida	Ford Escort RS	4h.25m.17
9	Borges/Bevilacqua	Opel Kadett GT/E	4h.25m.24
10	Colsoul/Lopes	Opel Kadett GT/E	4h.26m.08

52 starters, 19 finishers

ECR46 ALGARVE RALLY (P) 2-4 November 1979 *Coeff 2*

1	Schweizer/Dartsch	Opel Kadett GT/E	7h.40m.56
2	Fontainhas/Seromenho	Ford Escort RS	7h.51m.52
3	Roldao/Marcelino	SEAT 1430/1800	7h.52m.56
4	Santos/Alegria	Opel Kadett GT/E	8h.09m.54
5	Cabecadas/Conde	Ford Escort GT	8h.34m.12
6	'Ojuara'/Branco	Ford Escort RS	8h.43m.15
7	Melo/Teles	Ford Escort Sport	10h.00m.49

58 starters, 7 finishers

ECR43 Lackinger

ECR44 Morelli-Bertier

ECR45

ECR46 Slick

Major rally results

Ford Forum

Reynecke's winning Ford F100 Custom pick-up truck — Barberspan 500 rally

Archives

Shekhar and Yvonne Mehta winners of the Rothmans Kuwait Rally

Morelli-Bertier

Susset's Strakit SCII in action winning the Rallye Tout Terrain Causses-Rouergats

Non-Championship International rally results

DECEMBER 1978				
2-18	Tour de la Mediterranee F	Tchubrikov/Hino	Lada 1300	189h.37m.40s.
15-16	S. Giacomo di Roburent I	cancelled		
16-17	Russian Winter Rally* SU	Antropov/Kukoviakin	Moskvitch	6791.9
JANUARY 1979				
18-19	Bahrain Rally KWT	Kallstrom/Billstam	Datsun 160J	2h.45m.
18-21	Safari du Zaire ZAI	Vincens/Giallolacci	Mitsubishi Lancer	883m.
27	James Povoa de Varzim P	Santos/Tristao	Opel Kadett GT/E	1h.09m.04s.
FEBRUARY				
3	Perce Neiges CDN	Heinonen/Burgess	Toyota Celica	2h.46m.41s.
3-4	Rally Vasco-Navarro E	Etchebers/Etchebers	Porsche 911	3h.06m.47s.
9-11	Rally Stomil PL	Stawowiak/Lewandowski	Polonez 2000	7694.6
10-11	Rallye Das Camelias P	'Meqepe'/Vilar	Vauxhall Chevette 2300HS	1h.33m.35s.
10	Rallye Sjuharadsnatta Opel Rally Jamboree S	Johansson/Bonving	Saab 99EMS	4185
16-17	Molyslip Rally ZA	Van der Merwe/Boshoff	Ford Escort RS	3h.42m.54s.
17	Ontario Winter CDN	Perusse/Belanger	Triumph TR7	1h.31m.23s.
23-24	Barberspan 500 ZA	Reyneke/Fourie	Ford F100	7h.42m.52s.
23-25	Mintex Rally GB	Blomqvist/Cederberg	Saab 99 Turbo	2h.33m.54s.
24-25	Ronde de la Giraglia F	Beguin/Lenne	Porsche 911	3h.23m.26s.
MARCH				
2-4	Kempen Rally B	Delbar/Lux	Porsche 911	2h.22m.32s.
2-4	Rallye San Marino 'Fernet Tonic' RSM	'Tony'/Mannini	Lancia Stratos	3h.50m.30s.
7-9	Kuwait Rally KWT	Mehta/Mehta	Datsun 160J	7h.04m.10s.
10	Rallye de Femmes YU	Prihic/Lukic	Zastava 750	831
10-11	Rally 'Earinon' GR	'Siroco'/Fertakis	Lancia Stratos	2h.00m.44s.
10-11	Westfalen-Lippe-Fahrt D	Mayendorf/Gronau	Opel Kadett GT/E	6420
10-11	Rallye Lyon — Charbonnieres F	Mouton/Conconi	Fiat Abarth 131	3h.55m.04s.
10-14	Rallye Maspalomas E	Bagration/Llopis	Lancia Stratos	1h.51m.21s.
16-18	Circuit des Ardennes B	Dumont/Rorife	Vauxhall Chevette 2300HS	2h.50m.49s.
17	Rallye Schinderhannes D	Uhl/Schmidt	Ford Escort RS	
17-18	Sachs Rallye Unterfranken D	Heller/Jestaett	Ford Escort RS	6335
17-18	Rallye Yonne Morvan F	Fray/Boni	Opel Kadett GT/E	2h.33m.22s.
17-18	Rallye Mistral — gravel F	Therier/Vial	Toyota Celica	1h.12m.05s.
18	Rallye 'Megas Alexandros' GR	Hambis/Mavridis	Ford Escort RS	52m.18s.
24-25	Criterium Montseny Guilleries E	Bagration/Llopis	Lancia Stratos	2h.07m.59s.
24-25	Criterium de Touraine F	Beguin/Lenne	Porsche 911	2h.16m.32.7s.
25-26	Rallye Trifels D	Smolej/Hopfe	Audi 80	9768

*As a result of this rally, Sedivy became 1978 Peace and Friendship Champion

APRIL				
30/3-1/4	Rallye Figueira da Foz P	Silva/Nobre	Ford Escort RS	1h.42m.26s.
31/3-1/4	Lavanttaler Mitternachts Rallye A	Haider/Pattermann	Opel Kadett GT/E	10420
31/3-1/4	Castrol Rally AUS	Carr/Gocentas	Ford Escort RS	48m.07s.
31/3-1/4	Werraland Rallye D	Rack/Ufer	Porsche 911	3823
31/3-1/4	Rallye Dome-Forez F	Teilhol/Teilhol	Porsche 911	2h.24m.04s.
31/3-1/4	Rally 'Olympiacon' GR	Moschous/'Simetra II'	Datsun 160J	1h.33m.24s.
7-8	500km d'Andenne B	Moortgate/De Coninck	Porsche 911	2h.29m.27s.
7-8	Rallye Jean Behra F	Vincent/Huret	Porsche 911	3h.56m.40s.
7-8	Rallye Tout Terrain Champetre de Nancy F	Susset/Hannard	Strakit SCII	1h.10m.20s.
8	Rallye de San Telmo Tuy E	Goncalves/Oliveira	Porsche 911	35m.10s.
14-15	Rallye Tout Terrain Causses Rouergats F	Susset**	Strakit SCII	1h.04m.52s.
19-21	Rallye Zwickau DDR	Heimburger/Weitz	Wartburg 353	5515
21-22	Rallye 'Stemweder Blerg' D	Huthwelker/Ricken	Ford Escort RS	
21-22	Ronde D'Armor F	Begiun/Huret	Porsche 911	3h.07m.41.7s.
21-22	Rallye des Vosges F	Meny/Lienere	Renault-Alpine A310 V6	2h.48m.37s.
21-22	Rallye Futebol Clube Do Porto P	Silva/Nobre	Ford Escort RS	1h.44m.56s.
27-29	Asean IV Philippin Rally PI	Asterhag/Gullberg	Toyota Corolla	4h.52m.50s.
28	Vogelsberg-Rallye D	Gunther/Ricken	Ford Escort RS	
28-29	Rallye Police Gendarmerie B	Runestig/Bakke	Opel Ascona	285.3
29-30	Ronde Luronne F	Hazard/Tassel	Porsche 911	2h.44m.30s.
MAY				
5-6	Raika Rallye A	Wittmann/Nestinger	Porsche 911	8499
5-6	Rallye Teplice CS	Kvaizar/Kotek	Skoda 130RS	5520
5-6	Roland-Rallye D	Hainbach/Fabisch	Ford Escort RS	4707
5-6	Rallye tout terrain du Haut-Bugey F	Iribaren**	Punch	1h.17m.48s.
10-12	Trans Kalahari Endurance Race ZA	Marais/Woods	Kartcraft Sprinter	11h.06m.26s.
12	Pacific Forest CDN	Heinonen/Burgess	Toyota Celica	60m.25s.
12-13	Rallye de Pays Basque F	Dubert/Maroni	Simca Rallye 3	2h.49m.25.9s.
13	Stockholm Rally S	Liljeborg/Liljeborg	Opel Kadett GT/E	991.3
18-20	Rally de Ploegsteert B	'Gustavson'/De Coninck	Porsche 911	2h.42m.03s.
19-20	Lübeck Rallye D	Schnoor/Liske	BMW 2002	
20-26	Duckhams Rally ZA	Pond/Leeke	GM Chevair	19412
25-27	Haspengouw Rally B	'Didi'/Pauly	Fiat Abarth 131	4h.51m.30s.
25-27	Lauriacum Rallye A	Wittmann/Nestinger	Porsche 911	5470
25-27	Volan Rallye H	Ferjancz/Tandari	Renault 5 Alpine	5927
26	Trail of the Bison Rally CDN	Heinonen/Burgess	Toyota Celica	1h.20m.58s.
26-27	Metz Rally D	Rohrl/Geistdorfer	Fiat Abarth 131	8265
26-27	Criterium Luis de Baviera E	De Bagration/Llopis	Lancia Stratos	1h.57m.26s.
26-27	Ronde Cevenole F	Andruet***	Fiat Abarth 131	3h.24m.33.6s.
26-27	Rallye du Touquet F	Probst/Royer	Opel Kadett GT/E	1h.42m.41s.
JUNE				
1-4	Rallye Wolfsburg Berlin D	Brusch/Schaller	Opel Kadett GT/E	
1-4	Gunaydin Rally TR	Kocibay/Markopoli	Ford Escort RS	12179
2-3	Ronde de la Premiere Terre F	Therier/Vial	Toyota Celica	1h.21m.15s.
2-3	Rally Rota Do Sol P	Silva/Nobre	Ford Escort RS	1h.38m.31s.
8-9	Ele Rally NL	Van der Lee/Vogt	Opel Kadett GT/E	7262
9-10	Rallye du Forez F	Beguin/Lenne	Porsche 911	3h.22m.12s.
9-10	Nordwestdeutsche ADAC-Leistoungsprufung D	Nikola/Hartwigsen	Ford Escort RS	
15-17	Eurally B	Moortgat/De Coninck	Porsche 911	3h.28m.01s.
16-17	Rallye Pistons les Wapitis CDN	Buffum/Shepherd	Triumph TR7V8	1h.27m.54s.
20-23	Castrol Rally ZA	Asterhag/Van Heerden	Toyota Corolla	8h.04m.25s.
20-24	Rallye do Brasil BR	Alen/Kivimaki	Fiat Abarth 131	7h.30m.25s.

**No co-driver nominated

Barta

The Kvaizar/Kotek Skoda 130RS in the Rallye Teplice

Fekete

Ferjancz winning in Hungary on the Volan Rallye

Kocibay's early Escort on Turkey's Gunaydin Rally

Europeans Alen/Kivimaki in a factory Fiat in Brasil

APN

The winning Holden Commodore on the Australian Repco Reliability Trial

Sator

Radio 5 Rally winner Asterhag in his Toyota Corolla in South Africa

Fekete

Another win for the Renault 5 Alpine, this time on the Rallye Tatra

June continued

23-24	Ronde de Sallanches F	Carron/Jacquemet	Porsche 911	2h.30m.11.9s.
23-24	Rallye Bordeaux Sud-Ouest F	Therier/Vial	Autobianchi 1500	2h.04m.03.5s.
30	Rallye Baie des Chaleurs CDN	Heinonen/Burgess	Toyota Celica	1h.16m.00s.
JULY				
29/6-1/7	Volta Ilha Sao Miguel P	Borges/Bevilacqua	Opel Kadett GT/E	4h.50m.07s.
30/6-1/7	Rheinhessen Rallye D	Smolej/Hopfe	Audi 80	2577
6-8	Rally de Las 24 hrs MEX	Arnstein/de Silva	Renault 5 Alpine	791
7	Rally Lesbos GR	Gallo/Petropoulos	Datsun 160J	
7-8	Rallye Vorderpfalz D	Fritzinger/Hopfe	Toyota Celica	
7-8	Rallye des 1000 Pistes F	Therier/Vial	Toyota Celica	3h.51m.10s.
7-8	Trofeo Colline di Romagna I	Vudafieri/Barban	Fiat Abarth 131	2h.26m.15s.
14-15	Rallye Cuidad del Ferrol E	Etchebers/Etchebers	Porsche 911	1h.31m.49s.
21-28	Rally de la Codasur RA	Guichet/Todt	Peugeot 504	10h.34m.22s.
24-25	Rallye Sachs E	Sunsundegui/Larrinaga	Porsche 911	1h.18m.41s.
28-29	Rallye Delle Valli Piacentine I	'Tony'/Mannini	Lancia Stratos	1h.30m.59s.
AUGUST				
4-5	Lobster Rally CDN	Millen/Bellefleur	Datsun 510	1h.13m.03s.
5-18	Repco Reliability Trial AUS	Brock/Philip/Richards	Holden Commodore	3h.39m.18s.
10-12	Bayerwald Rallye D	Rohrl/Geistdorfer	Fiat Abarth 131	3h.01m.15s.
10-12	Rallye Rias Bajas E	Etchebers/Etchebers	Porsche 911	6442
18-19	Mountain Trials Rally CDN	Heinonen/Burgess	Toyota Celica	3h.03m.23s.
24/8-9/9	Tour de la Mediterranee F	Frequelin/Briet	Renault 5	15h.6m.51s.
25-26	Rallyes des Deux Bottes B	Moortgat/De Coninck	Porsche 911	1h.01m.35s.
25-26	Rallye Hebros BG	Petkov/Gourlev	Lada 1600	3h.17m.57s.
25-26	Rocky Mountain Rally CDN	Millen/Bellefleur	Datsun 510	1h.08m.28s.
31	Scorpion GR	Kounanis/Petropoulos	Ford Escort RS	35m.56s.
SEPTEMBER				
1-2	Barum Rallye CS	Haugland/Bohlin	Skoda 130RS	17185
1-2	Rallye Uri CH	Haldi/Sandoz	Porche 934 Turbo	4139
1-2	Rallye Dacia R	Olteanu/Scobai	Dacia 1300	10817
6-8	Radio 5 Rally ZA	Asterhag/Van Heerden	Toyota Corolla	4h.37m.55s.
8-9	Rallye Tout Terrain des Cimes F	Aguerre**	Pachiaudi-Porsche	40m.34s.
8-9	Cornix Th Rallye B	Van Peer/Delie	Opel Kadett GT/E	2h.20m.49s.
8-9	Principe de Asturias NL	Martinez/Lopez	SEAT 124/2100	2h.06m.21s.
14-15	Coppa Liburna I	'Tony'/Mannini	Lancia Stratos	2h.26m.17s.
15-16	Rallye Tatra CS	Pavlik/Jiratko	Renault 5 Alpine	11072
15-16	Ronde du Point d'Alencon F	Nourry/Royer	Porsche 911	2h.40m.48s.
19-20	Salonica Fair GR	Moschous/'Simetra II'	Datsun 160J	1h.55m.27s.
22-23	Endrust Forest Rally AUS	Portman/Runnalls	Datsun 1600	53.02m.
22-23	Rally rac 1000 MEX	Jourdain/Jourdain	Ford Fairmont	246
22-23	Limburgia Rally NL	Droogmans/Malais	Ford Escort RS	2h.07m.01s.
27-29	Roof of Africa ZA	Harcus***	Mazda Special	7h.10m.02s.
29-30	Rallye el Coste Ingles E	Etchebers/Etchebers	Porsche 911	1h.14m.53.9s.
28-30	Atrium Sauna Rallye A	Wittman/Nestinger	Porsche 911	16924
29-30	Rallye Jeanne D'Arc F	Nusbaumer/Lafitte	Porsche 911	1h.33m.22.6s.
29-30	Rallye Ain Jura F	Krucker/Lovey	Porsche 911	3h.14m.02.2s.

***No co-driver for this event

OCTOBER

5-7	Rally 'Mil Millas' EC			
5-7	Volta a Portugal P	'Meqepe'/Vilar	Vauxhall Chevette 2300HS	6h.10m.23s.
6	Prupungfahrt Stuttgart D	Haider/Entress	Opel Ascona	12252.2
6-7	Heures de Lessines B	Droogmans/Malais	Ford Escort RS	1h.40m.55s.
6-7	Rallye du Rhin F	Meny/Lienere	Renault Alpine A310 V6	2h.26m.20s.
6-7	Cork '20' Rally IRL	Buckley/Caplice	Ford Escort RS	16419
6-7	Rallye Isla de Tenerife E	Perez/Alonso	BMW 320	1h.32m.6s.
7-20	Tour d'Europe D	Fritzinger/Wunsch	Toyota Celica	195h. 25m.
12-13	AMAC Tulpen Rally NL	Danielsson/Booth	Ford Escort RS	5393
12-14	Trans Chaco PY	Silguero/Molas	Toyota Celica	
17-21	Southern Cross Rally AUS	Fury/Suffern	Datsun Stanza	20h.34m.50s.
19-20	Ulster Rally GB	Airikkala/Virtanen	Vauxhall Chevette 2300HS	3h.27m.05s.
19-20	Hepolite Rally ZA	Mortimer/Leeke	GM Chevair	6h.15m.58s.
19-21	Munich-Vienna-Budapest Rally D	'Lucky'/Pons	Fiat Abarth 131	1614
20-21	Omloop van Vlaanderen B	Droogmans/Malais	Ford Escort RS	2h.40m.19s.
20-21	Rallye Mont-Blanc F	Krucker/Baud	Porsche 911	3h.46m.15s.
20-21	Rallye 100,000 Trabucchi I	'Tony'/Mannini	Lancia Stratos	2h.52m.35s.
20-21	Rallye Monte-Carlo Junior MC	Ballet/Barjou	Porsche 911	1h.45m.24s.
20-25	Giro d'Italia I	Moretti/Schon/Radaelli	Porsche 935 Turbo	3h.56m.34.9s.
22-23	Achaeos Rally GR	Macris/Chaveles	Lada 1200	53m.56s.
25-27	Wartburg Rally DDR	Stawowiak/Rozanski	Polonez 2000	4755.2
26-28	BAC Rally NL	Van der Marel/Van Traa	Vauxhall Chevette 2300HS	7076

NOVEMBER

1-4	Tour du Senegal SN			
2-4	Rallye della Lana I	Bettega/Serra	Fiat Abarth 131	2h.20m.17s.
3-4	Rallye 2000 Virajes E	Etchebers/Etchebers	Porsche 911	1h.34m.31s.
9-10	Mavro Rodo Rally GR	Moschous/'Simetra II'	Datsun 160J	1h.40m.46s.
9-10	Monsanto Rally ZA	Van der Merwe/Boshoff	Ford Escort RS	4h.00m.05s.
9-11	Rallye Court CH	Haldi/Santoz	Porsche 934 Turbo	6207
9-11	Ronde de Chamarel MS			
10-11	Repco Alpine Rally AUS	Carr/Gocentas	Ford Escort RS	2609
10-11	Rallye du Condroz B	Colsoul/Lopes	Opel Kadett GT/E	2h.05m.13s.
13-18	Safari Caledonien F	Bedas/Gauzere	Toyota Celica	122280
17	Tall Pines Rally CDN	Heinonen/Burgess	Toyota Celica	2h.03m.06s.
17-18	Criterium des Cevennes F	Beguin/Lenne	Porsche 911	5h.08m.57s.
17-18	Rallye Autodromo di Monza I	Pinto/Penariol	Ferrari 308GTB	1h.43m.53s.
22-24	Rally Acapulco MEX	Salas/Martinez	Ford Fairmont	38
30/11-2/12	Rallye du Var F	Bondil/Brunel	Porsche 911	4h.27m.31s.

DECEMBER

1-2	Trofeo Vallee d'Aosta I	Bettega/Mannucci	Fiat Albarth 131	4h.18m.14s.
1-2	Rallye Toute-terrain Plaines et Vallees F	Garcia/Fontanet	Punch 2000	1h.20m.09s.
5-6	Peloponnisos Rally GR	'laveris'/Stefanis	Ford Escort RS	1h.07m.13s.
7-8	Oman Rally UAE	Kallstrom/Billstam	Datsun 160J	4h.48m.18s.
7-9	Saalbacher Eis-und-Schnee Rallye A			
15-16	Russian Winter Rally SU	Goltzor/Schtinn	IZS-Moskvitch	7206.6
23/12-1/1 '80	Rallye 5/5 Echappement F			

Loerakker

Droogmans' Ford Escort RS on the Dutch Limburgia Rally

Hogie

George Fury's Datsun Stanza on Southern Cross Rally

Rallying at its best. Moretti's Porsche 935 Turbo on the Giro d'Italia

International and National Champions

International Series Champions
Rothmans Middle East Harry Kallstrom S
Mitropa 'Lucky' I
West Europe Guy Colsoul B
Peace and Friendship Jan Trajbold CS
North America Cup John Buffum USA
Balkan Stojan Kolev BG

National Champions
Austria (A) Franz Wittman
Belgium (B) Guy Colsoul
Bulgaria (BG) Radislav Petkov
Switzerland (CH) Claude Haldi
Czechoslovakia (CS) Svatopluk Kvaizar
Cyprus (CY) Kypros Kyprianou
West Germany (D) Reinhard Hainbach
Denmark (DK) Jens-Ole Kristiansen
Spain (E) Jorge de Bagration
France (F) national series Bernard Beguin
  gravel series Jean-Luc Therier
Greece (GR) George Moschous
Hungary (H) Attila Ferjancz
Italy (I) 'Tony' Fassina
Japan (J) Shinya Yamauchi
Luxembourg (L) Alain Beauchef
Holland (NL) Jan van der Marel
Portugal (P) Jose-Pedro Borges
Panama (PAN) Rodriguo Teran
Poland (PL) Blazej Krupa
Romania (R) Ilie Olteanu
Sweden (S) special cars Bror Danielsson
  standard 'A' cars Bjorn Johansson
Finland (SF) Kyosti Hamalainen

Jan Trajbold Fekete

Guy Colsoul

Kypros Kyprianou

Claude Haldi

Alain Beauchef

Bjorn Johansson

Blazej Krupa

Jean-Luc Therier

Jens-Ole Kristiansen

Jan van der Marel Loerakker

Reinhard Hainbach

Shinya Yamauchi Autotechnic

'Lucky' Fekete

English Speaking National Champions

Australian National Championship

ROUND 1 Akademos '78 17-18 March Melbourne

1 Fury/Suffern	Datsun Stanza	48m. penalty
2 Dunkerton/Beaumont	Datsun Stanza	52m.
3 Carr/Gocentas	Ford Escort RS	1h.06m.

31 starters, 18 finishers.

ROUND 2 Commonwealth Bank of the West 13-15 April Western Australia

1 Carr/Gocentas	Ford Escort RS	27m. penalty
2 Bond/Dawson-Damer	Ford Escort RS	28m.
3 Dunkerton/Beaumont	Datsun Stanza	44m.

49 starters, 25 finishers.

ROUND 3 Lutwuche Shopping Village 5-6 May Queensland

1 Dunkerton/Beaumont	Datsun Stanza	36m.56s. penalty
2 Portman/Runnalls	Datsun 1600/710	41m.53s.
3 Carr/Gocentas	Ford Escort RS	46m.53s.

50 starters, 16 finishers.

ROUND 4 Ampol Bega 16-18 June New South Wales

1 Bond/Dawson-Damer	Ford Escort RS	1h.31.18m. penalty
2 Fury/Suffern	Datsun Stanza	1h.37.56m.
3 Dunkerton/Beaumont	Datsun Stanza	1h.03.35m.

53 starters, 19 finishers.

Ross Dunkerton Hogie

ROUND 5 Endrust Forest 22-23 August South Australia

1 Portman/Runnalls	Datsun 1600/710	53.02m. penalty
2 Carr/Gocentas	Ford Escort RS	55.45m.
3 Dunkerton/Beaumont	Datsun Stanza	1h.03.32m.

55 starters, 25 finishers.

Australian National Champion Ross Dunkerton 27 points
2nd Greg Carr 23
3rd Colin Bond 22

Canadian National Championship

ROUND 1 Perce Neiges 3-4 February Maniwaki, Quebec

1 Heinonen/Burgess	Toyota Celica	2h.46m.41s.
2 Leverton/Craig	Datsun 510	2h.55m.46s.
3 Choiniere/Buffum	Saab 99EMS	2h.57m.22s.

23 starters, 17 finishers.

ROUND 2 Ontario Winter 17-18 February Toronto, Ontario

1 Perusse/Belanger	Triumph TR7	1h.31m.23s.
2 Heinonen/Burgess	Toyota Celica	1h.31m.27s.
3 Skowronnek/Arthur	Datsun 710	1h.37m.06s.

47 starters, 18 finishers.

ROUND 3 Pacific Forest 12-13 May Chilliwack, British Columbia

1 Heinonen/Burgess	Toyota Celica	1h.00.25m.
2 Vanderwall/Edwardes	Datsun 510	1h.05.57m.
3 Roberts/Gibson	Mazda RX2	1h.06.60m.

25 starters, 14 finishers.

ROUND 4 Trail of the Bison 26-27 May Winnipeg, Manitoba

1 Heinonen/Burgess	Toyota Celica	1h.20m.58s.
2 Perusse/Belanger	Triumph TR7V8	1h.27m.53s.
3 Jones/Seiling	Datsun 510	1h.29m.31s.

22 starters, 11 finishers.

ROUND 5 Pistons les Wapitis 16-17 June St Jerome, Quebec

1 Buffum/Shepherd	Triumph TR7V8	1h.27m.54s.
2 Millen/Black	Datsun 510	1h.28m.48s.
3 Heinonen/Burgess	Toyota Celica	1h.29m.41s.

32 starters, 19 finishers.

ROUND 6 Baie des Chaleurs 30 June-1 July New Richmond, Quebec

1 Heinonen/Burgess	Toyota Celica	1h.16m.00s.
2 Boyce/Edwardes	Saab 99EMS	1h.23m.48s.
3 Millen/Howard	Datsun 510	1h.24m.50s.

25 starters, 13 finishers.

ROUND 7 Nova Scotia Highlands 28-29 July Dartmouth, Nova Scotia

1 Buffum/Shepherd	Triumph TR7V8	1h.48m.08s.
2 Heinonen/Burgess	Toyota Celica	1h.48m.43s.
3 Millen/Howard	Datsun 510	1h.50m.55s.

25 starters, 16 finishers.

ROUND 8 Lobster 4-5 August Dieppe, New Brunswick

1 Millen/Bellefleur	Datsun 510	1h.13m.03s.
2 Heinonen/Burgess	Toyota Celica	1h.13m.33s.
3 Boyce/Edwardes	Saab 99EMS	1h.22m.14s.

30 starters, 16 finishers.

Taisto Heinonen Cannell

ROUND 9 Mountain Trials 18-19 August Kamloops, British Columbia

1 Heinonen/Burgess	Toyota Celica	3h.03m.23s.
2 Boyce/Edwardes	Saab 99EMS	3h.16m.48s.
3 Jones/Hoyer	Datsun 510	3h.17m.50s.

25 starters, 15 finishers.

ROUND 10 Rocky Mountain 25-26 August Calgary, Alberta

1 Millen/Bellefleur	Datsun 510	1h.08m.28s.
2 Boyce/Edwardes	Saab 99EMS	1h.15m.45s.
3 Vandervell/Adams	Datsun 510	1h.16m.06s.

32 starters, 29 finishers.

ROUND 11 Tall Pines 17-18 November Peterborough, Ontario

1 Heinonen/Burgess	Toyota Celica	2h.03m.06s.
2 Leverton/Humphrey	Datsun 510	2h.07m.22s.
3 Powe/Craig	Datsun 510	2h.11m.31s.

44 starters, 22 finishers.

Canadian National Champion Taisto Heinonen 177 points
2nd Doug Leverton 80
3rd Rod Millen 79

East African (Kenya) National Championship

ROUND 1 Nyanza 800 27-29 January Kisumu

1 Collinge/Levitan	Alfa Romeo Alfetta 2000	29m. penalty
2 Kirkland/Haworth	Datsun 160J	57m.
3 Nandra/Chager	Datsun 160J	1h.53m.

17 starters, 7 finishers.

ROUND 2 Safari 12-16 April Nairobi
See the results of World Championship round number 4 on page 70.

ROUND 3 Sanyo Kenya 2000 26-27 May Nakuru

1 Collinge/Levitan	Alfa Romeo Alfetta 2000	1h.17m. penalty
2 Manjit/Panesar	Daihatsu Charmant	4h.35m.
3 Green/Pilford	Ford Escort RS	4h.36m.

22 starters, 8 finishers.

ROUND 4 African Safari Airways 16-17 June Nairobi

1 Kirkland/Mehta	Datsun 160J	1h.46m. penalty
2 Manjit/Bhalla	Daihatsu Charmant	2h.53m.
3 Muigai/Khan	Colt Lancer	3h.08m.

15 starters, 10 finishers.

Mike Kirkland

ROUND 5 Coast 800 4-5 August Mombasa

1 Collinge/Levitan	Alfa Romeo Alfetta 2000	44m. penalty
2 Kirkland/Doughty	Datsun 160J	56m.
3 Hellier/Hope	Datsun 160J	57m.

24 starters, 13 finishers.

ROUND 6 Coca-Cola Bottlers' 25-26 August Nairobi

1 Hellier/Sellick	Datsun 160J	1h.30m. penalty
2 Tundo/Hope	Ford Escort RS	2h.13m.
3 Shah/Soin	Datsun 160J	2h.19m.

33 starters, 17 finishers.

ROUND 7 Raymond 15-16 September Eldoret

1 Kirkland/Doughty	Datsun 160J	39m. penalty
2 Collinge/Levitan	Alfa Romeo Alfetta 2000	1h.11m.
3 Choda/Choda	Colt Lancer	1h.15m.

19 starters, 13 finishers.

ROUND 8 Rift 300 27-28 October Nakuru

1 Collinge/Levitan	Alfa Romeo Alfetta 2000	51m. penalty
2 Ulyate/Street	Fiat Abarth 131	55m.
3 Hellier/Sellick	Datsun 160J	58m.

26 starters, 16 finishers.

ROUND 9 Malindi 17-18 November Mombasa

1 Kirkland/Lyall	Datsun 160J	2h.45m. penalty
2 Ulyate/Street	Fiat Abarth 131	3h.57m.
3 Nandra/Chager	Datsun 160J	7h.02m.

22 starters, 4 finishers.

ROUND 10 Jamhuri 8-9 December Nairobi

1 Ulyate/Street	Fiat Abarth 131	33m. penalty
2 Collinge/Levitan	Alfa Romeo Alfetta 2000	43m.
3 Kirkland/Barnard	Datsun 160J	49m.

29 starters, 14 finishers.

East African National Champion Mike Kirkland 124 points
2nd Robert Collinge and Anton Levitan 120

New Zealand National Championship

ROUND 1 Victoria University Car Club 26-27 May Upper Hutt

1 Jennings/Cook	Ford Escort RS	2h.04.62m.
2 Street/Robb	Ford Escort RS	2h.05.57m.
3 Teesdale/Smith	Ford Escort RS	2h.05.66m.

87 starters, 64 finishers.

ROUND 2 Marlborough Car Club 16-17 June Blenheim

1 Adams/Franchi	Ford Escort RS	3h.09.90m.
2 Robson/Halls	Ford Escort RS	3h.11.54m.
3 Woolf/Whittaker	Mazda RX3	3h.13.23m.

69 starters, 39 finishers.

ROUND 3 Northern Sports Car Club 28-29 July Auckland

1 Donald/Lancaster	Ford Escort RS	1h.44.81m.
2 Adams/Franchi	Ford Escort RS	1h.45.83m.
3 Woolf/Whittaker	Mazda RX3	1h.47.98m.

131 starters, 83 finishers.

ROUND 4 Rotorua Car Club 29-30 September Rotorua

1 Donald/Lancaster	Ford Escort RS	2h.15.81m.
2 S. Millen/Garner	Vauxhall Chevette 2300HS	2h.22.43m.
3 Adams/Franchi	Ford Escort RS	2h.22.83m.

122 starters, 76 finishers.

New Zealand National Champion Paul Adams 50 points
2nd Jim Donald 40
3rd Tony Teesdale 35

South African National Championship

ROUND 1 Molyslip 16-17 February Johannesburg-Pretoria

1 Van der Merwe/Boshoff	Ford Escort RS	3h.42m.54s.
2 Mortimer/Leeke	GM Chevair	3h.46m.13s.
3 Fekken/Swanepoel	Datsun 120Y 2.0	3h.56m.11s.

66 starters, 21 finishers.

ROUND 2 Tour de Valvoline 9-10 March Durban

1 Van der Merwe/Boshoff	Ford Escort RS	11313
2 Sanders/Ridden	Datsun 160Y	11453
3 Hettema/Joubert	Fiat Abarth 131 V6 2.4	11611

56 starters, 32 finishers.

ROUND 3 Valvoline 6-7 April Johannesburg-Pretoria

1 Van der Merwe/Boshoff	Ford Escort RS	3h.42m.24s.
2 Sanders/Ridden	Datsun 160Y	3h.46m.45s.
3 Mortimer/Leeke	GM Chevair	3h.46m.45s.

65 starters, 38 finishers.

ROUND 4 Castrol 1000 27-28 April Pietermaritzburg

1 Van der Merwe/Boshoff	Ford Escort RS	4h.45m.30s.
2 Klaver/Kriek	Mazda 323	4h.56m.07s.
3 Hettema/Joubert	Fiat Abarth 131	4h.59m.13s.

53 starters, 25 finishers.

Paul Adams

Sarel Van der Merwe

Sator

ROUND 5 Duckhams 25-26 May Wilderness

1 Pond/Leeke	GM Chevair	19412
2 Sanders/Ridden	Datsun 160Y	19497
3 Van der Merwe/Boshoff	Ford Escort RS	19598

58 starters, 20 finishers.

ROUND 6 Castrol 20-23 June Johannesburg

1 Asterhag/van Peerden	Toyota Corolla	8h.04m.25s.
2 Rainio/Liddon	Toyota Corolla	8h.10m.31s.
3 Mortimer/Leeke	GM Chevair	8h.12m.23s.

63 starters, 22 finishers.

ROUND 7 Fiat 2000 17-18 August Middelburg

1 Sanders/Ridden	Datsun 160J	3h.18m.59s.
2 Fekken/Swanepoel	Datsun 160Y	3h.36m.34s.
3 Keizan/Hawkins	Fiat Abarth 131	3h.39m.52s.

61 starters, 21 finishers.

ROUND 8 Radio 5 6-8 September Johannesburg

1 Asterhag/van Heerden	Toyota Corolla	4h.37m.55s.
2 Mortimer/Woodhead	GM Chevair	4h.44m.49s.
3 Hettema/Gerichi	Toyota Corolla	4h.47m.44s.

39 starters, 19 finishers.

ROUND 9 Hepolite Rally 19-20 October Ermelo

1 Mortimer/Leeke	GM Chevair	6h.15m.58s.
2 Hettema/Joubert	Toyota Corolla	6h.31m.35s.
3 Miller/Dahms	Ford Escort 1600	6h.50m.30s.

49 starters, 10 finishers.

ROUND 10 Monsanto 9-10 November Pietersburg

1 Van der Merwe/Boshoff	Ford Escort RS	4h.00m.04s.
2 Mortimer/Woodhead	GM Chevair	4h.06m.24s.
3 Hettema/Joubert	Toyota Corolla	4h.11m.53s.

45 starters, 15 finishers.

South African National Champion Sarel van der Merwe

United States of America (NARRA) Championship

ROUND 1 Olympus 14-15 April Olympic, Washington

1 Blok/Trimble	Plymouth Arrow	25253
2 Kraushaar/Gilley	Datsun	27823
3 Parker/Compton	Datsun	28584

39 starters, 16 finishers.

ROUND 2 20-stages 5-6 May Cadillac, Michigan

1 Millen/Howard	Datsun 510	11256
2 Blok/Trimble	Plymouth Arrow	11267
3 Walker/LeBeau	Fiat Brava 131	11567

47 starters, 25 finishers.

ROUND 3 Chisum Trail 26-27 May Paris, Texas

1 Buffum/Shepherd	Triumph TR8	13386
2 Goodwin/Sorensen	Fiat Brava 131	13576
3 Schmidt/Andreini	Dodge Colt	14877

27 starters, 18 finishers.

ROUND 4 Mendocion Forest 2-3 June Willows, California

1 Millen/Howard	Datsun 510	16241
2 Goodwin/Sorensen	Fiat Brava 131	16666
3 Buffum/Adams	Triumph TR8	17921

32 starters, 20 finishers.

Rod Millen

ROUND 5 24 Horas de Mexico 7-8 July Mexico City

1 Buffum/Shepherd	Triumph TR8	7044
2 Salas/Herrera	AMC Gremlin	7120
3 Van Buren/Name	Ford Mustang	7278

65 starters, 25 finishers. (Note: these positions are based on stage times only.)

ROUND 6 Northern Lights 22-23 September Alma, Michigan

1 Buffum/Shepherd	Triumph TR8	13784
2 Millen/Howard	Ford Escort RS	14289
3 Walker/Reese	Fiat Brava 131	15307

26 starters, 16 finishers.

ROUND 7 Norwester 6-7 October Rainier, Washington

1 Millen/Priest	Ford Escort RS	5523
2 Buffum/Shepherd	Triumph TR8	5724
3 Walker/Reese	Fiat Brava 131	5974

35 starters, 28 finishers.

ROUND 8 Forest Hill Divide 10-11 November Auburn, California

1 Millen/Howard	Ford Escort RS	14888
2 Woodner/Hinkle	Triumph TR8	15525
3 Mellon/Duhon	Plymouth Arrow	15912

24 starters, 15 finishers.

NARRA Champion Rod Millen 95 points
2nd John Buffum 87
3rd Hendrik Blok 45

United States of America (SCCA) Championship

ROUND 1 Big Bend Bash 10-11 February Alpine, Texas

1 Blok/Trimble	Plymouth Arrow	14121
2 Millen/Howard	Datsun 510	14413
3 Jones/Sieling	Datsun 510	14434

24 starters, 14 finishers.

ROUND 2 100 Acre Wood 10-11 March Rolla, Missouri

1 Buffum/Shepherd	Triumph TR7	13660
2 Blok/Trimble	Plymouth Arrow	13966
3 Smiskol/Krafft	Datsun 260Z	14577

41 starters, 27 finishers.

ROUND 3 Tour de Forest 24-25 March Shelton, Washington

1 Millen/Howard	Datsun 510	6395
2 Blok/Trimble	Plymouth Arrow	6425
3 Heinonen/Burgess	Toyota Celica	6437

33 starters, 22 finishers.

ROUND 4 Susquehannock Trail 10 June Wellsboro, Pennsylvania

1 Millen/Howard	Datsun 510	15542
2 Buffum/Shepherd	Triumph TR8	16198
3 Tolles/Rizor	Volvo 142S	17790

67 starters, 35 finishers.

ROUND 5 La Jornada Trabajosa 23-24 June Bakersfield, California

1 Buffum/Gallagher	Triumph TR7	11417
2 Goodwin/Sorensen	Fiat Abarth 131	11714
3 Millen/Howard	Datsun 510	11852

45 starters, 29 finishers.

ROUND 6 Happiness is Sunrise 11-12 August Coudersport, Pennsylvania

1 Buffum/Shepherd	Triumph TR8	1h.58m.20s.
2 Walker/Reese	Fiat Abarth 131	2h.02m.28s.
3 Tolles/Rizor	Volvo 142S	2h.03m.50s.

60 starters, 15 finishers.

John Buffum

ROUND 7 Sunriser 400 8-9 September Circleville, Ohio

1 Millen/Howard	Ford Escort RS	13949
2 Buffum/Shepherd	Triumph TR8	14062
3 Tolles/Rizor	Volvo 142S	14812

72 starters, 40 finishers.

ROUND 8 Valvoline 20 Mule Team 20-21 October Ridgecrest, California

1 Goodwin/Sorensen	Fiat Abarth 131	12832
2 Gibeault/Allison	Datsun 510	13543
3 Woodner/Hauge	Triumph TR8	13736

29 starters, 19 finishers.

ROUND 9 Press-on-Regardless 3-4 November Houghton, Michigan

1 Heinonen/Bellefleur	Toyota Celica	19794
2 Harvey/Graves	Dodge Aspen	21801
3 Schmidt/Andreini	Dodge Colt	22031

65 starters, 28 finishers.

ROUND 10 Nevada 17-18 November Las Vegas, Nevada

1 Millen/Howard	Ford Escort RS	24786
2 Stewart/Warren	Ford F100	26435
3 Smiskol/Krafft	Triumph TR7	27428

55 starters, 17 finishers.

ROUND 11 Snodrift 8-9 December Grayling, Michigan

1 Heinonen/Burgess	Toyota Celica	9894
2 Leverton/Wilkinson	Datsun 510	10223
3 Harvey/Graves	Dodge Aspen	10322

47 starters, 31 finishers.

Note: since going to press, it was confirmed that these events held International status, so that the names of the winners should have also appeared in the relevant section in this book.

SCCA Champion John Buffum 460 points
2nd Rod Millen 440
3rd Hendrik Blok 290

British Champions and Championships

British Club Champions

Sedan Products overall
Pentti Airikkala 49 points, 2 Russell Brookes 45, 3 Stig Blomqvist and Hannu Mikkola 35
group 1
Alan Carter

Castrol/*Autosport* overall
Malcolm Wilson 88 points, 2 Jimmy McRae 85, 3 David Stokes 82
group 1
Ivor Clark

Esso BTRDA Gold Star
Geoff Simpson

Rally Sport
Harry Hockly

Two's Company
John Green

Motoring News
Mick Bryant

***The Scotsman*/British Airways**
Drew Gallacher

Ford Escort 1300
Christopher Atkinson
(note: last year's winner was John Simpson, not as stated in *World Rallying 1*)

Mazda Hatchback
Fred Almond

Tudor Tarmac
Brian Nelson

British Championships

Sedan Products Open Championship

ROUND 1 Mintex 23-24 February 1979 Harrogate

1 Blomqvist/Cederberg	Saab 99 Turbo	2h.33m.54s.
2 Eklund/Broad	Triumph TR7V8	2h.39m.22s.
3 Toivonen/Harris	Ford Escort RS	2h.40m.17s.

72 starters, 46 finishers.

ROUND 2 Circuit of Ireland 13-17 April
Carrickfergus/Newcastle
See the results of European Championship round number 13 on page 142.

ROUND 3 Welsh 10-12 May Cardiff
See the results of European Championship round number 19 on page 143.

ROUND 4 Scottish 9-12 June Glasgow/Aviemore
See the results of European Championship round number 23 on page 143.

ROUND 5 Manx 14-15 September Douglas
See the results of European Championship round number 38 on page 146.

ROUND 6 Ulster 19-20 October 1979 Craigavon/Larne

1 Airikkala/Virtanen	Vauxhall Chevette 2300HS	3h.27m.06s.
2 McRae/Main	Vauxhall Chevette 2300HS	3h.28m.06s.
3 Blomqvist/Cederberg	Saab 99 Turbo	3h.34m.36s.

125 starters, 71 finishers.

ROUND 7 RAC 18-21 November Chester
See the results of World Championship round number 11 on page 112.

Castrol/*Autosport* National Championship

ROUND 1 Gwynedd 10 February Llandudno

1 McRae/Nicholson	Vauxhall Chevette	1h.41m.07s.
2 Stokes/Warner	Ford Escort RS	1h.41m.43s.
3 Brookes/White	Ford Escort RS	1h.41m.57s.

72 starters, 59 finishers.

Pentti Airikkala

Alan Carter

Geoff Simpson

North

Harry Hockly

Davies

North

Mick Bryant

Drew Gallacher

ROUND 2 York 7 April Tees-side

1	Wilson/Thomas	Ford Escort RS	1h.29m.01s.
2	Hill/Varley	Vauxhall Chevette 2300HS	1h.33m.06s.
3	Stokes/Warner	Ford Escort RS	1h.33m.11s.

108 starters, 76 finishers.

ROUND 3 Granite City 28 April Aberdeen

1	Wilson/Harryman	Ford Escort RS	1h.24m.27s.
2	McRae/Nicholson	Vauxhall Chevette	1h.25m.03s.
3	Heggie/Dean	Ford Escort RS	1h.26m.02s.

92 starters, 60 finishers.

ROUND 4 Peter Russek 18 August Llandrindod Wells

1	Elsmore/Gallagher	Triumph TR7V8	2h.09m.26s.
2	Stokes/Warner	Ford Escort RS	2h.12m.34s.
3	Kaby/Rainbow	Triumph TR7V8	2h.13m.23s.

68 starters, 34 finishers.

ROUND 5 Lindisfarne 1 September Newcastle upon Tyne.

1	McRae/Nicholson	Vauxhall Chevette	1h.50m.40s.
2	Dawson/Gormley	Datsun 160J	1h.53m.08s.
3	Stokes/Warner	Ford Escort RS	1h.53m.46s.

83 starters, 45 finishers.

ROUND 6 Tour of Cumbria 29 September Carlisle

1	Wilson/Harryman	Ford Escort RS	1h.15m.32s.
2	Rutherford/Harris	Mazda Hatchback	1h.18m.04s.
3	Gallacher/McHarg	Ford Escort RS	1h.18m.16s.

76 starters, 51 finishers.

ROUND 7 Castrol 13 October Aberystwyth

1	Vatanen/Richards	Ford Escort RS	1h.52m.18s.
2	Wilson/Thomas	Ford Escort RS	1h.55m.53s.
3	McRae/Nicholson	Vauxhall Chevette	1h.56m.53s.

125 starters, 82 finishers.

ROUND 8 Bovis 3 November Ross on Wye

1	Wilson/Harryman	Ford Escort RS	1h.33m.43s.
2	Elsmore/Harrold	Triumph TR7V8	1h.34m.01s.
3	McRae/Nicholson	Vauxhall Chevette	1h.34m.09s.

107 starters, 65 finishers.

Malcolm Wilson North

Ivor Clark North

Fred Almond North

John Green Motofoto

Christopher Atkinson Archives

Brian Nelson

International Calendar for 1980

January
1-24 Oasis-Paris-Dakar F
4-6 Polar-Bergslags S
5 Finnskogsvalsen S
11-13 Janner Rally A *Coeff 2*
12 Aruikanatta S
12 Finspangsrundan S
12-13 Tout Terrain Infernal F
17-18 Bahrain KWT
19 Snösvängen S
19-20 James-Povoa de Varzim P
19-26 MONTE CARLO MC
26 Ullerudsdansen S
26 VMS-Kannan S
26 Granrisrundan S
26-28 Veneto-Scuderia Padova Corse I

February
1-3 Boucles de Spa B *Coeff 2*
1-3 Arctic SF *Coeff 3*
2-3 Perce Neiges CDN
2-3 Ronde Hivernale Serre-Chevalier-Briancon F
2-3 Veneto I
2-3 Camelias P
6-10 19 Capitales U
2 Bergslagsrundan S
8-10 Galway IRL *Coeff 1*
8-10 Costa Brava E *Coeff 4*
8-10 Safari Du Zaire ZAI
9-10 Kalkberg D
9 Sjuhäradsnatta S
9 Skilling 500 S
9 Nordmarksnatta S
9 Taunus Wiesbaden D
15-17 SWEDISH S *(Drivers championship only)*
16-17 Ontario Winter CDN
16-17 del Sole I
16-17 Big Bend Bash USA
21-23 Mintex GB
22-23 Sachs Winter D *Coeff 2*
23-24 Ronde du Nouveau Namur B
23-24 Vasco Navarro E
23-24 Ronde de la Giraglia F
23 Nobelsvängen S
23 Dalbyrundan S
29/2-2/3 Snow F *Coeff 2*
29/2-2/3 Kempen B
29/2-3/3 Total Oil Economy Run AUS

March
1-2 Lyon-Charbonnieres F
1-3 Storforsnatta S
4-9 PORTUGAL P
7-8 Sicily I *Coeff 2*
7-9 Westfalen-Lippe-Fahrt D
8-9 San Marino RSM *Coeff 1*
8 Bergslagsloppet/Kopparsväugen S
8 Wiking D
8-9 100 Acre Wood USA
12-14 Kuwait KWT
14-16 Circuit des Ardennes B
15 Schinderhannes D
15 Sachs-Rallye Unterfranken D
15-16 Criterium de Touraine F
15-16 Criterium du Luxembourg L
15-16 Terre Mistral F
20-22 Pneumant DDR
22-23 Castrol AUS
22-23 12 Uren Van Tielt B
22-23 Criterium Montseny-Guillerias E
22-23 Tour de Forest USA
28-30 Costa Smeralda I *Coeff 2*
29-30 Yu YU *Coeff 1*
29-30 Lavanttaler-Mitternachts A
29-30 Jean Behra F
29-30 Figueira da Foz P
30 Trifels D

April
3-7 SAFARI EAK
4-6 500 km d'Andenne B
4-8 Circuit of Ireland IRL *Coeff 2*
5-7 Zlatni Piassatzi BG *Coeff 3*
11-13 Saarland D *Coeff 1*
12 Lahn D
12-13 Sachs E
18-20 Arbö A *Coeff 1*
18-20 AMAC Tulpen NL
19-20 Biarritz Pays Basque F
19-20 des Vosges F
19-20 Ronde D'Armor F
19-20 Tour du Luxembourg L
19 Sjöbosvängen S
24-27 Isola d'Elba I *Coeff 3*
25-27 Criterium L. Bianchi B *Coeff 2*
25-26 Mobil Economie Run F
26 Kuastadansen S
26-27 Wittekind D

May
1-4 Terre de France ESSO F
2-3 Teplice CS
3 Silverratten S
3-4 Criterium Alpin F *Coeff 2*
3-4 Kurhessen D
3-4 Tout Terrain du Haut Bugey F
3-4 Rota do Sol P
3 Olof Trätälja Rundan S
9-11 Raika Tirol A
9-11 Eurally B
9-11 Smalands S
10-11 Pacific Forest CDN
10-11 Maspalomas E
14-18 4 Regions I *Coeff 4*
16-17 Metz D
16-18 Haspengouw B
17-18 Lorraine F *Coeff 2*
17-18 Lübeck D
17-18 Ciudad de Sta. Cruz E
18 Stockholm S
23-24 Duckhams ZA
23-25 South Swedish S *Coeff 1*
23-25 Wolfsburg-Berlin D
24 Finnskoga-Specialen S
24-25 Trail of the Bison CDN
24-25 Ploegsteert B
24-30 ACROPOLIS GR
30/5-1/6 Bosphorus-Gunaydin TR *Coeff 1*
31/5-1/6 Police-Gendarmerie B
31 Dalslands S
31/5-1/6 Touquet F
31/5-1/6 Ronde de la Premiere Terre F
31/5-1/6 Mont Blanc F

June
1-6 Amålsspecialen S
5-8 Hessen D *Coeff 2*
6-8 Danube-Dacia R *Coeff 2*
6-7 Ele NL
7 Munkrandan S
7-8 12 h. de Marche B
7-8 Diepholz D
7-8 Gargano I
7-8 Forez F
7-8 Susquehannock Trail USA
7-10 Scottish GB *Coeff 4*
13-14 Rododendri I
13-14 KNA/VG Economy Rally N
14 Midsommardansen S
14-15 Pistons les Wapitis CDN
14-15 Volta Ilha Sao Miguel P
15 OLW-Trofen S
18-21 Castrol ZA
20-21 Antibes F *Coeff 3*
21-22 Valvoline-Rheinhessen D
21-22 Ronde de Sallanches F
21-22 Terre des Charentes F
21-22 La Jordana Trabajosa USA
21-22 Orense E *Coeff 1*
23-29 Maghreb F
26-28 Ciocco I *Coeff 2*
27-28 Jamt S
28-30 24 h. Ypres B *Coeff 4*
28 Karlskrona Pokalen S

July
4-6 Las 24 h. de Mexico MEX
5 Julirundan S
5-6 Skoda CS *Coeff 1*
5-6 Vorderpfalz D
5-6 Criterium de Rioja E
10-13 Polish PL *Coeff 4*
10-13 Trofeo Colline de Romagna I
12-13 Terre des 1000 Pistes F
14 12 h. Tout Terrain d'Ordiarp F
18-20 Firestone E *Coeff 2*
19-20 Tour Terrain Des Chemins Creux F
19-20 Sunriser 400 USA
21-28 CODASUR RA
25-26 Serengeti-Safari-Rethem D
26-27 Nova Scotia Highlands CDN

August
1-3 Valli Piacentine I
2 Karlstad S
2 Ekratten S
2-3 New Brunswick Lobster CDN
8-10 Rias Bajas E
8-10 Hunsruck D *Coeff 3*
9 Killingen S
9-10 Happiness is Sunrise USA
10 Morskogabacken S
10-12 Taurus H
12-16 Brasil BR
15-17 Volta Ilha da Madeira P *Coeff 2*
16 Snapphane S
16 Smesvängen S
16-17 Mountain Trials CDN
22-23 Ulster GB
23-25 Warsaw PL *Coeff 2*
23-24 Rocky Mountain CDN
23-24 Ciudad del Ferrol E
23-24 Alto Alpennino I
28-29 Hebros BG
29-31 1000 LAKES (Drivers championship only) SF
30 TV — Svängen S

September
1-2 Valli Pordenonessi I
3-6 Radio 5 ZA
4-6 Sachs Baltic D *Coeff 1*
6 Westerwald D
6 Reichsstadt Esslingen D
6-7 Dacia R
6-8 Halkidikis GR *Coeff 3*
6-7 Cornix Th. B
11-13 Manx Trophy GBM *Coeff 1*
12-13 Coppa Liburna I
12-17 NEW ZEALAND NZ
13-14 Omloop Van Vlaanderen B
13-14 Tatry CS
13-14 Rheinland D
13-14 Ronde du Point d'Alencon F
13-14 Tour Terrain des Cimes F
13-14 Principe de Asturias E
13 Gränsloppet S
13 Falköping S
14-21 Tour de France F *Coeff 4*
14 Gellerasspecialen S
18-21 Criterium du Quebec CDN
20 Welfen D
20-21 Limburgia NL
21 Acu U
21 Edsvalla S
25-27 Roof of Africa ZA
26-28 Cyprus CY *Coeff 3*
26-28 Atrium Sauna A
26-28 RAC 1000 MEX
27-28 Herkules D
27-28 Isla de Tenerife E
27-28 Yonne Morvan F
27-28 Ain Jura F
27-29 Trans Chaco PY
27-28 Champion Nordic SF
27-28 Barum Gottwaldov CS
28 6 Heures de Vise B

October
2-5 Volta a Portugal P
3-5 Vin CH *Coeff 1*
4 Kong Christian Race S
4 Fotorundan B
4-5 Prüfungs-Fahrt Stuttgart D
4-5 Neustadt D
4-5 Corte Ingles E
4-5 Terre du Quercy F
4-5 Picardie F
4-5 Rhin F
4-5 Cork '20' IRL
4-18 Tour d'Europe D
7-11 SAN REMO I
11 Dynamitsvängen S
11-12 Chataigne F *Coeff 1*
11-12 Forest CDN
11-12 Wiehengebirge D
11-13 Öasc A *Coeff 1*
13-14 Forest Hill Divide USA
15-18 Europa-Partnerstadt-Mainz D
16-18 Hepolite ZA
17-19 Spanish E *Coeff 3*
18-19 'Kohle und Stahl' D
18-19 Monte Carlo Junior MC
18-19 20 Mule Team Stages USA
18-22 Southern Cross AUS
18-25 Himalayan IND
22-24 Economy Run GB
23-25 Wartburg DDR
23-26 Tunisia TN
24-26 Munich-Vienna-Budapest D
24-26 Bac NL
24-26 100,000 Trabucchi I
24-26 TOUR DE CORSE F
25 Vildmarksnatta S
25-26 Teboil SF
30/10-2/11 Algarve P *Coeff 2*

November
1 Novemberskolden S
1 Ramerspokalen S
1-2 Autodromo di Monza I
1-2 Nordmark D
7-8 Press on Regardless USA
8-9 Condroz B
8-9 Court-Franche Comte CH
8-9 Köln-Ahrweiler D
8-9 2000 Virages D
12-16 Sesquicentenario de la Republica Oriental de Uruguay U
15 Knutstorpssvangen S
15-16 Tall Pines CDN
15-16 Hunsrück-Eifelfahrt D
15-16 Lana I
16-20 RAC GB
22 Solstanatta S
21-23 Cataluna E *Coeff 1*
22 Lill Swängen S
22-23 Criterium des Cevennes F
28-29 Acapulco MEX
29-30 Tout Terrain Plaines et Vallees F
29-30 Aveiro P
29-30 Northern Lights SF
29-30 Nevada USA

December
6-7 Var F
6-7 Aosta I
6-7 Sno-Drift USA
10-14 IVORY COAST CI
12-13 Russian Winter SU
13 Uddeholmsrundan S
13-14 Tropheo Valle d'Aosta I
20 Sista Möjligheten S
20 Nuttevalsen S
20 Knäckebrödsvängen S
22/12-14/1 Raid Afrique F
26 Tomtedansen S
27 Säffle Natta S
27 Explo-Safe S